Praise for
MOUNTAINS TO CROSS

"*Mountains to Cross* is a must-read for anyone who believes in the power of long-term commitment to social change. Dr. Abraham George's story demonstrates how one person's vision and perseverance can transform an entire community, turning generational poverty into hope and opportunity. His life's work is a shining example of aligning business acumen with a profound dedication to social justice, yielding inspiration for leaders and citizens alike."

—**NARAYANA MURTHY**; Philanthropist; Founder and Chairman Emeritus, Infosys

"Dr. Abraham George is a very special man—with a very special vision and a very special heart—who has written a very special book."

—**THOMAS L. FRIEDMAN**; Opinion Columnist, *New York Times*; Author of *The World Is Flat*

"Dr. George's story proves that the greatest return on success is to spend it on others. *Mountains to Cross* is a deeply human memoir and a guide for anyone seeking to turn privilege into purpose. Disruption is the story of our age, but conviction is the story of Dr. George's life. *Mountains to Cross* is proof that real progress rests not in what we build for ourselves, but in what we build with—and for—others."

—**ANEESH RAMAN**; Former Presidential Speechwriter; Chief Economic Opportunity Officer, LinkedIn

"*Mountains to Cross* is an astounding book, and you won't be able to put it down until you get to the end."

—**KARAN THAPAR**; Author of *Devil's Advocate*; Leading Journalist, *The Wire*

MOUNTAINS

to

CROSS

FINDING LIFE'S PURPOSE
IN SERVICE

ABRAHAM M. GEORGE

GREENLEAF
BOOK GROUP PRESS

Published by Greenleaf Book Group Press
Austin, TX
www.gbgpress.com

Distributed by Greenleaf Book Group

For ordering information or special discounts for bulk purchases, please contact Greenleaf Book Group at PO Box 91869, Austin, TX 78709, 512.891.6100.

Design and composition by Greenleaf Book Group
Cover design by Greenleaf Book Group and Brian Phillips
Cover photo used under license from ©Shutterstock.com/ Mohammad Bayoumy

Publisher's Cataloging-in-Publication data is available.

Print ISBN: 979-8-88645-409-3

eBook ISBN: 979-8-88645-410-9

26 27 28 29 30 31 32 33   10 9 8 7 6 5 4 3 2 1

First Edition

To my loved ones

CONTENTS

PREFACE

The path to accomplishing life's
purpose is paved with challenges,
but the journey is always worth taking.

MOUNTAINS TO CROSS chronicles my experiences in the pursuit of purpose through social service. More than a memoir, this book is to inspire those who wish to address systemic poverty and inequality but are uncertain about where or how to start. Drawing upon vivid personal stories and hard-earned lessons, I invite readers to reflect on what it truly means to live with conviction and make a meaningful contribution to the world. For social entrepreneurs, educators, philanthropists, policymakers, and those interested in grassroots change, this book offers practical insights and guidance to help transform good intentions into impactful action.

In my early years in India, I was troubled by the social and economic injustice that had entrapped an entire section of society for centuries. Caste-based prejudice and discrimination have hindered the progress and welfare of the lower strata of society. Despite prevailing oppressive practices, I remained steadfast in my conviction that everyone deserved a fair chance to succeed and enjoy a life of dignity.

From the age of twenty-one, I studied in the United States and pursued a successful business career. Consistent with my mission to help those in need, I returned to India after a twenty-five-year absence to fulfill my life's purpose, which I had long sought. Accordingly, I undertook several diverse yet interconnected projects aimed at improving the living conditions of marginalized communities. I focused on education, women's rights, access to health care for the poor, promoting a free and independent press, and environmental health. As a result of our work, thousands of families have been able to break free from generational poverty and oppression.

Of these projects, I am most proud of the pioneering approach we took to alleviate poverty by empowering children through education and a nurturing environment from a very young age. I was fortunate to find like-minded individuals who shared this vision and dedicated their lives to the cause. With great enthusiasm and care for one another, we worked together to overcome insurmountable challenges to accomplish our goals. In my pursuit of change, I encountered both unforeseen resistance and unexpected support from the communities I worked with, which challenged my impressions of the rural population. It has been an emotionally charged journey of profound self-discovery with a transformational impact.

I have learned many valuable lessons over the past 30 years of my social work career. First, I recognize that humanitarian projects call for passion and drive. Before embarking on them, sufficient thought must be given to the reasons for being involved, whether they be a moral, social, or religious duty. Only if those motivations are compelling is one likely to devote the energy to make the effort successful. Patience and perseverance are crucial for overcoming obstacles in social endeavors.

I have observed that poverty is not inherently due to a lack of resources but often the result of societal practices that prevent certain groups of individuals from achieving upward mobility. Social equality that offers fundamental rights is essential to improving the economic status of those at the bottom of society.

Social justice cannot be achieved when the upper class has the power to oppress those below. Those who are discriminated against find it challenging to overcome prejudices and improve their financial situation. Only with economic strength can they challenge long-standing practices and attain equality. The path to social justice lies in economic opportunity, and there is no better way to achieve it than through an excellent education of young people.

Oppressed people often have limited expectations for their future, as they lack a clear path out of their predicament. They tend to believe that nothing good will ever happen in their lives and no one will help them. Trust is a rare commodity in those who struggle to make ends meet each day and cannot think of tomorrow. Social projects succeed only when beneficiaries recognize the longer-term value of the service provided and derive hope from it for a better future.

Significant wealth remains in the hands of a relatively small minority. At the same time, billions of people continue to suffer because of their deplorable economic conditions. If some excess wealth is channeled to its proper use for the benefit of those in need, poverty can be significantly reduced. The most effective use of financial resources is for enhancing knowledge and developing skills. The precondition for a satisfying outcome is an excellent education that supports the progress of children from disadvantaged homes.

I offer my story not as a blueprint for service but as an invitation to consider your path of purpose to find joy and a world surrounded by compassion. Written in a storytelling style, I have shared my life experiences to provide insights into social work for those who wish to help the impoverished.

PART I

CHAPTER 1

A FATEFUL DAY

M Y REGIMENT WAS POSITIONED AT the northeastern border of India, high in the Himalayas, close to the Tibetan Plateau. The threat of conflict had loomed ever since the Sino-Indian War ended three years earlier, in 1962.

A week had passed, and there was still no sign of the delivery trucks. Bad weather had cut off our radio signals, making it impossible to contact the base camp. Food supplies were running low, and so were the fuse wires to light detonators for guncotton and dynamite. Without them, my soldiers and I couldn't continue blasting boulders to build the artillery gun positions and bunkers necessary to withstand an attack by the Chinese army.

Usually, a ten-inch fuse wire provided a soldier twenty seconds to seek cover, but we used fuses shorter than five inches and frantically sprinted to safety. Under normal circumstances, my *subedars* and *jemadars*—junior-commissioned officers who were senior among the soldiers—oversaw the blasting. With short fuse wires, I decided to do the blasting myself to avoid the risk to others.

"No, *Sahib*! We won't let you!" the subedar protested. "It's too dangerous. Let this soldier do it. He's quick and brave." His candidate was a seasoned Second World War veteran.

"No. I won't permit that," I replied. "If he makes a mistake, he could get killed."

Strangely enough, the possibility of injury or death didn't dissuade me. I blew the shrill whistle to warn the soldiers, and, as usual, they scattered to their positions. I struck the match and lit the wire. Before I noticed, the spark whizzed by and neared the detonator, giving me little time to take cover. I pivoted as swiftly as I could and leaped.

The shock wave catapulted me and slammed me hard onto the rugged ground. Rock and shrapnel pierced my clothing and limbs. The scorching heat burned my skin. I lay motionless, covered in dirt and rocks. A terrifying silence followed the thunderous blast. Had the explosion shattered my eardrums?

A frantic voice cried, "Quick! Start the jeep."

I could hear! I felt movement around me as strong arms scrambled to unearth me. The soldiers carried me into the jeep and gently placed me on the rear seat. One of the subedars brushed the dust from my face and gently pulled my eyelids back. My eyes stung and watered; his face was a blur as he hurriedly bandaged my head.

"Are my eyes all right?" I rasped, barely able to speak without retching from the pungent, toxic fumes stinging my throat. I couldn't bear the thought of being blind for the rest of my life.

"Yes, Sahib, don't worry," the subedar reassured me.

I drifted in and out of semiconsciousness through the two-hour drive down the treacherous mountain to the nearest military field hospital. The doctors removed rock fragments from my body and face and swathed me in bandages. To my relief, internal bleeding, organ injury, and concussion were ruled out.

I remained under observation for two days, sore and dazed. The explosion replayed again and again in my mind. If I had reacted a fraction of a second later, I would have died. Somehow, my careless mistake had not been the end for me.

I questioned why.

CHAPTER 2

HOME SWEET HOME

THE REGIMENTAL HEADQUARTERS ordered me home on six weeks of medical leave. I sent my father a telegram, withholding any details that might worry him.

On the day of departure, my driver and a senior subedar dropped me off at Missamari, the last station at the Himalayan foothills. "I'm sad to go," I told them. We sat together silently for a few moments, struggling with our emotions. I feared my soldiers might think less of me for not noticing the lighted fuse wire in time, and my superior officers might fault me for having violated protocol. My only consolation was that no one else had been injured. I bade them farewell, with tears in my eyes. We shook hands, and I affectionately patted their shoulders. I felt guilty for leaving my men mid-mission in the harsh environment while I returned to the comforts of my home.

My long journey took me across the country, from the far northeast to the southern tip of India. The narrow-gauge train with twin locomotives belched dark clouds as it chugged along, gradually picking up speed. Passengers perched uncomfortably on broken wooden benches as roaches and rats scurried about. My forehead had peeled

like a snakeskin, and my bluish, frostbitten fingers and bandaged eye
drew pitying looks. Stiff from sitting for hours in the packed third-
class compartment, I inched closer to the coach's doorway to stretch
my legs. The cool breeze, though refreshing, brought with it coal soot
that stung my unbandaged eye.

The ticket collector came by occasionally, looking for bribes. If
you paid him, he would let you know of a comfortable vacant seat,
possibly in first class, and at the next stop, you could run with your
luggage to the new seat. Sometimes, the rightful ticket holder for the
new seat would arrive, and you would have to return to your old seat,
hoping another eager traveler wasn't occupying it.

On the second day, the train traversed the breadth of Assam,
crossed the lordly Brahmaputra River, and headed close to Nagaland.
It was not uncommon for the Naga rebels to attack trains or sabotage
the tracks. In my current state, I couldn't handle another mishap.

Early the following day, we reached Calcutta, where I changed
trains and headed south. At every stop, food vendors hustled through
overcrowded compartments, calling out their tempting wares. I could
determine our location by the food they served: as we approached
Tamil Nadu, curd rice with pickle or a crispy lentil fritter called
medu vada with coconut chutney as a dipping sauce; closer to Kerala, it was *ethakka*, the local name for large plantains, in every form
imaginable—steamed, fried, and cooked in milk and sugar.

Passengers could get off at any station to buy a snack—a newspaper cone filled with roasted peanuts and a cup of *chai*, all for a few
paise. It was worth the price to watch the skilled vendor pour the
aromatic liquid from the height of his shoulder into the cup below
to mix and cool it without spilling a single golden drop. As soon as
the vendor handed over my goodies, I raced to catch the departing

train, and passengers sometimes offered a hand to pull me in. I had become rather good at boarding running trains, although attempting it then wasn't prudent.

The train snaked through small villages and thick vegetation as it entered Kerala State, in South India. At the sound of the train, children playing on the tracks scooted aside. Inured to its constant, noisy presence, adults performed daily chores without a glance. I wondered if the waste and fruit peels travelers carelessly tossed landed straight on the thatched huts lining the tracks.

Finally, I was on the home stretch to the seaside town of Trivandrum, the capital of Kerala State. Barely fifteen thousand square miles, Kerala is sandwiched between the Arabian Sea and the lush green mountains of the Western Ghats, where coffee, tea, rubber, cardamom, cloves, and other spices are grown. When teak and rosewood trees—the world's best timber—are legally felled, trained elephants transport them down the mountains. Kerala has exotic fish from its extensive backwaters, and tropical vegetables and fruits. It rains for almost nine months, with two annual monsoons eroding the mountain soil and carrying it downriver.

• • •

Despite being a busy and vital hub, the Central Railway Station in Trivandrum had only one platform. As the train neared the station, passengers jockeyed to be first, only to find me blocking their way, having occupied the steps as I usually did when I couldn't get a seat in the compartment. No one dared push past an army officer in uniform, least of all an injured one.

I spotted my father and two sisters amid the buzzing crowd. Overwhelmed with joy, I hurried toward them.

My father stood transfixed. "My God, *Monu!*" he cried, endearingly addressing me as "darling son" in our native Malayalam. "What happened to you?" He was expecting the twenty-year-old sturdy man who had left home a year earlier—not a wounded, weathered soldier.

I put my arm lovingly around his shoulders. "I'll tell you everything, *Achachan*," I said, referring to him as Father. "Don't worry. I'm all right."

My sisters couldn't hold back their tears. "*Kochetta*, what happened?" they insisted, addressing me fondly as the younger of their two elder brothers.

"I'm okay, *Molu*," I replied, calling them "my beloved girls." I hugged them tightly and kissed their cheeks.

Questions followed questions.

How did I get injured?

Why hadn't I written to them all these months?

How long was I going to stay?

It saddened me that I had no gifts. I usually brought them *salwars* and colorful shawls from local markets of recently visited cities. Once, I gave my mother a Kashmiri sari that she would treasure for the rest of her life.

"Thank God your mother isn't here to see you in this condition," Achachan said, shaking his head. She was in the US, working at the National Bureau of Standards in Washington, DC, after a two-year postdoctoral fellowship in physics at New York University.

"Yes. *Ammachi* would have been so upset. Where's Bijoy?" I asked, referring to my brother, older by two years.

"There isn't room in the car—he's waiting at home," my father replied.

Our driver, Joseph, who had been with us for over twenty years, reached for my large suitcase. "It's not good to see you like this," he said worriedly.

Touched by his concern, I patted his shoulder.

"You're finally going to see Bella Vista, Kochetta," Vinita said excitedly, referring to our recently constructed house.

"I can't wait. Is it beautiful?" I asked, settling into the back seat of the car. Rolling down the window, I greedily took in the smells and sights of my hometown. Nothing had changed since I had last been there. Old red-brick government buildings marked much of the city, a striking reflection of the official bureaucracy that had been in place for years.

We turned onto the grand road leading to the former Maharaja's palace in the upscale Kowdiar area of Trivandrum, lined with traditional British metal streetlamps. Sitting atop a quarter-acre property was our elegant two-story house, painted a glorious shade of rose pink with contrasting white trim.

I sprinted up the rosewood stairs to see my room, next to Bijoy's. It was furnished to my liking, with a wooden cupboard and cot. I stepped onto the expansive terrace and scanned the view. The ocean beckoned in the distance.

As news of my injury spread, anxious relatives and friends dropped by. "God saved you," one of my aunts said, reverently making the sign of the cross on my forehead and praying softly under her breath.

"How did you live there, *Aniyan*?" Bijoy asked, referring to me by my pet name, which meant the younger of two brothers in our native language. Having spent his entire life in tropical Kerala, he couldn't fathom how I had endured the extreme cold for months.

"Do you think we can repel another attack?" Achachan inquired in a serious tone.

I reassured everyone that we could stop the Chinese from breaking through our defenses, but I secretly worried our outdated weapons might not be a match for their modern army.

"Were you afraid of the Chinese, Kochetta?" Lekha asked one evening as we strolled along the beach.

Vinita inquired, "Did you ever shoot and kill anyone?" She scanned my face closely. She probably couldn't imagine her doting brother harming someone, even an enemy.

It was a joy to have the girls pepper me with questions. I regretted that my days in the army had kept me away from them. I enjoyed spending time with them, whether it was picking them up from school in our car, shopping, or going to the movies. Happy memories like these with my family had sustained me while I was away.

. . .

Our family tells the story that my paternal grandmother's ancestors had likely married Syrians who were among the first foreigners to have arrived in Northern Kerala from the land of Jesus Christ. Ancient churches in Kerala, particularly those of the Jacobite Syrian faith, are as old as Christianity. It is said that during his stay in Kerala, St. Thomas converted some local Nambudiris of the Malabar region from their faith to be followers of Jesus. Achachan's sharp features and coveted fair complexion were probably the result of a Syrian intermarriage to a native.

Achachan was the eldest of seven children born to a rural landowner in Northern Kerala, who grew coconuts and rice on the outskirts of a quaint, sleepy village called Ayyampilly. My father wasn't sure of his birth date because no one had recorded it. As a result, when he was first admitted to school, the authorities assessed his age and assigned a birth date based on his physical appearance.

One of two siblings who had attended college, he was among the first lawyers in Kerala State to earn a master's degree, which later helped him become a professor. His understanding of the world beyond his village was limited to what he had observed while studying at Banaras Hindu University in North India, where he was discriminated against for being a Christian from the South.

Even though Achachan was dignified, his studied manner intimidated no one. Fluent in English, he had a refined oratorical style; however, a pronounced stammer severely handicapped him, especially when he argued court cases. He nevertheless bravely fought his way through this disability, first as a lawyer and later as a college lecturer.

Ammachi's father, whom we called *Appachan*, was born in Kumarakom, a remote village on Vembanad Lake in the backwaters of Kerala. He had risen from modest means to the prestigious position of a High Court judge of Kerala State. His accomplishments enabled him to marry Ammachi's mother, the daughter of my great-grandfather, who held the highly respected title of *Rao Sahib*, meaning "king leader." Awarded by the Viceroy of British India, this honor was bestowed on those who rendered faithful service or contributed to public welfare.

The family joke was that Achachan had married Ammachi, an urbanite, to advance his career with Appachan's help. As an ambitious young man, Achachan perhaps saw marriage as a stepping stone for his legal career, even though my mother and her sister were "unmarriageable" because their mother was suffering from an unknown, dreaded disease.

Grandmother's illness progressed over a decade, her body ravaged by terrible sores, her skin sticking to the bedsheet when she turned over on her side. Some believed she had contracted leprosy in her early twenties from a beggar who frequented her place for food. Because she was given mercury injections, it seems that whatever her illness, it had likely been aggravated by poor medical treatment. Bedridden and kept in a secluded section of the house for much of her married life until her death, she became a living ghost.

My grandmother wouldn't touch her children or let them be close to her. Ammachi couldn't recall ever being held or kissed by her. She told me that just once, on her wedding day, her mother stretched out her hand and made a sign of the cross on her forehead.

"Every evening when my father returned home from court, he would go straight to her room and pick her up, wrapped in the bedsheet. Those in the living room watched as he carried her in his arms up the winding stairs to his upstairs bedroom. Soon, we could hear their resounding laughter as he recounted his humorous and sarcastic exchanges with lawyers who appeared before him in court. Sometimes, we overheard her chastising him for the arrogant way he treated junior lawyers. In those moments together, they found their joy," Ammachi recalled.

Shortly after my parents' wedding in 1941, Ammachi's mother passed away. To everyone's surprise, Appachan remarried soon after. Ammachi resented that another woman had taken her mother's place so quickly. She didn't understand then that her father needed a woman's care and companionship, especially in his later years, when his children had married and made their own homes. Grandfather grew angry toward his children for their open disapproval of his new wife, and a lasting rift developed.

Those were difficult days for the country as well. Famines were frequent, and over the radio, the government announced rice rationing, limiting how much a family could purchase from local shops. We were used to wholesome rice grown in Kerala, but when shortages arose elsewhere, our rice was shipped out, and we settled for macaroni imported from the United States.

Ammachi struggled to manage our household expenses with her paltry salary teaching physics at the local women's college, but when things turned desperate, she reached out to her father, despite fearing that he might not help. He promptly replied, "Tell your husband to pay for it!" His terse words conveyed his annoyance at the request from his daughter, who had shown resentment toward him.

Achachan struggled to establish himself, though the state capital offered aspiring lawyers opportunities to secure business contacts and develop their practice. Unable to get steady clients to earn enough to support the family, Achachan swallowed his pride and approached his father, requesting a small sum to clear bills. Instead of the hoped-for help, he received a curt handwritten note: "Don't stretch your legs before you sit"—an old Indian proverb meaning that one should live within his means.

My father was humiliated. Grandfather disapproved of borrowing from anyone, and he did not understand that Achachan had many expenses, especially as a lawyer living in the city. Unwilling to seek a job outside his profession, his financial condition worsened by the day.

Eventually, we moved 130 miles north up the coast to Cochin, a major commercial center, where Achachan sought better work prospects. Large populations of Christians and Jews lived in Cochin, and the city is home to one of the world's oldest synagogues. Locals were pleased to discover that Achachan was from Northern Kerala, which they surmised by his family name, Mazhuvencheril Parambath. But Achachan didn't succeed as a practicing lawyer in Cochin, either. I wonder if his stammer or restrained nature had something to do with it. He might have succeeded if he had received a helping hand from someone who referred clients to him. As the family struggled, he received an offer of a lecturer position at the law college back in Trivandrum; so, once again, the family moved back.

Ammachi took up teaching at the Government College for Women in Trivandrum. Women from wealthy and middle-class families didn't work outside their homes then, but Ammachi was determined to pursue higher studies for a promising career. With no formal PhD programs in physics in Kerala at the time, Ammachi submitted her dissertation to three European universities for evaluation. She was awarded the degree, becoming the second woman in India to obtain a doctorate in physics.

I was blissfully oblivious to our parents' hardships. They shielded us from their worries by remaining outwardly content and happy. They neither spoiled us by pretending to be rich nor restricted us by implying we were poor. Our parents kept our spirits and needs balanced, and the freedoms they afforded us nurtured the independence I prized in the years to come.

• • •

My parents settled into teaching positions, and life became manageable. Bijoy and I enjoyed the comforts of our modest home, which consisted of two rooms and a kitchen where cooking was done with firewood. Bijoy's and my bedroom had a round dining table for the four of us. Our parents' bedroom had a wooden wardrobe called an *almirah*, which held Achachan's court papers and clothes. I have no idea how he ever found anything in there.

A large bamboo mat hung in front of the veranda. Ammachi rolled it up every morning to admit light and rolled it back down by noon to keep the heat out. Old homes in tropical Kerala were typically designed around a central courtyard that opened to the sky, letting in fresh air, sunlight, and rain, and ours was no different. A few yards behind the house was a well and a bathroom with an adjoining toilet that didn't have running water.

Since labor was cheap, we employed two servants who tended to us children and helped with house cleaning, fetching well water, washing clothes, and buying groceries from the local open market. With Ammachi's help, the younger servant cooked. She was happy to join Bijoy and me in the evenings as we chased a rubber ball or played cricket with a coconut-branch bat.

My young life was all about play, fun, and mischief. I had enough energy and curiosity to try my mother's patience. To juggle her duties at home and as a college lecturer, she sent me off at five to a nearby school. She was so desperate to be rid of me for at least a few hours that she changed my birth date, moving it forward by one year to make me eligible for first grade. Certain that my rambunctious five-year-old self would fail and repeat the year, my mother was pleasantly surprised when I was promoted to the next grade.

"Look at this fellow. How could he possibly have passed? The boy plays all the time and never studies!" she exclaimed.

Our simple pleasures were watching black-and-white television and listening to Hindi and English music and cricket commentary on the radio. During test matches, our ears were glued to the radio for five days of cricket commentary broadcasting on Radio Colombo or the BBC. Bharath Vani aired classical regional music, but the weak signal made it barely audible.

Evening entertainment occasionally included card games at neighbors' homes, where some revealed their stingy habits. One family set out a plate with fewer sweets than the number of guests. My mother would whisper, "*Idukanda,*" meaning "don't take," which was hard for me to obey. We were compelled to decline politely to avoid the awkward moment of the last guest going without. Later at home, Ammachi would laugh at their miserly ways and tease me for staring gluttonously at the sweets I couldn't have.

On weekends, we frequently went to the beach five miles away. Ammachi would pack a picnic of meat cutlets, biscuits, and fresh bread. After frolicking in the waves, we would sit on a large mat spread out on the warm sand, enjoy snacks, and watch the sunset over the sea.

In the distance, returning fishermen called out to their wives and families waiting with baskets to take the day's catch to the city market before dawn. The men dragged their *vallam*—wooden canoes that could barely seat two people—and tethered them to coconut trees lining the shore or to jutting rocks to keep the incoming tides from carrying them away. There, the boats remained until the wee hours of the following day when they were once again steered out to sea.

Ammachi also took Bijoy and me for evening walks to the public gardens, where a group of local musicians played drums and flutes. I chased dragonflies and butterflies, keeping my captives in a glass jar. I was disappointed they survived only a day or two, no matter how often I tried feeding them sugar water. Ammachi disapproved of what I was doing and told me it was cruel.

"You must let them free. Every creature has the right to live, Monu," she explained.

She would sit me beside her on the wooden bench in the park and talk about the virtues she considered essential, especially humility. "False or pretentious humility is worse than the absence of humility," she would caution us. As the night turned dark, she would direct my gaze to the glorious, starry night and say, "The universe is enormous and deep. There are hundreds and millions of stars and planets beyond what our eyes can see."

I didn't realize that my mother was trying to inspire me to be curious about science, physics, and the mysteries of our planet. She urged me to think imaginatively, see beyond the obvious, and appreciate the universe's wonders. Talking about the kind of person she wanted me to be, she often emphasized truthfulness and humility. She seldom talked about my progress in studies but showed interest in my school activities and motivated me. The lessons I learned from her and the values she instilled in me have lasted my lifetime.

• • •

While in middle school, every day, Bijoy and I set off after breakfast carrying our backpacks. Unable to afford shoes, we walked barefoot in the scorching sun, avoiding the scalding, liquefied tar on the road that stuck to the soles of our feet.

At school, groups of boys routinely battled each other. Sometimes, my friends and I would confront that week's "enemy" and their friends; other times, there was hand-to-hand combat. After every field hockey match against St. Joseph's, their team sent out their gang to fight us if they lost. Being an outstanding hockey player, Bijoy was a prime target. He relied on me to defend him, even though I always failed in my combat against him. Coming home from the field with a black eye, I still felt great pride in having protected my brother.

Then came the most miserable part of my day: settling down with him for homework. Bijoy was studious; he never looked up from his books to see what I was doing. In no time at all, I would be snoring. Sometimes, to my bad luck, my mother or father would catch me napping with my head on my palm in a pathetic attempt to hide my slumber. Achachan rarely raised his voice, but Ammachi's furious scolding jolted me awake: "If you keep this up, you'll be sweeping Bijoy's house and cleaning his latrine when you grow up."

Despite spending more time playing than studying, I still achieved good grades on tests by cramming just before an exam and guessing what questions would likely be on it. Still, Ammachi was unsatisfied with my academic performance. If I got a ninety-five in math, she would ask, "What happened to the other five?"

I longed to be at the center of things, and I begged to become an altar boy, reasoning that it might make the boring church service more tolerable. But the priest quickly regretted his decision to accept me. I couldn't stand still for long, and once, I enthusiastically swung the incense-filled thurible so high it nearly hit his face. "This boy is no good," he declared to my mother, releasing me from my spiritual duties.

Ours was not a particularly religious household, yet I remember annual visits with my mother to the cemetery to pluck weeds around my grandmother's grave. "My mother suffered for all of us, so nothing bad will ever happen to us, our children, or our grandchildren," she would say. It surprised me to hear her, a scientist, speaking of karma as though she believed in it. As a family, we prayed every evening before dinner and went to church on Sundays, although we never discussed heaven, hell, or other Christian beliefs. But something happened one day that altered my outlook toward religion forever.

A dispute arose between two factions in our local church. One group broke away and established a separate congregation. The *ramban*, a bishop-to-be, came to our house with some dissenting rebels to seek a donation.

Achachan told them he wasn't interested in a new church.

Angered, the ramban admonished, "God will certainly punish you!"

"Who are you to speak for God? Take off your gown and cap, go to the slums, and work for the poor," my father replied indignantly.

I understood he wasn't indifferent toward poor people's living condition, even though we hadn't done much to help them. I had often heard my parents talk about service to those in need as an essential duty. This incident profoundly affected my emerging views on religion and social work.

CHAPTER 3

AYYAMPILLY

As CHILDREN, WE ANTICIPATED spending the summer with Achachan's parents in Ayyampilly, one of the exotic Vypeen Islands in Kerala, raised from the sea from volcanic eruptions seventy million years ago. It was a long journey from the southern city of Trivandrum to the islands across the coastal town of Ernakulam in the north.

One could reach the Vypeen Islands only by hiring local fishermen and their *kattumaram*, a raft made from three or more tree trunks tied together. If travelers came by car, the fishermen linked two or three such rafts and covered them with planks for a wooden platform. It was a tricky business to drive a car onto this rickety surface, despite the boatmen's careful guidance. Armed with long bamboo poles, four boatmen expertly plied the brackish backwaters as they pushed off from the head of the bay and passed several verdant islands en route to Ayyampilly.

Upon reaching the island, we would pile back into our car and drive along muddy roads. After a certain point beyond which no vehicle could pass, we walked on dark topsoil, decaying coconut shells, and wild vegetation. A labyrinth of small channels and larger canals crisscrossed the sandy island, with footbridges made of long coconut trunks. The scariest canal was over ten feet wide. Using our luggage for balance, we wobbled across the narrow makeshift bridge over snake-infested waters. Bijoy and I thought of ourselves as brave high-wire artists, though we were anything but graceful, and the village boys laughed heartily at us—the tottering, clumsy city folk.

At the end of this arduous journey, we were relieved to see my grandparents' house. It could accommodate their only daughter, six sons, wives and children, and a gaggle of relatives who came to spend the summer.

On the property's border, the servants lived in huts that Grandfather had built for them. They hailed from historically poor families, called *Pulayas*, who had likely served the family for generations as kitchen helpers, sweepers, and field laborers. For reasons I didn't understand back then, we children were not allowed to visit those huts scattered across the extensive property at a reasonable distance from the main house.

Another clan of dependents, called *Parayas*, lived at the corners of the property. For centuries, the Pulayas and the Parayas were treated as slaves: bought, sold, and shared among their owners' family members. In addition to working hard all day in the fields, they performed jobs considered degrading, like cleaning communal latrines.

During my father's younger days, the underclass customarily announced their arrival loudly when they approached the landowner's residence, remaining at least one hundred feet away. When their masters presented themselves, the underclass removed the thin cotton shawls from their shoulders, tied them around their waists, and bowed subserviently, nearly touching the ground, saying, "*Adian*," meaning "I am an untouchable."

The upper castes did not allow men and women who belonged to the poorest stratum of society—the *Dalits*, formerly called the "untouchables"—to enter their houses. Their one daily meal was composed of rice and a watery vegetable curry, served on banana leaves, either by the well or in the shade of nearby trees.

Resigned to their fate, these unfortunates fed themselves mostly on what their owners doled out. They were forbidden to touch household utensils for fear of contaminating their masters' food. When a cow or bull died, they dried some of the meat to be eaten later and skinned the animal to sell its hide. None of my family or our circle of friends ever openly acknowledged or discussed this indignant practice of subservience. As a youngster, I accepted it as the way life was, always had been, and always would be.

· · ·

In the late 1950s, communist parties with Stalinist and Leninist philosophies emerged in Kerala. A spirit of revolution brought people into the streets as rallies and demonstrations swept through the state. Mao Zedong's philosophy of empowering the working class added fodder to political and social upheaval as peasants realized their power and demanded control they had never enjoyed under the Maharajas who had previously ruled the state.

A controversial piece of legislation in Kerala State required that landlords divide and distribute their land among the peasants who lived and worked there. This sudden and unexpected land reform, a just measure, empowered peasants who had remained landless to break free from their masters' domination and gain opportunities.

Thus, my paternal grandfather had to relinquish ownership of a significant portion of his land and distribute it among fifty or more peasant families who had faithfully worked for him and his ancestors for generations. Panicked, he struck deals to buy back a portion of the land he had transferred to laborers under the new law. By paying small sums, he secured twenty to thirty acres, enough to bequeath an inheritance to his sons, who supervised the fieldwork and made their living off it.

All the sons, except my father, gathered in Grandfather's room every evening. I watched them assemble in submissive, respectful postures—shoulders slightly bent and arms folded across their chests. While questioning them about the day's work, Grandfather would roll fresh tobacco leaves, lime paste, and areca nut, pop it into his mouth, chew, and transfer it from one cheek to the other with his tongue. When done, he would spit the mass into his polished brass spittoon. A servant would refill a bronze container with fresh tobacco leaves and lay it by his armrest.

The sons dutifully updated their father on the coconut harvest, the state of the paddies, or his other considerable ventures. They said nothing that might upset him. They handed over money from selling produce in the local market. Grandfather would count the cash and carefully stash it in the small jute bag he hung around his waist, under his shirt. As the family patriarch, Grandfather had absolute authority in all affairs affecting the family's welfare. I never saw anyone argue with him on any matter.

Grandfather would return at noon from teaching two hours at the local primary school. Grandmother and we children were free to enter his chamber, unlike the other adults who had to be summoned or invited. Sometimes, Bijoy and I curiously peeked into

Grandfather's room to find him lying comfortably in his wooden easy chair, his legs raised high on the long armrests. With a loving smile, he would gesture us to approach him. Gently holding our hands, he would inquire about our day.

"Why are you so dirty?" Grandfather would ask, noticing our muddy legs or the soiled clothes we had tried so hard to clean before coming indoors.

If I told him I had spent the day playing in the fields, he would ask if I had climbed any trees or caught any crabs. If I had, as a reward, he would call for Grandmother to give me some homemade sweets. He seemed to enjoy our interactions, even my foolish answers to his questions.

· · ·

Grandmother had a commanding presence paired with effortless elegance. She dressed impeccably, in a white *mundu* with a matching loose blouse over her ample bosom, which sagged from nursing her seven children, each for over two years. The heavy gold earrings she wore stretched long holes in her earlobes.

I never knew exactly how old she was; Grandmother might have been giving birth from fifteen until she was forty. The age difference between my father, the eldest son, and the youngest was about twenty-three years. Grandmother was a formidable delegator, who brooked no laziness. As quartermaster and drill instructor, she barked orders to the servants, closely monitoring the cooking and cleaning. The household was a tightly run ship, with her steering everyone's daily activities. She had a considerable crew of daughters-in-law to command.

For women, life here was all about childbearing, household chores, and serving their men under Grandmother's hawklike gaze.

She sequestered them in a separate block of the family's traditional house, called *nalukettu*, where they remained during their menstrual cycle. During the latter part of their pregnancies, they were sent to their parents' homes. After giving birth, they remained there for twenty-eight days, with servants or midwives attending.

The daughters-in-law belonged to well-to-do families from nearby villages. Ammachi was the only urbanite among them. All had wed into my grandparents' family through arranged marriages. To Grandmother, their families' wealth meant little. A woman's duty was to her husband and children, and Grandmother ensured that every daughter-in-law lived up to this expectation.

As the eldest son's wife, Ammachi was highly regarded. Grandmother didn't scold her directly. She would mutter under her breath loudly enough for my mother to hear that Grandmother was unhappy or dissatisfied with her. "Look at this city girl! She doesn't know the first thing about running a house," Grandmother would mutter. If she spotted Achachan heading toward the kitchen area, Grandmother would immediately lower her voice to avoid trouble for disrespecting her eldest son's wife.

Grandmother mocked my mother for having a darker complexion than her husband, though hers was no different from most others, as many South Indians have the dark skin common to people of Dravidian lineage.

"You're too white for me!" Ammachi lamented to my father, wishing they could trade complexions.

"You are not dark," Achachan would reassure her.

Ammachi didn't seem good enough for Grandmother, who never paid her a compliment. Achachan would listen sympathetically when Ammachi complained to him about his mother, but he wouldn't respond, and she didn't expect him to. She never provoked her husband to react or interfere in any way. Although he enjoyed the prerogative as the firstborn son to confront any woman in the household, including his mother, he never brought up his wife's unhappiness with either of his parents.

Grandfather would listen patiently to Grandmother's tirades about her daughters-in-law, but his quiet dignity prevented him from saying anything rude or hurtful about his sons' wives. Out of respect, the daughters-in-law didn't converse with Grandfather, and he wouldn't ask them anything directly, either. Grandmother was the intermediary if he wanted the women to do something for him.

The precedents dictating the family hierarchy were firmly established, and peace in the household was maintained by strictly adhering to them. No one dared question them. Perhaps that was why there were no loud or heated confrontations. Grandmother was the only one who could raise her voice. While the rules differed for men and women, as a child, I was oblivious to their unfairness.

· · ·

No fewer than ten people were tasked with preparing the day's meals. Each day, a servant went into the backyard to collect eggs, catch four or five roosters, and cut and clean the birds before handing the raw meat to another servant waiting to start cooking.

Cooking was done in large bronze or brass vessels and clay pots, all handmade by visiting tradespeople. The kitchen fire burned on firewood and dry coconut stems, belching out clouds of choking smoke that engulfed the entire room. Women weren't allowed near the fire; that work was entrusted to two male cooks who had been with my grandparents for years.

Grandfather took his meals alone in his room, and Grandmother served him special dishes the rest of us didn't get. The children were served next. I would look to see if they favored Bijoy, the first grandson, with a better portion. He was always served the best part of the fish or meat during meals, which I wasn't happy about.

After feeding and sending the children out to play, Grandmother served her sons their breakfast. Achachan sat at the head of the table with his brothers lined up on either side. The others wouldn't sit down to eat until my father, the eldest brother, had seated himself. Female servants and daughters-in-law scurried around, carrying food-laden vessels into the dining room and returning empty ones to the kitchen for replenishment. Wives tried to sneak their husbands a little extra when Grandmother wasn't looking.

At last, the women gathered around the table and shared what remained after the men and children had eaten. But even then, Grandmother wouldn't leave them in peace. "You are eating too much! You didn't serve the men enough," she would scold. The women would start preparing lunch soon after the breakfast dishes were cleared.

Bijoy and I took advantage of Achachan's status as the most senior of his siblings to anoint ourselves as the chieftains for our generation. Except for Mary and Varghese, all other cousins were much too young to give us company. Our leadership status was enhanced because we were urbanites, more sophisticated than our country cousins. Despite being the eldest cousin, Bijoy rarely wielded his authority.

I was my boss, with my secret agenda and bravado, trying to turn everything into a grand adventure. We competed with our cousins to see who could catch the most mice with two large traps, using roasted coconut pieces with a strong odor for bait. With all its dark nooks and crannies, Grandfather's house had no shortage of rodents, especially in the attic storage room full of grains, coconuts, and plantain bunches that were hung by ropes tied to the ceiling.

Unlike us, laborers' children grew up with nature; they were familiar with climbing tall coconut trees barefoot to harvest the fruits, fishing in canals and rivers, and working in paddies. They returned in the afternoon with plenty of catches and produce for the day. Everything appeared natural and easy for them; their seemingly carefree, languid lifestyle was simple yet enchanting. Like them, Bijoy and I tried to climb the tall coconut trees or chase the large, stately herons that feasted on the banks of the backwaters. We never succeeded.

The day's excitement was in discovering nature and its creatures—colorful butterflies on flowers, tiny insects on plants, chameleons running up coconut trees to escape us, scary spiders in every corner, water snakes swimming beside fish in shallow canals, an army of black ants fighting red ants, and beautiful birds on tree branches. We knew what to avoid, like walking into beehives or getting bitten by scorpions.

On sunny days, a few crawfish or lobsters emerged from the waters during high tide to nap on the muddy shores, but they were too big for my small, bare hands. Small crabs didn't scare me as much. As soon as I spied a big one, I tried to sweep it away from the banks of the canal with a stick, but the clever creature would rush back into its hole or the water before I could get near enough.

When the sun was too hot, we would sit quietly under the shade of trees, surveying the fishermen's boats setting out to sea in small *vallams*, boats manually rowed by two or more men. They would return bearing abundant catches in the iridescent hours of dawn. The locals placed nets in the canals to snag a bounty of shrimp when the sea receded at low tide. They flung the excess from the fish harvest to fertilize coconut groves, giving the air a distinct reek and attracting countless flies.

Days seemed to pass quickly, and we were forever looking forward to the next meal. Upon returning to the house, we attempted to wash off the slush that covered us up to our waists. Seeing us trying to clean up hastily, Ammachi and our aunts would scold us: "Look at your clothes! Do you have to go so deep into the mud?"

The servants lined us up naked on the pavement encircling the well, doused us with buckets of water, and scrubbed us with coconut fiber. One elderly servant took these responsibilities far too seriously; if I dared protest that her scrubbing hurt, she scrubbed even harder. She had worked for my grandparents for over twenty years, so all the mothers listened to her. I had no choice but to keep still and patiently endure this well-intentioned torture.

This practice was altered on Sunday mornings. Our mothers helped the female servants to oil our hair and bodies and stood us naked once again in the sun for an hour before they bathed us in water, wrapped us in cotton towels, and carried us into the house so our feet wouldn't collect dirt. These practices continued until we were old enough to wash ourselves in a private bamboo shed adjoining the house.

The daily ritual I hated most at Ayyampilly was the morning ablutions before sunrise. Stories of ghosts, monsters, and snakes told to us by relatives preyed on my mind as we picked our seemingly never-ending way through the coconut grove to the family's make-shift toilet at the farthest end of the field. Afraid of snakes, I let Varghese lead us, and he happily obliged, excited to be in charge. If the matter proved too urgent for the long trek, Ammachi allowed us to use the coconut grove. Later in the day, the bright sun acted as a natural disinfectant for the stench.

The ghastly dug-out toilet pit was about six feet deep and half full of filthy water and human waste. It stank horrifically, and gigantic flies buzzed noisily around it. We straddled the two coconut branches over it while praying that we didn't lose our balance and fall into this disgusting hellhole. I tried to avoid the morning ritual by valiantly holding my bowels in check for two or three days, but we ate so much food that this became impossible.

Without major illnesses to worry about, there was no need for a trained doctor in the village. As far as I knew, no one suffered from serious ailments or trauma; everyone appeared outwardly balanced. No one in the family took illnesses seriously; it was just the way of rural life. For us city folks, however, the unfiltered salt water gave us perpetual diarrhea, forcing us to rely on herbal medicine. Achachan occasionally took a ferry back to Cochin to fetch large containers of fresh drinking water. Everyone sympathized with us city folks who couldn't stomach the salty water. I wasn't spared other problems, either.

Ammachi told me the story of the severe eye infection I contracted at three years old. My eyes oozed with thick, yellowish pus, and I could barely open them. Throughout the night, she anxiously wiped my eyes with her sari and brushed away the cockroaches drawn to the infection while praying for my eyesight to be spared. At daybreak, she begged Achachan's cousin to take me to a doctor in the nearby city. He carried me on his shoulders and hurried across the bay to a doctor who saved my eyes.

• • •

As evening set in, the servants would light kerosene lamps in every room. A special lamp with a ball of brightly burning filament was lit in Grandfather's room. At eight o'clock, the children and adults would gather in his room to pray, the young ones standing beside their parents. Grandfather would remain seated in his chair. He or Grandmother would recite from memory or read in Malayalam from the family Bible. The rest followed their lead in a saintly chorus.

If any of the women failed to follow the prayer lines, Grandmother would scold them later. "God won't protect you, even if he wants to," she would tell them. These poor women couldn't seem to do anything right. They had no choice but to stay alert and fight the temptation to doze off. No one ever rebuked the men for not keeping up with the recitation or for falling half asleep—after all, they had worked in the fields. Never mind that the women had been on their feet all day attending to the entire family's needs.

I looked around, eagerly seeking ways to doze unnoticed while standing during this tedious ritual. As the worship progressed in earnest, hymns and chanting prayers lulled me into a trance. My swaying body sometimes gave me away, and a grown-up would pinch my arms or twist my ears. Sometimes, I woke up on my own with a jolt and joined in the chorus, desperately hoping to cover up my sin. But I only further embarrassed myself by singing too loud or out of tune.

At last, we dispersed for supper, famished from the day's play. We children sat around the dining table on long benches of thick wooden planks. It would be well after ten o'clock when the women could finally get to eat what was left.

After dinner, the children gathered on the veranda to enjoy the cool night breeze and our uncles' terrifying stories of *dacoits* who terrorized the villagers. It was frightening to learn that dacoits raided wealthy neighborhoods late at night, wielding machetes and sometimes setting homes ablaze. They were looking for grains stored in granaries and cellars, behind thick wooden doors supported by iron bars, just as at Grandfather's house. Most people surrendered rather than fight the attackers, so it was a relief that Grandfather was among the few who could buy protection by paying a group of local men to defend him from attack.

When I recall vacations with my paternal grandparents, only joyful memories come to my mind. I hardly think of the uncomfortable living conditions we had to endure—humid summer nights, sleeping on a mat on the floor, fighting off flies and mosquitoes, and those scary, disgusting early morning routines. Instead, the friendship I cherished with our cousins, marked by shared childhood memories, would last a lifetime.

Our peaceful, healthy lifestyle in Ayyampilly blended with nature. The harmonious give-and-take rhythm within our multigenerational family made life enjoyable for us children. The grown-ups left us alone to roam freely and discover for ourselves the mysteries of nature. Through it all, Ayyampilly exposed me at a young age to rural India, with its caste-based society. I could see that much of Indian society was built on different levels of privileges and duties, and no one seemed to question them. Those experiences would linger in my subconscious and offer me the familiarity I would need with village life years later.

CHAPTER 4

THE MAKING OF
A SOLDIER

MY INTEREST IN THE MILITARY began at age ten. Watching soldiers marching in their green uniforms and heavy boots at my hometown army cantonment, I felt drawn to follow in their choreographed footsteps. I wished upon falling stars, prayed to God, and even offered the holy Virgin Mary a boyish bribe to pass the entrance exam at the National Defense Academy (NDA), a premier officer training institute. My parents and I were overjoyed at my selection in 1961, unaware of what lay ahead.

The NDA occupied several hundred acres in the beautiful, secluded Khadakwasla Valley, commanding a majestic view of its namesake's lake amid the surrounding mountains. Over a dozen hilltops had been leveled to create soccer fields, and bridle paths wound up the slopes for horseback riding.

We enjoyed our meals in a beautiful dining hall with exquisite, solid Burmese teak paneling. In a land as poor as India was then, such opulence seemed out of place. Prime ministers, presidents, and foreign dignitaries occasionally visited, and when they did, we enjoyed traditional delicacies from their native lands. Yet I preferred the homemade sweets Ammachi occasionally mailed me in nicely wrapped packages.

The pain of my first separation from family and the incessant ragging by seniors in the initial months were hard for me. I frequently wrote home, begging my parents to let me return. "I promise to study hard at the college in our hometown," I vowed. My parents wrote back, encouraging me to endure hardship and stay strong.

My fellow cadets hailed from northern states like Punjab and Uttar Pradesh and were physically more robust than I was. Unlike me, nearly all of them had family members in the military and were quite familiar with its ways and its glory. Cadets from South India were seen as docile, perhaps not aggressive enough to be soldiers. The relatively peaceful conditions that the South had enjoyed for centuries had probably shaped our gentle demeanor. After all, the North had repeatedly invaded the South for over two thousand years or so—from Cyrus II, the founder of the Achaemenid Persian Empire in ancient Iran, to Alexander the Great of Greece.

We tended to form friendships with boys from our states, who spoke our native language and shared our customs. I made friends with a senior named Rajan, from the southern state of Madras. He carefully watched over me, ensuring I was okay and protecting me from excessive ragging.

Rajan joined the Air Force after graduating from the NDA. Unlike me, he was a daredevil, with a rebellious, crazy streak. After a few years of training and serving as an Air Force pilot, he flew a military aircraft under a bridge for the sheer thrill of it. He was instantly discharged from service, but I was happy to find out later that, true to character, he had charmed his way back to active duty.

Throughout our training, tardiness was never tolerated. If we were late, the seniors punished us by making us somersault over the gravel. I lost some hair in the initial three months but learned the hard way to be punctual—a habit that would stick with me for the rest of my life.

Our days were filled with the usual academics, but my favorite courses were Battle Strategy and Tactics. The games of my youth were replaced with gymnastics, cross-country hikes, horseback riding, and sailing. One day in gymnastics, I fell from a high bar and hit the lower bar on my way down, badly injuring my thigh. The academy's medical officer placed my leg in a plaster cast and asked me to lift weights with it. When the cast came off a month later, my entire thigh muscle was rock hard yet without agility.

They immediately rushed me to the brigade hospital with better medical facilities. The colonel who examined me diagnosed my condition as myositis ossificans and explained it as having "dead muscles." The hospital sent my parents a telegram informing them that my leg might require amputation. My parents and I were terrified by the possibility of me losing a leg.

To add to my horror, there was no treatment beyond total bed rest. The only hope was that the blood running through my thigh might absorb the clot that had hardened the muscle. Amazingly, the muscle softened in a few weeks, and I could bend my knee a little. The doctor kept me in the hospital for two more months for the muscle to recover.

By the time I was released, my leg had miraculously regained much agility but was still noticeably weak. I worried about losing a semester if I failed the required physical tests: climbing ropes, navigating obstacle courses, and performing mat exercises. Through sheer determination, I met the minimum physical requirements within a month or so and advanced to my last semester in the academy.

Although my performance at the NDA wasn't exactly stellar, I graduated after three years of training and moved on to the Indian Military Academy (IMA) for another year of specialized army training in the tradition of England's prestigious Royal Military Academy, Sandhurst. I was seventeen and did not know then that my star was about to rise and shine.

. . .

By Mussoorie hill station lay a quaint city called Dehradun, where the IMA was located. With my health restored and my spirits up, I trained hard in every activity and performed well. I excelled at marching drills and was among three cadets honored with carrying the academy's flag at the passing-out parade.

As one of the top twenty cadets in my class, I could choose my preferred army branch. Artillery was an easy choice since I didn't want the marching required of infantry. While it was glamorous to be a tank officer, I didn't fancy being stuck inside an armored vehicle. As I had hoped, they assigned me to the 34 Medium Artillery Regiment, which comprised the Maratha soldiers.

I vividly recall marching through the venerable Chetwoode Hall in the Academy's main building and receiving my commission as a second lieutenant at age eighteen. The four years of vigorous training and discipline had taught me valuable lessons like discipline, punctuality, commitment to excellence, and loyalty. My immense pride in wearing a star on each shoulder brought to mind an officer's responsibilities to soldiers, leadership, and courage in the face of danger.

I was disappointed that my parents couldn't witness this momentous occasion, because of the long travel distance. Still, I was keen for them to see me in an officer's uniform, imagining how impressed they would be with my more polished, sophisticated manners and brisk military walk. I was sure everyone would see that my mischievous old self had been replaced somewhat by my newly disciplined ways. My parents were proud to introduce me to neighbors, friends, and relatives as an officer in the artillery—a rare accomplishment among young people in my state.

After a brief vacation, I left for my new posting in northeast India. The regiment was camped in a secluded place on the outskirts of Bomdila, a small tribal settlement nestled at an altitude of eight thousand feet in the eastern ranges of the Himalayas. Anyone would be awed by its mountainous terrain and history. It was through this remote town that the current Dalai Lama crossed on foot in 1959 when he fled from the Chinese persecution of Tibetans.

My regiment's illustrious history dated back to battles fought as part of the British army in the Italian and North African campaigns of World War II. Its official battle cry was "*Shivaji Maharaj Ki Jai*," exhorting victory for Shivaji, the great Maratha warrior of centuries ago. I felt humbled to be joining such a legendary unit.

I wasn't the only officer who had newly arrived at Bomdila. Gupta and Kashyap were also fresh fodder for ragging. I had naively expected my fellow seniors to greet us warmly and considerately, but they didn't give us time even to freshen up. They ordered us to toss our luggage into the assigned tent and report for duty.

At an evening party to celebrate our joining the regiment, the seniors handed us tall glasses of what they said was tea. "Down it in a single gulp. It's the tradition," one of them instructed. Bringing the glass to my lips, I smelled the rum and the deception. I took a few small sips before feigning that the glass had slipped from my hand. The seniors yelled at me for messing up the table. My friends swallowed theirs in one go and were quite drunk within minutes.

Gupta, Kashyap, and I decided we wouldn't let the seniors continue to bully us. Rather than confront them directly, we practiced passive resistance by acting like fools and pretending to misunderstand their instructions. We knew insubordination was an offense, but being stupid wasn't.

Instead of standing at attention in front of the senior barking orders, I plunked down on the floor and removed my boots. "Something is biting my feet, sir!"

"Put those boots back on!" the senior shouted.

We took all the fun out of their ragging until they finally quit. Such silliness aside, I was thrown into leading troops in complex battle simulations and practices for mountain warfare. During overnight marches through hills and valleys, with a fifty-pound bag on my back, I pushed myself to keep up in front, determined to make a good impression on my men. I wanted them to see that the officer assigned to lead them into battle and protect their lives was brave, physically strong, adept, and capable.

The lessons learned from those experiences gave me the confidence to lead my troops and earn their trust and loyalty. My attention to their welfare and winning over their loyalty were the cornerstones of my leadership. I was transparent and direct in my communication and relied on humor to lighten things up. My men knew when I was serious and didn't take advantage of my playful ways. I could tell from their smiles that they were glad to see me whenever we met.

. . .

Barely three months later, Lt. Colonel Surinder Singh, the commanding officer of my regiment, summoned me to his office. I marched in with apprehension and saluted.

"Lieutenant George! I'm sending you to Se La," he began in his crisp yet kind baritone voice. He looked imposing yet gentle, his beard neatly tied and a turban wrapped around his head.

"You must establish the camp, dig the bunkers, and correctly place the gun platforms." He emphasized the need to position the guns behind hills with a clear line of fire toward the strategic route the Chinese army had taken to invade the Tawang–Se La region.

"Yes, sir!" I responded without hesitation.

He promptly dismissed me, and I marched out of the office, feeling confused.

Why had the commanding officer selected me? Had he observed me enough in such a short time to be so confident in my abilities? Or was this just another order to a junior officer? Colonel Singh likely relied on my initial training at the NDA, but I still didn't have the experience to lead a large contingent of soldiers on a risky, critical assignment in unknown terrain. Besides, I didn't even know where Se La was!

In the days that followed, Colonel Singh briefed me further. "Lieutenant George, setting up the position will take many more months. Medium artillery guns had never before been deployed at such a high altitude. When you're ready to receive the guns, the road should be passable for heavy trucks."

Army engineers were using explosives to blast through big boulders and construct a road across high mountains, clearing a path from peak to peak to Se La and beyond. Former trading paths winding through the hills enabled jeeps and light vehicles to pass, but the engineers needed more time to ensure that the road was navigable for hauling large artillery guns to higher altitudes. The first three years of constructing this strategic passage had already claimed the lives of several soldiers in the engineering corps, and the next phase was exceptionally perilous.

We spent two weeks loading our vehicles with supplies while I received training in rock blasting. When the day came for our departure, Colonel Singh stood by the assembly ground with a dignified, serious expression, watching us leave on our arduous journey. I had never imagined that I would be the first officer to take medium-range heavy artillery to the highest battleground on earth.

It took two days to make the ascent, giving our bodies time to acclimate to the dizzying altitude and near-freezing temperatures. The road led us to Se La's breathtakingly exquisite passage, with views of deep valleys and towering mountaintops reaching for the sky. The Nuranang River carried melted ice and snow from mountain slopes and flowed into the large frozen Se La Lake. In every direction, snow-covered rocks and ice stretched out in timeless vastness. It was like coming to the end of the world.

We set up our camp on level ground by the pebble-covered riverbanks at an altitude of over fourteen thousand feet. Camouflaged against snow, each of the ten tents housed twenty men, with just enough space for sleeping bags. When night fell, I huddled in my one-person tent and quickly burrowed in my sleeping bag to warm myself from the excruciating cold.

A small kerosene lamp burned feebly, its glow too weak to cast my shadow. Loud and ominous, the howling wind kept me awake; it was as though the mighty Himalayas were angry with us for having invaded their territory. My insignificance before the grandeur of the mountains only added to my loneliness and fear.

I woke to find my tent buried under thick snow. Thankfully, my young orderly found me and brought a most welcome gift of hot coffee. Swathed head to toe in warm clothing, I emerged to survey the strange surroundings. *Where have I come to?* I asked myself. A blanket of white covered everything as far as I could see. To make matters worse, the thin air severely lacked oxygen, making me gasp for breath while I walked even a short distance. An unshakable feeling of displacement gripped me.

On the second day, I assembled the soldiers outside my tent at 6:30 a.m., per standard military practice. The sun had barely risen, and all of us shivered. I immediately changed our schedule: We would wake two hours later and end our workday an hour before the early sunset. This revised timing boosted the soldiers' spirits and brought some comfort, and they worked twice as hard in the reduced work time.

We prioritized building underground ammunition bunkers and platforms for large-caliber guns and worked feverishly to construct them before deep winter descended. We dug with picks and shovels, but when we encountered boulders, our only option was dynamite. Using crowbars, we broke into solid rock to place guncotton and plastic explosives. All day long, the mountains echoed with deafening detonations. Without heavy machinery, it took at least a dozen soldiers to roll away the enormous chunks of rock loosened by the blasts.

"With all this blasting, we are moving the mighty Himalayas!" I proudly exclaimed.

Subedar Amar, one of the senior soldiers, chuckled. "No, Sahib, the mountains are unconquerable."

After the initial months constructing underground storage for munitions, bunkers for lodging were built, each with funnels to direct air inside. My bunker had a *bukhari*—a traditional drumlike iron cylinder for burning charcoal and wood—to warm me. A hole in the ground under a separate small tent served as a latrine, the snow our toilet paper. I avoided bathing in the bitter cold for two to three weeks at a stretch, but when it could no longer be put off, I would heat enough snow to produce a bucket of water for bathing.

Alone in my tiny tent, tucked inside the sleeping bag, I spent hours imagining the good times when I would be posted elsewhere, hopefully to a warm city. I longed to enjoy the company of my family and friends, drive a fancy car, go to movies, and experience other joys. These distant dreams kept up my spirits and made me long for the good times to come.

Over the next eight months, we prepared for a possible Chinese invasion from the direction of Tawang, the last border town north on the way to Tibet. Cut off from everyone else, we learned little about activities across the border. Rumblings about preparations by the Chinese army to cross the line of control near us and occasional Chinese skirmishes with Indian troops elsewhere kept us nervous and alert. Despite being close to enemy territory, we worried more about surviving the harsh weather than about being attacked.

Eventually, we finished our platforms, and our guns would be set a few miles behind the front line to support our infantry. Incorrect bearings or hills in the line of fire could endanger our soldiers ahead. After ensuring the new base was well prepared, I left for Bomdila to fetch our medium guns from the base camp.

Although the climb from our base camp to Se La was only six thousand feet, we had to navigate miles of newly carved winding roads over mountain ranges. The heavy guns were towed by powerful, eighteen-wheeled Mack Trucks with manual steering wheels. Every truck had a primary driver to steer the wheel and a codriver by his side; another driver stood outside on the running board to assist them.

The codriver pushed the steering wheel while the other pulled, and the main driver controlled the process while making sharp turns. If they couldn't fully navigate a hairpin turn, the driver stopped, rolled back slightly, and repeated the process incrementally. Such maneuvers were dangerous on unpaved roads because the truck could skid, fall off, and plunge into the valley thousands of feet below.

I dispatched men to walk alongside the trucks. If a truck halted, the men would rush to place chocks behind each wheel to prevent it from sliding. They adjusted the chocks to allow the driver to reverse a little when needed. These operations required immense concentration and coordination to avoid critical mistakes.

Once a truck got so close to the road's edge that the earth gave way underneath one of its wheels. "Stop. Look where the tire is!" a soldier accompanying the truck shouted, waving frantically. The situation was precarious. The gun could fall off the side of the road; worse, if the truck turned over, the drivers would surely die.

"I can't make the turn!" The main driver was too frightened to try navigating any farther. His codrivers were equally terrified.

"Don't worry. Stay calm," I called out, running from my jeep to his truck. Concealing my fear, I shouted instructions to the men placing the chocks. Climbing onto the running board beside the main driver, I yelled instructions into his ear, directing him how far to turn the wheels and when to inch forward and backward. I held my breath as he nervously gripped the wheel.

Finally, after many to-and-fro maneuvers, he made the turn. The soldiers clapped and cheered, "Sahib is a hero!" I laughed with relief and embarrassment and signaled the soldiers to continue our journey, lumbering up the serpentine route to our forward position at Se La.

My ability to uphold the soldiers' confidence was tested on other occasions when fierce winds, heavy snowfalls, and subzero temperatures threatened our camp. When a vehicle broke down, the driver would call us on the wireless for help. If the signals couldn't reach anyone, the convoy could be in danger of exposure. Once, I had to bear freezing temperatures all night when my jeep was stuck in heavy snow by a mountain pass.

I unreservedly embraced the responsibility of looking after soldiers who were decades older than me and attending to their safety and comfort. I cared for them deeply and believed they cared for me even more. The unforgiving climate, demanding work, and extreme isolation bolstered our mental and physical toughness while nurturing camaraderie. We were connected by the fraternal bond of brothers-in-arms.

. . .

Our base camp at Bomdila delivered food rations every week but was often delayed due to bad weather. Meat supplies frequently ran out, and we made do mostly with lentils. Luckily, on our way up to Se La, I had noticed flocks of chickens and herds of goats in a Monpa tribal village below our camp at an altitude of about nine thousand feet.

"Let's go and get some fresh chicken for dinner," I cheerfully proposed one morning.

"Sahib, we'll make you a good curry with tasty masala!" laughed one of the subedars.

We parked the jeep at the village entrance. Clusters of huts with mud walls and thatched bamboo roofs dotted the mountain slopes, frozen in tranquility and time. There appeared to be very little activity. Yak and sheep grazed among the chickens beside a barley field, and the village ended at the edge of a deep valley covered with dense conifers.

I didn't know the Monpa's language or what to expect, but I knew not to show up unannounced and arrogantly demand chicken. With a smile and hand gestures, I approached the first person I met and asked for the village chief. He directed me to a rugged hut where women and young girls were weaving woolen shawls outside. I had my customary pistol, and the two soldiers with me carried rifles, but we had nothing to fear—these locals were welcoming.

The chief bade me sit on a handwoven mat on the mud floor of his hut. His friendly demeanor and constant smile put me at ease. With hand gestures, I quickly overcame the language barrier to transact our business. Pointing to the XXX labels on the rum bottles I had earlier brought along from the base camp to emphasize their high quality and then pointing to his chickens, I made my offer clear.

The chief ordered an older woman, probably his wife, to bring me a drink. Pouring from a metal jar, he generously filled my cup with a homemade liquor called *ara*. When his attention was elsewhere, I emptied the glass over my shoulder, fearing it might sicken me. Gentle brown eyes watched me from behind the curtains, and I heard soft giggling.

I asked the chief for a few chickens, and he turned to a male villager. In short order, six chickens were brought, but I thought two bottles of rum would have paid for more than a half dozen. Despite being disappointed, I wasn't about to haggle and appear ungrateful.

At the camp, the soldiers laughed hard at hearing that I had gone to the village and returned with chickens, as promised. "Sahib has become a Monpa," they joked. That evening, the senior-ranked soldiers and I enjoyed a dinner of chapattis and parathas with delicious, fresh chicken curry.

Subsequently, we made four more trips to the Monpa village for chickens. On one such visit, the entire village was assembled in an open field. Both men and women were chanting prayers, their attention transfixed on something laid out in the field's center. An elder explained in broken Hindi, "We're preparing to take a dead man's body to the river."

Following the religious custom among this Monpa Buddhist tribe, they cut the corpse into 108 pieces—equal to the beads in a Buddhist rosary—and placed them on a wooden plank covered with flowers. The men carried the plank half a mile to the river, and the women followed, chanting hymns. At the bank, the villagers threw the pieces into the river for the fish to feed on, like the Parsis leaving their dead in the Tower of Silence for the vultures.

I was awed by their ritual. *This is a much nobler way to dispose of bodies. What is the use of burning or burying our dead?* I thought. The simplicity of their lives and the spirituality in their death led me to reflect on the purpose of my being. Lessons like these went into a diary I had been carrying for over a year before coming to Se La. I had sketched in it my interpretations of virtues like truthfulness, compassion, and humility. I consciously guarded myself against jealousy, a vice I had observed to be the cause of much infighting even among family members.

Sometimes, I found a virtue such as honesty conflicting with another. Was telling the truth justified at the cost of betraying a friend's confidence? Should a child reveal a parent's misdeeds to someone outside the family? Was stealing justified to feed a hungry family? I finally concluded that nothing was absolute. Right and wrong could not be so rigid; every virtue or lesson might have situations that required exceptions. This moral and ethical dilemma still challenges me.

On breaks from work, I wandered away from the camp to climb the nearby hills and watch the sea of clouds drifting away below me. This had become a daily practice, until heavy snowfall made it hard to get to my favorite spot. Sitting amid majestic, solemn mountains and valleys sprawled out far below, I pondered my future and my purpose.

I considered the poverty-stricken lives of the Monpa tribes and the caste-ridden societal evils in the far corners of my country. I was wrong to remain indifferent in the face of such social discrimination and economic deprivation. These people could do nothing to overcome their deplorable condition but live with their faith in God to save them. This explanation didn't satisfy me, and I felt compelled to fulfill my duty. I wanted to find a way to use my humanity to serve others, but I didn't yet know how to accomplish that.

CHAPTER 5

A HEART DIVIDED

A FTER THE SIX-WEEK LEAVE resulting from my near-death
experience at Se La, I received orders to rejoin my regiment. It
amazed me that in such a short time, the regiment had crossed the
entire breadth of India and relocated to Pathankot, a dusty town in
the northwest that served as a military base in Punjab State en route
to the Jammu–Kashmir sector.

Being close to the border with Pakistan, the Indian army was
always on high alert. Both countries had already fought two wars over
Kashmir following their independence in 1947, the most recent being
just two years prior to my assignment. Tensions ran high between the
countries, and armed skirmishes occasionally broke out.

I wasn't looking forward to a posting in a "field area," the army
term for a conflict zone. I longed to be stationed at an exciting
metropolis like Delhi or Bangalore, with fashionable restaurants,
movie houses, and—not far from my thoughts at the time—pretty
girls to watch.

Upon arrival, I was greeted by loud cheering from the soldiers
I had left behind in Se La. They cried out, "George *Sahib ki jai!*"

meaning "Victory to George Sir." This was a big relief, because I was concerned that they perceived me as weak for having left the mission midway after the dynamite blast. The first few evenings I reminisced with fellow officers about our times in the Himalayas, singing old Hindi songs and teasing each other. Some remarked humorously that I had blown myself up deliberately to escape the harsh weather.

Our days were filled with strenuous training exercises to prepare for imminent war with Pakistan, which materialized a few years later. We practiced frequent battle deployments and set up gun positions behind short hills to conduct artillery fire drills.

Our regiment's new commanding officer, Colonel S. L. Rege, would suddenly appear at battle practices to inspect and encourage the officers to prepare for difficult situations. His distinct no-nonsense personality and style appealed to me, and I compared his decisiveness to that of Field Marshal Montgomery of the British Army. Observing my diligence and dedication, Colonel Rege entrusted me with key tasks, like surveying the border with Pakistan for suitable gun positions in case war broke out.

Colonel Rege tried to lift our spirits by reminding us that we belonged to one of India's oldest artillery units, carrying forward the illustrious traditions of the Marathas. "It was a glorious history that shouldn't be tarnished by fears and failures," he would say.

Ever since the accident in Se La, I was more defensive, anticipating others' mistakes. When the soldiers practiced grenade throwing, I delivered my instructions from the relative safety of a makeshift pit a reasonable distance away. My new caution wasn't misplaced. A few tragic incidents occurred during those field exercises. Two of our officers were electrocuted when their jeep's tall antenna hit an overhead high-voltage line. Another soldier had a mental breakdown, shot an officer, and fled the camp but was caught later. Unexpectedly, the adjutant of our regiment, a senior captain, met with an accident and was hospitalized with severe injuries. With the regiment's morale deeply shaken, officers tried hard to motivate the soldiers.

Barely two weeks later, Colonel Rege called me into his office. He was seated behind his massive desk, and I stood at attention and saluted him.

"Congratulations, Lieutenant George. I'm promoting you to captain," he announced with a smile, scanning my face to gauge my reaction. He noted my disbelief with some amusement and continued, "I obtained special permission for your promotion. As of now, you are the adjutant of this regiment. If you're not the youngest captain in the Indian Army, you're certainly the youngest adjutant!"

I was stunned. It was rare for a lieutenant at twenty-one to become a captain. The position of adjutant was usually reserved for a senior captain, but these norms didn't seem to trouble Colonel Rege, and it was not my place to argue. He instructed me to occupy the adjutant's office that evening and start my new assignment the following morning. As the custodian of top-secret documents, such as maps of enemy positions and initial deployment plans, I would be the first to receive communications from brigade headquarters via the red hotline, should hostilities break out.

One evening, the subedar-major and I passed the makeshift temple the soldiers had built to worship their Hindu gods and Chhatrapati Shivaji Maharaj. I heard them chanting and saying my name in their native Marathi. Perplexed, I turned to the subedar-major. He explained that the soldiers were praying for my well-being, something they did every day. He added, "Sahib, they are grateful that you are looking after them and helping their families."

Whenever the soldiers had informed me of their concerns on the home front, I had petitioned senior government officials or the head of police of their village to intervene. Illnesses, disputes, and threats of violence against families from local gangs were valid concerns for them. If we were lucky, a positive response from an official promised to rectify the situation.

Before the soldiers went home for vacation, I was required to educate them about birth control. Not yet having experienced intimacy with a woman, I sought the resident medical officer's advice. He demonstrated barrier contraception by unrolling a condom on my finger, and I relayed this information to my men as though I were an expert. Despite my instructions, I subsequently learned that some had impregnated their women. The joke was they had gone to bed with condoms secured on their fingers!

. . .

Every morning, I updated Colonel Rege on what had transpired the previous day, followed by a briefing on the day's activities. He gave me instructions and offered wisdom on being an exemplary officer and, more importantly, a good person.

"I've had difficulties with my superior at the brigade headquarters because we disagreed on several issues," he once revealed. "Captain George, you must always stand up for the right thing and express your views honestly if you truly believe they're important." He was the first to advise me to never execute an unlawful order and to always remain true to what is right.

Reporting directly to Colonel Rege profoundly influenced me. He emphasized looking after the needs of the soldiers and their families and valuing their loyalty to the officers and the regiment. I strove to emulate his hard work, dedication, and personal integrity. I knew that Colonel Rege and others saw a bright future for me in the army, with the potential to become a general someday. Without knowing my frame of mind, he nurtured every element of the better angels of my nature, and I aspired to be like him.

Having successfully established the gun positions in the Himalayas, I was highly regarded in the regiment, and my men valued my leadership. But despite the recognition and the excitement of my new responsibilities, something felt amiss. More than two years had passed since my dynamite blasting incident, and it was becoming increasingly difficult for me to resign myself to a career as a soldier.

I asked myself whether I could spend the rest of my life pursuing the ideals of the military. The writings of Bertrand Russell, a renowned philosopher, and Dr. Albert Schweitzer, a Nobel laureate, contributed to my internal dilemma. Each impacted my evolving convictions on moral courage and social justice.

"War does not determine who is right—only who is left," a saying commonly attributed to Bertrand Russell, captures war's absurdity and horror. Even though I was a proud soldier, this thought made me question the futility of war and living a life preparing for it.

Dr. Albert Schweitzer's medical service in the jungles of Gabon, Africa, deeply moved me. He founded a clinic and then a hospital to treat natives who suffered from tropical diseases. Over time, people beyond the local community sought his medical help. Dr. Schweitzer overcame countless hardships living in the jungle and transporting medicine by boat through dangerous rivers.

His work was extraordinary and romantic—learning local languages, being amid elephants, and bonding with the local people. I dreamed of one day following in his footsteps and starting a school for tribal children in the jungles of Africa. I imagined the simplicity of living with nature, growing my food, learning the locals' ways, and, most importantly, improving their lives.

The youthful fantasy and glamour of the military had driven me to be a soldier, but having embraced Mahatma Gandhi's principle of *ahimsa*—doing no harm—I was no longer prepared to take life. Officers in my regiment constantly talked about the glory of sacrificing their lives for their country, but I wasn't willing to run into enemy fire and die young. My patriotism ended with my regiment and the safety of my soldiers. I saw no glory in death or sacrifice as demanded by the military. I wished political leaders would compromise and avoid war. The future the army offered didn't feel right, but a departure meant throwing away my hard work and turning back on the investment of my parents and the military.

Unsure of how to embark on a different future, I spent considerable time alone in contemplation, the solitude facilitating weighty introspection. It was then I conjured a 50-50 game plan to devote the first half of my life to professional ambitions and the latter half to making a difference in the lives of the most vulnerable. I further divided my expected life span into four components: the first twenty to twenty-five years toward learning, the next twenty to twenty-five years for professional pursuits, the third twenty to twenty-five years to seek purpose in life through contribution to others, and the remaining years to diligently pass the baton to the next generation.

Still, another critical issue would soon influence my future plans.

. . .

I started noticing that frequently I had to ask others to repeat themselves. At first, I blamed my gradual hearing loss on prolonged exposure to loud artillery gunfire, the blast that nearly killed me, and living in harsh, cold conditions for a year. The deterioration in my hearing bothered me enough to visit the Central Medical Headquarters in Delhi.

"You're developing otosclerosis," the ear specialist at the hospital declared after performing a conduction test. "Calcium deposits have formed on the stapes bone in your middle ear, causing it to harden and cripple its movement. Currently, only your right ear is affected, but in the future, the left one might develop the same issue."

I was terrified at the possibility of losing my hearing but should have known that nothing in life happens without a reason.

The medical officer recommended stapedectomy, a specialized microscopic surgery involving the middle ear that might remedy my condition, and referred me to Dr. R. Raman, the only doctor in India qualified to perform it. Ammachi was then in the US, but I immediately sent her a letter about my hearing defect. She was saddened but not shocked. "It is hereditary, Monu. I, too, suffer from it in my right ear." She also disclosed that her aunt was deaf in both ears, and many others in our extended family suffered from it too.

I wrote to Dr. R. Raman and immediately headed to Madras, where he had established his clinic following his training in the US. When we met to discuss the surgery, he smiled and said, "Abraham, your mother sent me a telegram from America instructing me not to operate on you. She said she is arranging for it to be done in the United States. What would you like me to do?"

I was not surprised, as this was absolutely in character for Ammachi. "How confident are you about restoring my hearing?"

Dr. Raman replied, "Very confident. You need not worry."

Desperate, I scheduled the surgery for the next day.

Post-surgery, I stayed at the clinic for two days and then moved into a nearby hotel. Food was arranged to be brought to my bed, as I was too off-balance to walk. After a few days in the hotel, I was well enough to return to the clinic for tests. Dr. Raman declared the surgery a total success. I was elated that my hearing was restored in the right ear. After three more days of recovery in the hotel, I boarded a train and headed back to Pathankot.

Not wanting Colonel Rege or the soldiers to know about my surgery, I removed the bandages from my right ear. Except for the pinkish outer layer of one earlobe from where some tissue had been grafted, there was no evidence of what I had undergone. I didn't want my medical condition to affect my duties, so I got straight to work.

While the surgery dramatically improved my hearing, problems lingered. The most troubling was the constant ringing in my ears— tinnitus—which intensified over time. The possibility of losing my hearing in the left ear worried me. Referring to the noise in my ear, I once told Ammachi, "It sounds like the screeching chorus of a thousand angry crickets!"

I asked her if my ear troubles could be a reason for seeking a medical discharge, and she agreed they were valid. Luckily, she knew the wife of the top general in the medical corps, General Joseph, who might get me a discharge from the army. They had studied together at the same college, and Ammachi wrote to enlist her help in getting me out.

Desperate for a discharge, I left for Delhi to meet the general. The military guard at the gate to his house initially refused to let me in, although I showed him my military ID card. "I am a captain, and I have an important matter to discuss with the general," I said sternly in Hindi. He reluctantly allowed me in.

I waited anxiously in the living room. The general appeared annoyed that I had come in without an appointment, but he listened carefully to my request. "I just had surgery in one ear, and it cannot take the loud sounds of artillery fire. I feel the other ear is deteriorating," I explained. Though he didn't commit, he appeared amenable to my request, and I hoped he would arrange my medical release. In the meantime, however, all I could do was continue my military responsibilities.

CHAPTER 6

FAREWELL TO ARMS AND COUNTRY

WHEN I RETURNED TO TRIVANDRUM on my next leave, no family member received me at the railway station. The driver took me home in uncustomary silence. My every attempt at conversation was met with unsettling quiet. My parents and sisters were waiting for me on the front veranda of Bella Vista, unusually subdued.

"How are you, Ammachi?" I asked, embracing her and giving her a loving kiss. I was so happy to see her again after her four years in America.

"I'm okay, Monu," she said in her usual soft voice.

"Why is everyone so quiet? What's going on?" I asked, turning to the others. Achachan said nothing, leaving it to Ammachi to reply. I followed my mother into the study.

"Monu, I have some bad news. They have suspended your father from his job." My mother explained in detail what had transpired against the backdrop of the political and social changes taking place in Kerala since my last visit a year before. In 1967, a coalition of political parties led by the Communist Party of India won the election. One minister in this new government had been a lecturer at the law college where my father had taught. Achachan had suspended him for instigating student involvement in political activities on campus. In retaliation, the minister orchestrated my father's dismissal from his position as the college dean on charges of "misappropriation of funds."

The college head clerk had withdrawn unauthorized funds from the state Treasury Department using duplicate invoices of earlier purchases. When Achachan discovered this misdeed, he notified government auditors. Nevertheless, using this incident as a pretext, the minister suspended him without further pay or pension.

"Why should they hold Achachan responsible for a crooked fellow's actions?" I protested, furious at the preposterous accusation. "Don't they know he had nothing to do with the theft?"

Ammachi shook her head sadly. "Your father feels betrayed by his staff. Others must have known about this much earlier."

Achachan had an honest and unsuspecting nature, which probably made him an easy target for deception. I could only imagine how shattered he was, having fallen from what was a much-anticipated promotion as a High Court judge just a few days prior.

"How could they expect Achachan to know what the head clerk was doing every minute?" I was indignant and defensive of my father, a man of complete integrity.

Ammachi rejected my argument. "He should have noticed earlier. He should have been careful not to sign duplicate invoices."

I disagreed. I easily saw how Achachan could have assumed that the duplicate invoices were necessary for the college's records.

Although we held different viewpoints, my mother and I were determined not to let this crisis defeat us. We talked late into the night, brainstorming how Achachan's suspension could be reversed. My parents knew several influential people, some within the government, but as we reviewed our options, it became clear that it would finally come down to a bribe. While paying off key politicians might work, we weren't prepared to do it.

"There's no end to the bribe game once you start down that road," Ammachi cautioned.

The next morning, I contacted Paneker, a good friend from my school days. He suggested I meet with a senior political leader he knew. Despite my apprehensions, I decided to give it a try.

Paneker drove me to a public guesthouse where members of the state legislature were known to spend their evenings. The place was filthy, littered with empty liquor bottles and cigarette butts. Some men lingered in the shadows with women who appeared to be prostitutes.

After we waited in the lobby for nearly an hour, a servant gestured to us to follow him to a private room. A shabbily dressed middle-aged man was reclining on a bed. Upon seeing me, he lazily raised himself and leaned against the wooden headboard. My friend stood beside me while I explained what had happened to my father. Before I could complete my narration, the politician interrupted me.

"What are you prepared to pay for what you want?"

I had suspected this outcome, but the politician's casual indifference to the truth angered me. With a clenched jaw, I stood in silence and glared.

Paneker nervously tapped my shoulder and whispered, "Let's go outside and discuss the matter, Abraham."

"I need time to think about it," I muttered to the politician and stormed out. This was my first serious encounter with bribery but surely not my last.

. . .

When word of Achachan's suspension inevitably spread, a steady stream of friends and relatives dropped by our house to hear the details and see how the family was faring in our sudden misfortune. Ammachi warmly welcomed the guests and led them to the lawn, where chairs had been placed.

Bella Vista shone brightly, with the lights turned on as though this were a joyous occasion. Ammachi instructed Lekha and Vinita, "You girls play the piano and go on as usual."

I moved about, passing snacks to the guests. My mother engaged everyone by initiating conversation on topics unrelated to the crisis. The normalcy of our family surprised a departing visitor, who remarked, "If I were in your shoes, I would have been devastated."

Ammachi smiled. Whatever she might have been thinking or feeling, she kept to herself.

Achachan remained contemplative throughout, answering the same questions from different guests repeatedly. Without exception, everyone wanted to know: "Why did you sign the duplicates?"

Achachan answered, "I assumed signed documents were needed for our records. I never suspected that the head clerk would use them to withdraw money a second time."

Visitors usually responded with expressions of pity, but we could discern those who genuinely accepted our explanation and those who secretly delighted in seeing my father a crushed man.

"Uncle, you should have looked into what the clerk was doing with the signed papers," my mother's cousin said, irritation clear in his tone. "Your careless mistake has brought disgrace to you and the whole family."

None of us took offense at his candid talk, although I sensed that my father was struggling to fight his severe disappointment at letting down his family. Feeling his pain, I tried to console him. "The Treasury Department knows very well that they can't make payments on duplicates. Someone in the treasury must be a part of this fraud."

My father nodded.

After our guests left, Ammachi remarked, "My cousin was the only honest man who came to see us today."

That night, Ammachi and I retreated again to the study. She clearly had no interest in seeking justice from officials. The present crisis had followed another disappointment for her just a year earlier when the state had turned down her proposal to set up a small laboratory in her college to continue the research she had begun at the National Bureau of Standards in Washington, DC.

Despite a strong recommendation from Dr. Vikram Sarabhai, the then chairman of the Atomic Energy Commission of India and a close friend of my mother's, the government was unmoved. The final decision was unequivocal: "The proposed research is too advanced for the needs of the State at present."

Hardly three months after his suspension, Achachan received a deanship offer from Osmania University Law College in the nearby state of Andhra Pradesh. The Kerala government declined his request to leave the state and take up the position while he was being investigated. The government had already canceled his salary and pension.

If we remained in Kerala, all our available savings would soon dry up, and we couldn't live on Ammachi's meager salary. If my father contested the government's decision, there would be mounting legal expenses and possible retaliation. His adversaries, now in power, wouldn't let the government reverse its unfair decision against him.

We had no choice but to leave India for good. Our plan could work only if Ammachi moved to America first and the rest of us followed. Bijoy was already in the US, doing his master's in engineering, but Achachan and I would have to overcome serious hurdles. To begin with, the state authorities wouldn't allow Achachan to leave Kerala because he was still under investigation, an obstacle that appeared nearly insurmountable.

Determined to overcome this terrible setback, Ammachi said, "I'm going to write to my friends in America and let them know I want to return and take up a teaching position. I'm sure at least one of them will respond favorably." She had formed many good relationships during her four years in the United States, and her long-term work visa was still valid. Looking back at my mother's decision, I can only marvel at her determination to overcome every obstacle the family faced.

To our relief, two months later, Ammachi received an offer to teach at a college in Alabama. My parents' next concern was how to care for my two sisters until they, too, could move to America. Vinita had just finished high school, and Lekha was a college freshman. We decided that the girls could live in the college hostel, as our father couldn't attend to their needs amid all his difficulties.

We feared the government might confiscate our house, especially if my father left Kerala. The income tax agency had earlier audited our finances, only to find that all the money for building Bella Vista had legitimately come from the savings my mother had sent from America between 1961 and 1965. My parents put out the word that they wished to rent Bella Vista, explaining that they couldn't afford to live there any longer.

My mother resigned from her teaching post at Kerala University, where she had served as a professor for over ten years and recently been promoted to head the Physics Department. I still remember the day I drove her to the university for the last time. Waiting anxiously in the car, I worried about her taking so long. Had someone discovered our family's plans?

Just as I was about to look for her, Ammachi came downstairs, escorted by her colleagues, who looked sad at learning of her decision. She told me she had used the same pen to accept her promotion and then immediately tender her resignation—a dramatic way of conveying her unhappiness and initiating the family's exodus. Our family would soon be broken apart, each one in a different place, and there was no knowing if and when we would be together again.

I then had to make plans to leave India. Soon after I received my medical discharge notice a month later, I went to Delhi to find a travel agent who could obtain an Indian passport. Some rules prevented an army officer from leaving India soon after his discharge if he had recently served in a conflict zone, as I had. However, once I mentioned that the general of the medical core had permitted me to visit the US for the ear surgery, my passport was approved. I received Ammachi's sponsorship letter for my US visa, which stated she would support me financially while I studied in America. With that letter and my Indian passport, I applied for a US visa.

Despite my unwillingness to continue in the military, the parting was painful. I met my fellow officers individually and bid farewell to the soldiers at the parade ground. It hurt to think I probably would never see them again. I felt guilty for escaping the hardships my comrades would experience. I prayed that life would be kind and merciful to each one.

Finally, the moment came that I dreaded the most. I walked into Colonel Rege's office and saluted him one last time. Sadness filled his face as he wished me a promising future. Overcome by my admiration and loyalty toward him, I broke down crying.

Discharged from the army, I returned to Trivandrum with an Indian passport, an American visa, and a plane ticket to the US. Achachan and the two girls knew nothing about my ear surgery or medical discharge. Except for Ammachi, I had kept this a secret from others to avoid creating more anxiety amid our other pressing troubles.

For the first time in years, I disembarked from the train in civilian clothes.

My father was surprised to see me in such casual attire. "I love seeing you dressed as an officer."

"I'm no longer an officer," I announced. "I've been discharged from the army. I'm going to America."

Achachan was shocked. Despite the family's decision to leave for the States, he hadn't expected me to act so quickly. "Monu, you have been in the army all these years. You don't have the academic background or preparation for college."

"That's all right, Achachan. I'll start over and study very hard." I couldn't tell him exactly what I would study because I didn't yet know. Despite being unsatisfied with my answers, he didn't dissuade me, aware that I had Ammachi's backing.

"Achachan, you must get out of India. And we must start the process now," I advised.

"How? The government won't allow me to leave the state without police clearance," he replied, frustrated. He was not in a frame of mind to act independently and navigate the bureaucracy.

I again sought out my friend Paneker, who had a high-level contact in the state police department. When he and I visited this senior official to seek clearance for my father, the official pretended to be unaware of my father's widely reported suspension. He informed us he would take care of the matter, including the payments to the passport office, which I understood were not official fees. I told Paneker, "Please find out what he needs. We will surely meet all the expenses."

Our travel plans had to be worked out undetected by the authorities. Achachan immediately applied for his passport and US visa, and in a few days, he received them, as did my sisters. The possibility of leaving India finally became real to my father, but he wasn't sure what he would do in America. He was giving up a familiar life for an unknown one and was nervous about starting all over. Before him lay the choice between an uncertain future in a distant land and guaranteed doom in his own country.

In December 1968, I departed for America, leaving behind my home and the country I had served with pride. I was consumed by excitement with the thought of studying at an American university and exploring the grandeur of a new country.

PART II

CHAPTER 7

MUCH TO DISCOVER

A RRIVING IN ANNISTON, ALABAMA, I was surprised to see Ammachi dressed in Western clothing and easily navigating the busy airport. She drove me to Talladega, where she was teaching in a predominantly Black college while doing research at NASA in Huntsville, Alabama.

India and its chaotic, congested streets seemed a world away, and thoughts of home were quickly displaced by the astonishing impressions of my new surroundings. Rolling west along Interstate 20, I was amazed at how clean and organized everything was. A glimpse of my favorite car, a convertible Chevrolet Impala, passing us on the broad, perfectly paved highway couldn't have excited me more.

My mother hadn't warned me that the Deep South was a hotbed of racial discrimination and persecution at the time. George Wallace, the segregationist governor of Alabama and a presidential hopeful, frequently made national news with his rhetoric denying African Americans their constitutional and civil rights. I would soon discover that America, too, had a "caste system" of its own.

Within a week of my arrival, my mother sent me for a haircut.

Accustomed to obeying military and maternal orders unquestionably, I set off to the town center. During the short drive, I had to remind myself to stay on the right side of the road. Downtown Talladega had a small public garden encircled by shops, police and fire stations, a diner, and a municipal building. Old folks occupied the park benches while a few shoppers strolled along the walkways in the central square. No one appeared busy, and the tranquility impressed me.

Back in Kerala, the barber came by our house every two months and sat us down on a sturdy stool placed on the porch. But here, I didn't know that the swirling red-white-and-blue stripes of a lamp identified barbershops. Walking past several stores, I saw a man in one sitting on an oversized swivel chair getting his hair cut. I entered the shop, sat on a side bench, and patiently waited.

The barber appeared grumpy and ignored me. Once he was done with the others, he turned toward me with an intimidating stare and motioned for me to occupy the now-empty big chair. "How d'ya want your hair cut?" he asked in his Alabama drawl.

Suspecting that haircuts had fancy names in America, like *rockabilly* and *mop top*, I uttered the first style that came to mind. "Oxford, please."

With a puzzled look, he asked me again.

This time, I thought I had guessed it right: "Uh, Cambridge?" I am unsure what possessed me to answer that way, but whatever it was—humor, mischief, or confusion—it fell flat with the confused and unamused barber.

With no further questions, he buzzed my head with an electric razor. In mere minutes, he was done and collected his money.

When I returned home, Ammachi exclaimed, "You haven't cut enough! Go back there and ask him to trim a little more."

Ever brave and dutiful, I soon found myself parked again in front of the shop. The barber watched me approach and met me at the door. "Whaddya want now?" he demanded.

"I'd like you to cut a little more, please."

"Ya wait right there," he said, retreating into his shop and emerging seconds later with a rifle.

Not wasting a second, I whirled around and scurried to my car as he hurled threats at my retreating back.

"Git outta here! If ya come back again, I'll shoot ya!"

Why was he so enraged? I could only imagine he felt insulted at being asked to cut a brown man's hair not once but twice. And once had been bad enough.

In another instance, on my way home from Birmingham after a late-night movie, a traffic cop pulled me over for failing to stop at an intersection. He ordered me to follow his car to the local courthouse. The front door of the small colonial building wasn't even locked, so the police officer went in without hesitation and turned on the lights. I stepped into the narrow hall behind him and found the judge fast asleep on a bench. The officer nudged him awake. The judge hurriedly sat upright and donned his black gown. The police officer briefed him on my crime in just one sentence.

The judge asked me, "Are ya guilty?"

As I started to explain, the judge turned to the police officer, jerked his thumb toward me, and asked, "What language he speaking?"

It didn't take him long to reach a verdict—I was fined twenty-five dollars.

"Your Honor, I only have twelve dollars with me."

"Y'wanna spend the night in jail?" the police officer snapped.

I pleaded with the police officer until he finally agreed to take whatever cash I had. As he led me out of the courthouse, I thanked him with minimal enthusiasm and asked, "Have you arrested other Indians before?"

"I don't see creatures like you," he replied with a scowl. Despite the insult, I chose to ignore the comment for my own safety. The implications of my presence in a White-dominated state gradually began to sink in.

A few months later, I was admitted to Samford University in Birmingham, Alabama, for a joint MBA and juris doctor program offered in association with the University of Alabama in Tuscaloosa. My diplomas from the military academies had convinced the university that I had earned the equivalent of a bachelor's degree. Except for three or four Black basketball players, everyone else was White, and mostly born-again Christians.

As a person of color, I would have to work harder to prove myself. Some professors assumed I was "not white, not bright." When my exam results became known, they were surprised that I had secured top grades in most subjects. "I didn't know you are so smart!" one professor remarked. Word of my academic performance spread on campus, and I was happy when a few students struck up conversations with me at the cafeteria.

Working at the law library, I saved enough money for an occasional date with a White female classmate brave enough to go out with me. But soon I stopped dining at restaurants, even low-priced ones, after noticing that servers glared at me, made me wait unusually long before taking my food order, and brusquely placed the plates in front of me. My date graciously pretended not to notice each time, but I sensed her unease.

None of the students were openly prejudiced or hostile, but they didn't invite me to their social events. The only exception was the evening prayer meetings my classmates held on the front lawn of the campus. They prayed and exchanged stories of how each one had seen God and been reborn, urging me to convert to Christianity. Feeling awkward, I repeatedly told them, "My family is Christian. I have taken my Holy Communion." They didn't appear convinced or satisfied.

Sandy, a White student in my class who befriended me, asked me to join her for service at the church her family regularly attended. Unlike the towering building where I had regularly attended services in my hometown, this one looked more like a white stucco home. Eyes followed us as Sandy led me to the front row. I would have preferred to sit in the back, safe from the congregation's scrutiny.

I listened to the pastor's fiery sermon proclaiming that the American Civil War was still being waged. His voice boomed like a cannon as he explained why God had created Black and White people, just as he had created Cain and Abel. Bewildered, I couldn't understand how this man of the cloth could use the Bible to condone bigotry. The silent reception of his message by those present unnerved me.

"Abraham, did you enjoy the service?" Sandy's father asked me as we stepped outside.

"Yes. I liked the choir very much," I replied cautiously.

After the church service, we lunched at an exclusive country club where I was, once again, the only Brown person present. There were no Black guests, only Black servers, who carved roast beef and pork for lunch. I was out of place in this all-white gathering, but people were friendly enough and used their limited knowledge of India to strike up a conversation.

"Are there snakes on the roads?" one asked.

"Dangerous, venomous ones," I emphasized.

"Are people starving?" another inquired.

"Yes, the majority are poor," I replied.

Poverty and snakes were all they seemed to know about India.

. . .

Months passed quickly. Ammachi and I continually wrote anxious letters home where, shrouded in secrecy, my father was trying to settle our family's affairs. He wrote that most household items had been sold, and he was still looking for a tenant to rent Bella Vista. In a stroke of good fortune, the Reserve Bank of India, a central government agency outside the state government's jurisdiction, agreed to rent the house for ten years.

A trustworthy travel agent booked Achachan and my sisters' airline tickets and kept the flight plans confidential. Unknown to even our close relatives and family friends, Achachan, Lekha, and Vinita left for Mumbai one night, where they caught the international flight to America via Germany to join us in Alabama.

With crippling anxiety, Ammachi and I reached the airport two hours before their arrival time and intently scanned the passengers as they slowly filed into the lobby.

"Where are they? Ammachi, do you think they have been detained in Frankfurt?" I asked.

"I don't know, Monu," Ammachi replied, not taking her eyes off the crowd.

Just as our anxiety levels were peaking, we spotted my father making his way along the airport hallway, with Lekha and Vinita right behind.

"My God! They made it!" Ammachi cried out, tears filling her eyes.

We ran toward them and fell into each other's arms. Their tender embraces had never felt more comforting.

"We were afraid something might have gone wrong," I exclaimed, holding my sisters tightly. At last, my family was free!

Our first weekend together, we picnicked by Talladega Lake and reminisced about our days in India. The girls wanted to explore their new town and countryside, and I was only too happy to show them around. They promptly put away their Indian clothing and purchased miniskirts and dresses.

"These girls aren't modest, Ammachi," I complained.

She laughed and replied, "They are young. Let them be."

In coming months, through letters from friends in Trivandrum, we learned the Kerala government hadn't taken Achachan's escape lightly and had launched an investigation. Desperate to clear his name, Achachan filed a lawsuit against the government for his unlawful suspension, a case that lingered for five years. We worried if we could ever set foot again in the land of our birth. We considered ourselves banished by our homeland, a country my parents had served honestly and one for which I had almost given my life.

Ammachi assured us we could do well in America if we worked hard, and she expected all her children to get PhDs, just as she had under challenging circumstances. Bijoy finished his MS in engineering and was admitted to the PhD program at the Courant Institute of Mathematical Sciences at New York University. She was equally elated at my completion of my MBA in 1970. I thought it would be a good idea to find a job in New York that offered better opportunities than what I might find in the South.

Bijoy supported my plan and drove to Alabama to pick me up. We loaded up his Plymouth Duster and set off on the long road trip north. We were fascinated by the vast countryside, the small towns, and West Virginia's beautiful Blue Ridge Mountains. Upon reaching Manhattan, we spent the night in Harlem with one of Bijoy's friends. The following day, Bijoy saw an ad on the college notice board for a small apartment in Washington Heights, Manhattan. It was within his meager means, so we promptly moved in.

Now that we had a place to stay, I had to find a job. I leaped at the first opportunity: a statistical analyst position at Standard & Poor's. The manager at the placement office told me it was a prestigious company, but I had no idea what the job entailed. It required starting early to capture corporate announcements in newspapers and enter them on computer punch cards. I was crammed in a room with others all day, knocking away on clunky Friden calculators. With my first paycheck, I excitedly bought an excellent sound system and vinyl records of my favorite Frank Sinatra and Nat King Cole songs.

Trying to impress my boss, I completed more analyses and finished them faster than anyone else, but in my haste I frequently missed a zero or added one, so ten million became one million or one hundred million. At the end of six months, my boss told me, "This job is not for you." It was embarrassing to let my parents know that I had been fired.

By then, following my mother's footsteps, I had already sought admission to the PhD program in business at NYU, though I had embarrassingly poor GMAT scores. Bijoy was amused when I received an interview offer from the college. "I can't believe this!" he exclaimed.

Dressed smartly in a blue blazer, white shirt, and gray slacks, I arrived at NYU's Stern School of Business. At that time, it was housed in Nicholas Hall, a ten-story building in the heart of the Wall Street financial district. As I made my way to the faculty offices, I thought about how my life would change if I could be a part of this inspiring place of learning.

The secretary smiled kindly and gestured toward the office of the chairman of the International Finance Department. Once inside, I carefully stepped over the books, notes, and manuscripts strewn over the floor.

"How are you?" Professor Hawkins asked, rising from his chair to shake my hand.

I guessed he was in his forties. His tidy crew cut would have been the envy of my first American barber in Talladega.

"Abraham, tell me what you've accomplished," he said, putting aside my résumé.

There was little to speak of on my academic accomplishments, so I relied on my military experiences to make an impression. I was pretty much at ease, having rehearsed the critical points in front of the mirror that morning.

"From nineteen, I served as an officer in the Indian Army for over three years, stationed in the Himalayan ranges and Kashmir, sir."

Professor Hawkins leaned forward, listening intently. "Tell me more."

"I established an artillery position at an altitude of fourteen thousand feet and lived there for eleven months."

"Fourteen thousand?" He sat back, his eyes wide and incredulous.

I shared my adventures in the Himalayas and told him I had completed my MBA at Samford University in Alabama.

To my surprise, he waved his hand dismissively. "That's not an education."

I wanted to get the bad news over with. "I'm afraid, Professor Hawkins, I don't have a good GMAT score."

Professor Hawkins smiled and thought for a moment before

replying, "Being a successful army officer on such perilous assign-
ments is very impressive for a young man."

I felt hopeful.

"It's interesting that you were in the middle of everything happening in the South."

I assumed he was referring to the civil rights protests that were
taking place there. I told him I wanted to pursue a PhD in developmental economics and international finance and eventually use this
education to help impoverished countries.

"Abraham, you're the kind of student we want here. I know you'll
do very well," he declared enthusiastically.

My days in graduate school were an exhilarating and transformative period. I studied international finance and developmental
economics and researched to prepare course reports—a far cry from
anything I had done until then. I frequently interacted with bright
young people, some working in nearby commercial banks and investment firms, and spent the next four years mostly in classrooms and
the library. In my final year, I served as the president of the PhD
student association, following a hotly contested election.

I found myself exposed to progressive ideas, like social responsibilities of citizens and human rights. I recall protesting in front of the
Waldorf Astoria Hotel in New York City when Ferdinand Marcos,
then the president of the Philippines, stayed there to attend a UN
session despite being accused of oppressing his own people.

To cover my living expenses, I taught finance and economics at
nearby colleges. My daily routine was to take an early morning bus
to Bloomfield, New Jersey, to teach at Bloomfield College and then
an evening ferry across the Hudson River to Staten Island to teach
at Wagner College.

Lekha and Vinita, now in their early twenties, came to live with me upon admission to NYU. They had completed their bachelor's at Samford University. I was shocked that they were no longer the docile teenagers who looked up to me for brotherly counsel and protection but had instead taken quickly to the American independent way of life.

What irritated me most was that they talked on the phone and received letters from male friends. They were annoyed when I stopped them from socializing, while I went on dates.

"You're so unfair, Kochetta. You keep us stuck in our rooms all weekend while you have fun," Lekha whined.

I didn't see anything wrong with what I was imposing on them. Girls of their age seldom spoke to boys in our hometown: After all, I, too, didn't get a chance then to talk to girls. "Ammachi, what has happened to these girls? Can you believe they want to go out with boys?" I once complained to my mother on the phone.

Ammachi sided with me and scolded my sisters, "You must listen to your brother. Unmarried women can't behave the same way as men." Achachan wouldn't voice his opinion openly, but we all knew he agreed with Ammachi and left the matter to her.

When my sisters refused to speak to me for a few days straight, I warned them, "I will not have such unruly girls in my apartment. You're going right back to Ammachi." I didn't carry out the threat, though.

My conservative upbringing in India undoubtedly conflicted with America's progressive outlook. It would take me years to reshape my ways to fit into America's liberal society. Over time, we would embrace the freedoms offered, and within a single generation, the family's traditional views on gender equality changed.

. . .

In late 1973, I began working on my dissertation: a detailed analysis of a managed float exchange rate system wherein currencies traded freely within a band set by central banks. To substantiate its implications for developing countries, I devised a mathematical model to estimate its impact on their employment, inflation, and growth.

Professor Hawkins summoned me to his office when I formally submitted my dissertation proposal. "Abraham, do you want to solve all the world's problems, or do you want to earn your PhD? I suggest you cut the scope of your project in half unless you want to work on this paper for the rest of your life." He seemed amused at my desire to address broader issues instead of confining myself to narrower, specific questions.

Meanwhile, I applied for a job at the World Bank because I thought working for an international organization would allow me to serve developing countries. To my disappointment, I was rejected. I considered a few other possibilities, such as the UN and the IMF, but those didn't work out either. My views on fair treatment of workers deterred me from applying to for-profit companies, and the only choice I saw was an academic career.

Like my mother, I was fairly enthusiastic about teaching and research. I thought it would give me sufficient time to formulate my ideas on poverty alleviation and eventually prepare myself for an advisory role in a developing country. I applied for a teaching position and received an offer from Syracuse University at an annual salary of $20,000.

But before I could accept the teaching position, I received a call from Alan Teck, a senior officer at Chemical Bank, now part of JP Morgan. "I'm impressed with your thesis on the new international monetary system. We want to consider you for a position in our consulting arm," he said in his initial call. This opportunity surprised me, and I met him at the bank in person. Following a brief interview, he suggested I start work soon after receiving my PhD.

My impulse was to turn down the banking position, as it contradicted my personal philosophy on a life of service. However, the annual salary of $30,000 was just too attractive to forgo, so I set aside my idealism and desire for nonprofit ventures and accepted the offer. My future looked bright; I was about to get my doctorate from a prestigious university and start a well-paying job.

Professor Hawkins was elated. I found time to drop by the business school to meet with him periodically. He had been my touchstone and mentor, guiding my education and career. We grew close through the years, and I fondly took to calling him by his first name, Bob, as he preferred.

A few months later, the US Immigration & Naturalization Department notified me of my American citizenship. Though delighted, I still valued my Indian heritage and struggled with my feelings about the end of my military tenure. I comforted myself by believing I had served my home country as best I could.

For the first time in America, I felt secure. I had submitted my dissertation for review, and in three to four months, I would start at Chemical Bank. Lekha and Vinita were nearing the end of their master's programs at NYU, and Bijoy was excelling academically, as usual. Achachan had taken up a teaching position in political science at the same college as my mother.

Our lawyer in Kerala informed us that the district court had partially exonerated Achachan, declaring that he had not committed a crime and that his suspension as dean of Trivandrum Law College was unlawful. They still declared him "negligent." It was a bittersweet victory for my father to partly reclaim his reputation.

To celebrate our good fortune, all of us got together for a special Sunday dinner at an Indian restaurant in Manhattan. "Our home is here now," Ammachi declared emphatically. Gratitude filled my heart. America, a land of seemingly boundless opportunity, had given us a chance to start over as a family.

CHAPTER 8

A NEW UNION

MY PARENTS RECEIVED MARRIAGE proposals and photos of eligible young women from relatives in India. They scoured them to find prospective matches for Bijoy, based on family status and physical attractiveness. My brother wasn't ready to consider them until he completed his studies and secured a stable job, so they passed these marriage prospects to me.

Despite living in America, my parents held onto traditional beliefs and customary Indian practices regarding marriage. They encouraged me to marry an Indian woman from a well-to-do Syrian Christian family, as our community discouraged marrying outside its own. Family status and background were less important to me than shared values, interests, and compatibility. Still, not wanting to go against my parents' wishes, I agreed to marry into our community. Since Syrian Christians in America were relatively few, I would have to find a bride in India.

My parents wanted an arranged marriage in which a third person —a relative or a friend—would introduce both sets of parents to each other, and they would determine if the proposed alliance was worth pursuing. The woman generally had little choice in the matter, as the parents expected her compliance with their wishes.

The thought of having someone else select a wife for me was disconcerting. "Ammachi, I don't want you to make the selection. Let me go alone," I insisted as respectfully as I could. "I know the practice is to parade the woman in front of the man and his parents. I find that demeaning. I would like to see her at some social event, church, or another place where she wouldn't even know why I am there."

"Monu, this is not how we do these things," Ammachi asserted, annoyed at my disregard for custom. She had already made plans to visit Kerala and meet with our relatives and friends who could introduce us. My parents would be disappointed if they couldn't participate in this critical search, but after deliberation, Achachan said, "Monu, I don't agree but go ahead."

Ammachi wrote to her contacts in Kerala, describing my quest and asking whether they might arrange introductions for me during my three-week stay. For some relatives, the request to see a woman before her parents and mine could meet was insulting and inappropriate. "He can't just walk into a respectable home and ask to see their daughter" one of my uncles angrily wrote back. I was relieved when a few agreed, though begrudgingly.

I was returning to Kerala for the first time in six years. On my way from the airport, I detoured to Bella Vista. Nostalgia choked me as I stood by the roadside, staring at our former home. I could still hear my sisters playing the piano and our happy chatter over a thousand family meals. I fondly remembered Ammachi asking Achachan after having slaved over a delicious meal how he liked it. His response usually was *tharakedilla*, meaning "it wasn't bad." If she expressed unhappiness at his answer, he would say, "Didn't you see I ate very well? If it was bad, would I have?" We'd laugh at this exchange, but Ammachi found this backhanded compliment incredibly infuriating. It was heartbreaking to think we would never again spend carefree days there as a family.

My uncles took turns shuttling me from one city to another to meet young women in informal social settings. To avoid embarrassing the woman's family if I rejected the proposal, I asked my uncles not to let them know about the purpose of my visit. Before each visit, they filled me in on the woman's family background, not withholding their views about her suitability based on her socioeconomic status.

But in every instance, the family welcomed me with their best savories and tea. As if on cue, an elder ushered a young woman into the room. Traditionally dressed in a sari and blouse, her face was usually over-powdered with talcum to lighten her complexion.

I could only briefly talk to the woman in prearranged settings, supervised by her parents. Most women didn't dare lift their heads. When I started a conversation, they replied in monosyllables. There was no way we could get to know each other freely.

Every family wanted an answer within a day or two of my visits. If my uncle found me unenthusiastic after a meeting, he would ask, "What was wrong with that one?"

"I'm looking for a well-educated woman who's sweet, fun to be with, and isn't afraid to speak her mind," I replied. I valued adventure and risk-taking and wanted to marry someone outgoing and free, like Grace Kelly in *To Catch a Thief* or Julie Christie in *Doctor Zhivago*. "What if I go to Africa to do social work? I want her to be excited to come along," I said, imagining her working beside me in the jungles of Gabon.

My uncle laughed uncontrollably. "Bah! This is real life, not some movie, Aniyan!" he said, shaking his head. He was frustrated and amused by my outlook, which he saw as naive and delusional, an unfortunate consequence of living in America.

To compound my problems, my time abroad had already erased my Indian accent. I couldn't tell if my Western speaking style fascinated or irritated people. "Has he forgotten his mother tongue?" one father asked sarcastically at a social gathering where everyone spoke Malayalam. He probably mistook my lack of fluency for arrogance.

My refusal to accept a dowry was another significant faux pas that irked almost everyone and sometimes disqualified me. To the richest families, the dowry was an essential element of their prestige within their community, but a woman having to pay for a husband offended me. I refused to budge, even when offered dowries that included large sums, properties, gold, cars, tea estates, and other enticing gifts.

"Is there something wrong with him? He wants a wife for no price at all," a few asked, suspecting I might be hiding a physical or mental disability. My relatives were losing patience, and I was growing disheartened. I wondered if there was more going on in the background of these meetings. Apparently to gain popularity, my uncles wanted to promote women only from their social circles.

Nearly three weeks passed, and I received impatient letters from my parents. Without further prospects, there was no point remaining in Kerala. Disappointed, I left for Madras to spend a little time with my aunt.

. . .

Two days before my return flight to America, Johnny *Chayan*, meaning uncle in Malayalam, called me from Cochin. His voice was full of warmth. "Aniyan, my wife has a niece named Mariam, in Jamshedpur. She is very attractive and well educated, and comes from a well-respected family," he said. "She has a master's degree in political science. If you'd like me to introduce you, meet me in Calcutta tomorrow, and I will accompany you."

"Sure, why not?" After numerous setbacks in finding a prospective wife, I wasn't hopeful.

From Calcutta, we flew to Jamshedpur, in the northeastern state of Jharkhand. It had a predominantly Hindi-speaking population and was the location of the headquarters for India's largest steel company, Tata Iron and Steel Company. Johnny Chayan briefed me that Mariam's father had been Tata's chief health officer for years. He had tried to run a trucking business with the help of a close relative but found himself defrauded. Having lost all his savings, his family lived in a modest home.

Mariam's parents, both Malayali Syrian Christians, were astonished when we turned up on their doorstep. I had finally gotten my wish for an impromptu visit!

"What a wonderful surprise, Johnny! We never thought you would come this far. Who is this young man?" the tall, kind-faced father asked with a welcoming smile. After a brief chat, my uncle drew me into the kitchen. He explained the reason for our visit to his sister-in-law.

"What! She's the youngest. Her two older sisters are still unmarried!" Mariam's mother exclaimed. As per custom, the eldest sibling always married first.

"You might regret turning it down," Johnny Chayan urged Mariam's mother.

She gave me a nervous look and went to talk to her husband.

I settled on the living room sofa and waited anxiously.

Nearly ten minutes had passed when a slim woman in her early twenties, modestly dressed in a colorful sea-green sari, was ushered into the room. I didn't know what her parents had told her, but she looked nervous. I noticed her gentle eyes and striking sharp features and found her fairer and taller than most women I had met in Kerala. Her parents questioned me about my life and career in America while she listened without speaking.

After a while, Johnny Chayan pushed his luck further. "Let the two young people have time to speak freely without us watching over them," he said. Surprisingly, everyone followed him to the front veranda.

Like all the other women I had met earlier, she didn't make eye contact or speak.

"My family is from Trivandrum, but we live in America." She had already heard this, but I felt it was only proper to tell her myself. "Would you like to study in America?"

She looked up, excitement in her eyes. "Yes," she said in a shy voice.

I asked her about her interests and college life, and she answered in short sentences. I did most of the talking, and she appeared to listen keenly.

Ten minutes turned to twenty before Johnny Chayan and Mariam's parents slowly filed into the living room. I caught them closely scanning our faces. Mariam blushed because it was the first time she had talked to a young man alone for so long.

I made a jovial remark. "We have been alone too long."

My uncle chuckled.

"It was very nice that I could meet all of you," I said with a smile. The parents thanked us for coming and walked us to the door. I glanced at Mariam, and our eyes met. The earnest gentleness in her face drew me to her. From her cheerful smile, I sensed that she probably liked me. And that smile, loving and sweet, sealed my fate.

On our way to the airport, I told my uncle I wanted to proceed with a proposal. "I'll ask for my parents' approval when I get home."

"That's wonderful. I'm delighted!" Johnny Chayan replied, beaming.

Waiting at the airport for my flight, I imagined a new life with this young woman. I was hopeful Mariam would accept. I wanted our relationship to differ from those practices in India that demanded women remain timid and submissive. A self-confident woman was perceived as immodest, but I wanted Mariam to express herself and enjoy personal freedom. I was eager to share my adventures and see her pursue a career she liked.

Upon arriving in America, I informed my parents of my choice. They knew Mariam's family through past connections and didn't object. They requested only that the wedding be in America—it was still unsafe for Achachan to return to Kerala. Ammachi wrote to Johnny Chayan, who contacted Mariam's parents for their consent, which they readily gave. She applied for her passport and visa and booked her flight.

Things were moving very fast. I couldn't believe that I would soon be a married man. My siblings were overjoyed for me. Lekha and Vinita were busy shopping and planning for the ceremonies. Ammachi requested Archbishop Mor Athanasius Samuel, a central figure in the discovery of the Dead Sea Scrolls, to bless the occasion. Having known my mother since her earlier visit to America in the 1960s, the archbishop readily agreed, and we were deeply honored.

In the days before Mariam's arrival, I worried about the hearing loss I had developed in my left ear. Even though it was a minor defect,

I wanted to be "normal" for her, so I underwent surgery by a highly reputed New York City doctor.

In retrospect, it was foolish to have the surgery just weeks before the wedding. A severe post-op infection irrevocably damaged the fine nerves in the inner ear. For days after the surgery, it felt like a volcano erupting in my ear. Each time I turned my head quickly, I was dizzy and unsteady, making crossing streets and driving difficult. I kept denying the reality of losing my hearing entirely in the left ear.

Ammachi tried to lift my spirits with her characteristic optimism and calm. "We'll fix it, Aniyan. There will be some new treatment soon."

"Not this time, Ammachi," I said, devastated. "The nerves are dead."

Luckily, the hearing in my right ear was nearly perfect, restored by my prior surgery. The Teflon wire the surgeon had implanted was holding up, miraculously, at least for now.

On the day of Mariam's arrival, Ammachi and I drove to Kennedy Airport in New York City. My mother smiled warmly at Mariam and inquired about her first journey on a plane. "Was the flight comfortable?" I closely watched Ammachi's face to discern her first impression of my future wife. I was relieved that she appeared pleased.

The next day, when I told Mariam what had happened to my hearing, she asked, "But you can hear me, so what's the problem?"

I laughed with relief. "If I don't hear you, please speak a little louder."

Within two weeks of Mariam's arrival, we were married in a formal but simple ceremony at a Syrian Orthodox Church in New Jersey, attended by about 150 guests. Her parents couldn't participate in the ceremony, but we sent them telegrams and photos.

The church service in Aramaic sprinkled with English seemed never-ending. Finally, Mariam and I exchanged rings, and I fastened a traditional gold chain around her neck to mark her as my wife, per the Indian custom. Ours was probably the first wedding among the Syrian Christian Indian community in America.

I didn't have much money to spend on a honeymoon, but there was plenty of time to explore New York City and show my wife the sights and places that had amazed me. We visited the Empire State Building, museums, and the Bronx Zoo; strolled through Central Park; and walked the nearby beaches hand in hand. I was keenly aware of having brought a young woman to a strange and faraway land and felt deep responsibility.

Those first years together were about Mariam exploring her new homeland's exciting possibilities. I had lived independently for many years, so adapting to American life and making cultural adjustments was easier. In contrast, Mariam had never lived away from her parents or been exposed to Western life. She found much to intrigue her: learning to drive, taking to Western clothing, discovering new foods, being exposed to the rock and roll music of Elvis and the Beatles, and living in freedom outside a rigid, patriarchal society.

She bought countless cookbooks, trying new recipes beyond the repertoire of curries her mother and aunt had hurriedly taught her before she came to America. "Everything imaginable is available in America," she would say, delighted by the ease of purchasing the vast array of vegetables, meat, and seafood necessary for the typical Keralan curries.

At the Fulton Fish Market in Lower Manhattan, we bought fresh fish at 2:00 a.m., when the boats arrived with their latest catch. Under the raised highway, the roadside stalls displayed varieties of fish, but we had trouble choosing after having tasted only those from the warm seas around India.

Mariam started taking sociology courses at the New School of Social Research in New York City. Then she tried different subjects at the New York City College to see what interested her most. She attended a design school for three months before settling on an MBA at Rutgers University, followed by a CPA degree.

She took to calling me Aniyan since my family addressed me by my childhood pet name, and I liked it. She once confessed that she would have hated me for the rest of her life if I hadn't married her. "How you looked at me so lovingly at our first meeting was like a promise. I couldn't have stood it if you had dashed that hope."

I laughed and hugged her. We were young and full of optimism.

CHAPTER 9

VENTURING INTO
THE UNKNOWN

WHEN I COMPLETED MY PHD and joined Chemical Bank in 1974, the US Financial Accounting Standards Board had just issued new rules on reporting the impact of currency movements on corporate financial statements. Companies were expected to manage their currency risk within those guidelines, and my department provided consulting to help them comply.

I wrote a paper on the subject for the bank, detailing the strategies that multinational companies could implement to prevent financial losses from adverse exchange rate changes. My suggested recommendations excited my boss, Alan Teck.

"Abraham, how long would it take you to implement your ideas if we provide you with the resources?" he asked. He wanted me to create a computer system for customers to manage their international financial risk, one that would distinguish us from our competitors.

"Six months, at least," I replied. I requested two good technical people to do the programming: Eric Roffman, who had a PhD in physics from Brandeis University, and Dietrich Fisher, a PhD student at the Courant Institute of Mathematical Sciences, New York University. Both were proficient in computer programming.

I wasn't sure what my button-down boss would think of Dietrich's college student appearance. "I know your style, but bankers are a little stiff. Would you consider wearing a tie to the interview?" I asked Dietrich.

"Sure, Abraham. I'll look for one," he replied with a smile.

He obliged me, although his tie was unstylishly pencil thin. But he turned up wearing a red sock on one foot and a blue one on the other. It hadn't occurred to me to recommend matching socks as well, but luckily my boss overlooked his unconventional dressing style, trusted my judgment, and hired him.

The three of us worked around the clock to develop the system, which was completed and tested after several months, and the bank then made it available to its international clients. Our novel approach successfully drew new clients. "We are the first bank to offer a computerized foreign exchange management system to corporate clients," my boss proudly announced at a staff meeting.

On the personal front, it was an exciting time with the birth of our first son, Ajit. My parents flew over to New York to meet their grandson. I had never felt this happy. Little did I know then how close I would soon come to losing it all.

One evening, I was home from work, waiting for Mariam to return from college. The phone rang.

A police officer on the other end introduced himself and asked, "Are you Abraham George?"

"Yes."

"Sir, your wife has been in an accident."

I gasped. "What?"

"It is best that you get to the hospital fast," he urged.

"How serious is it? Is she alive?" My heart pounded with overwhelming fear.

But the police officer wouldn't tell me more.

Frantically, I grabbed my infant son and ran next door where my friend Elizabeth lived. She was a nurse at the highly regarded Columbia Presbyterian Hospital in Manhattan. Luckily, she was home.

"I just got a call from the police. Mariam has been in an accident." I didn't have to explain more.

Elizabeth threw on a jacket and called out instructions to her housemaid, in whose care we left Ajit. We sped off in her car to a small hospital in Harlem. A flurry of frightening thoughts sped through my mind. I couldn't bear losing Mariam.

A police officer was waiting for us at the hospital entrance. "Your wife was hit by a speeding car while crossing a six-lane street." He explained that the impact had thrown her some twenty feet, and a bystander had called 9-1-1. "She was found unconscious, and an ambulance rushed her here."

A hospital attendant approached us.

"Can I see her?" I asked softly, struggling to find my voice.

The attendant directed me to the intensive care unit.

I waited nervously by the door. I found Mariam unconscious on a surgical table. Her right leg was turned in the wrong direction, and bloody bandages covered her arms and head.

Horrified, I asked, "What's her condition?"

One of the doctors replied, "We're trying to stabilize her. She's in a coma, but we're hopeful she'll come out of it soon."

Holding back my tears and questioning why this had to happen, I hurriedly stepped outside to call my parents.

Ammachi gasped. "Take care of what you need to do and call me back, Monu."

"I will," I assured them.

"Where is Ajit?" Achachan asked.

"With a friend."

"Don't worry. We'll come over to take him with us," Ammachi said.

Assured by their support, I rushed back to Mariam's side.

It felt like a lifetime before Mariam regained consciousness. Upon seeing me, she burst into tears.

"I'm here. You'll be okay. Don't worry," I said repeatedly, squeezing her hand. I fought back tears—I needed to be strong for both of us.

"How is Ajit?" she asked between sobs.

"Ammachi and Achachan will take care of him. Don't worry," I assured her, holding her hand.

The lead physician said, "We can address the leg injury only after a total scan. Any head injury must be ruled out first. Nothing more can be done until morning."

I found Elizabeth and expressed my concerns. "That's too long," she replied and immediately arranged for an ambulance to transfer Mariam to Columbia Presbyterian Hospital. Once we reached there, the emergency room doctor informed us, "No bed is available. She will have to be transferred elsewhere after she receives urgent care."

Elizabeth contacted her administrator, who allowed Mariam to remain in the hallway until a bed became available. I spent the night by her side as nurses attended to her. The following day, I met with specialists who described the nature of her injuries and medical needs. To our relief, scans revealed no brain injury, but her right femur and both shin bones were severely fractured, posing an imminent danger: Her lungs could clog from bone marrow seeping from the broken femur.

"She's still in physical shock. Her condition must stabilize before we operate on her leg fractures," the specialist said. The doctors needed to consult each other on how best to repair the leg without causing a permanent limp.

Two days later, an orthopedic surgeon operated on Mariam's leg and put it in traction. I balanced my work at the bank and attended to Mariam until late in the evening. She was in excruciating pain and relied on me to make her comfortable. Ajit remained in his grand-parents' care in Virginia.

Within three weeks, Mariam was sufficiently recovered to leave the hospital in a wheelchair. To my relief, her condition improved steadily with each passing day, and within two months, she could walk on crutches. The nightmare had finally passed, and I realized that fate was kind to save us from a terrible tragedy. It was my second time involving near-death experiences—the first in the dynamite blast and now a major car accident. Despite the seriousness of Mariam's injuries, I was immensely grateful that her life was spared, and the baby and I wouldn't be alone.

• • •

Bijoy announced his decision to proceed with a marriage proposal that Achachan and Ammachi had posed. He and my parents soon left for India, where the marriage ceremonies were to be held according to the wishes of the bride-to-be's family.

My parents worried that it might be risky for Mariam to undertake a rigorous trip to India three months after her accident. The doctors I consulted sided with them, cautioning that traveling in this early stage of recovery wasn't advisable.

But I disagreed. "It will be psychologically worse for her to miss the festivities," I said. Mariam was happy that I was on her side. "I will look after her," I assured everyone.

Taking care of a baby and an injured wife on a long flight to Calcutta, with a layover in London, was challenging. I must have been quite a sight descending the plane's stairs, cradling my son with one arm and supporting Mariam with the other as she struggled by my side on crutches.

Before proceeding to Trivandrum, we planned to visit Mariam's parents in Jamshedpur. We arrived at the overcrowded Howrah railway station in Calcutta in late evening, but the train's departure had been delayed until early the following day. Too exhausted and famished to search for a hotel in the middle of a stifling summer night, we hunkered down in a corner on the station's lobby floor, blending into a sea of refugees who had fled violence and political turmoil in East Pakistan in the early 1970s.

Poor Ajit cried nonstop.

"He's too hungry and uncomfortable in the heat, Aniyan," Mariam said, trying all she could to soothe him.

"Let me find hot water to mix his milk powder," I said, making my way through the masses, trying hard to not step on anyone.

At a small chai shop, the vendor gave me a dirty steel jar filled with hot water and an equally filthy tumbler. Offering him a few extra rupees to scrub the pot clean and boil the water in my presence, I asked in Hindi, "I need to make milk for our baby. Can you get me a clean glass?" I was glad my Hindi was still fluent enough.

By the time we boarded the train the following morning,

the sweltering heat had exhausted us, especially Ajit. We were panic-stricken—no matter how hard we tried, we couldn't wake him.

Sensing our parental anxiety, an elderly man across the aisle rescued us. "Don't worry. Just watch in a minute," he said in Hindi and emptied cold water from an earthen pot on Ajit. It was likely his drinking water.

Startled, our baby opened his eyes and looked around, drowsy and disoriented. Mariam cried out in relief, kissing Ajit and rocking him in her arms. I repeatedly thanked the kindly man for his thoughtfulness. Ajit went back to sleep and didn't wake up for hours until we reached Jamshedpur.

My in-laws' house wasn't air-conditioned, so we first checked into a modern hotel to recover from the heat and sleep for a while. Later, in the cool evening, we took a taxi to Mariam's parents' home. They were overjoyed to see us and to meet their grandson. But they were stunned to find Mariam on crutches, and I spent the first hour being interrogated.

"What was she doing outside the house in the evening anyway?" my father-in-law asked, making no effort to mask his disapproval.

"She was returning home after her evening class," I answered calmly.

"But why weren't you with her?" Mariam's mother asked, glancing first at me, then at her daughter, and back at me again.

Mariam's parents were shocked that she was out at night by herself—women in India wouldn't dare leave home after dark, and certainly not unaccompanied. Despite my efforts to explain how freely and independently women in America went about their business, they clearly found me guilty of not protecting their daughter. I gave up trying to justify myself.

Two days later, we traveled south to participate in Bijoy's wedding celebrations. Although Mariam hobbled on crutches throughout the long trip, she thoroughly embraced the event, helping plan the reception attended by over two hundred guests and reuniting with relatives and friends. I was glad that she hadn't missed this special family event. When it was over, we returned to America, exhausted but pleased that everything had turned out well.

• • •

Back at the bank from my overseas trip, I received a cordial welcome. Having introduced a new computer application that corporations found helpful, I earned the respect of my colleagues.

Recognizing how companies managed their foreign exchange risk, I saw market potential for another new system with numerous additional features. I gave considerable thought to creating an application superior to what Eric, Dietrich, and I had developed. Moreover, the bank's system was designed around the first set of regulations introduced by the Financial Accounting Standards Board, but just a year later, that same body proposed further rule changes. My planned software would incorporate those new rules and analytical tools to simulate risks and hedging strategies. It would be far superior to the previous one, and I could describe specifications for programmers to develop it.

If I was to make lots of money, working for a bank was not the career path I needed. I was impatient to start my own company and write a technical book on managing international financial risk. It wasn't prudent to announce my business plan, for fear that the bank might try to stop me. Instead, I cited having to work on my book as the main reason for my resignation.

"Abraham, the bank is prepared to give you a six-month sabbatical to write your book." Alan then offered me a substantial pay raise and promotion to persuade me to stay.

Although flattered and tempted, I didn't change my mind. "I don't want to rush the book. Moreover, I can't be sure how long it will take," I reasoned. He was dismayed by my firm decision.

A few days later, Mariam and I attended the bank's year-end party. She looked gorgeous in a colorful sari, drawing compliments from guests. I encouraged her to speak freely and introduce herself to everyone. As a young woman who hadn't socialized much in mixed company in a formal setting, she kept close to my side and shied away from conversation. As the evening progressed, she began to feel more at ease and chatted with my colleagues.

When we got home, Mariam said worriedly, "Aniyan, everyone thinks you shouldn't quit. Why do you want to walk away from such a good job? How do you know your plans will succeed?"

She had reason to be wary. I was proposing an audacious plan to start a computer software company that would offer a complex financial application and would compete with international banks providing related services. Such a business risk was too unnerving for her—perhaps memories of her father's failed trucking venture fueled her anxiety.

"This is an evolving field. It's a good time to move into it quickly. I have ideas no one else has implemented," I explained. But she wasn't convinced. It frustrated me that she couldn't relate to my ambition or see the potential I saw.

"Just trust me, Mariam. I have a good feeling about this," I said, confident I could financially support the family with part-time teaching jobs and future book royalties. I was moving practically alone into unknown territory. The challenges were formidable, but I was determined, daring to find out where this path would lead.

CHAPTER 10

CEASELESS PURSUIT

B Y 1979, I HAD COMPLETED the manuscript of my first book, *Foreign Exchange Management and the Multinational Corporation—A Manager's Guide.* Writing it had taken me four months, and Professor Hawkins encouraged me to submit it to Praeger Publishing. Being my first venture into authoring a book, I was skeptical about its acceptance.

"Why didn't you reference any other published works on the subject?" the editor at Praeger asked me.

"There's no other work on what I have written about," I explained nervously. "It's a brand-new field resulting from a change in the global financial system."

Bemused, he replied, "Well, then, others will reference you!"

I stared at him. Was he accepting my book for publication?

It turned out he was. To my amazement, the book soon became known as the "bible" among practitioners in banks and corporations seeking definitive steps to manage their companies' currency risk. Authoring the book helped me crystallize the necessary calculations for developing my planned software application. Methodologies and formulas were derived to analyze the impact of currency movements on corporate finances.

I reached out to Bijoy, who had completed his second master's in computer science at Courant Institute of Mathematical Sciences, NYU, to be the lead programmer. He jumped at the idea, and we jointly formed Multinational Computer Models Inc., or MCM for short. Having consulted for Bell Labs at AT&T, Bijoy knew other programmers and recruited three systems developers to work for MCM during their after-office hours.

At our first meeting in my apartment with the programmers, I sketched out the proposed system's enormous commercial potential but acknowledged our financial limitations. "I can't pay you now, but you will receive a stake in the new company," I said. Trusting my optimism, the programmers accepted the risk of the project. My apartment basement served as our head office, where we met on weekends for planning and coordination.

We spent the first two years designing and creating an initial product that could be presented to potential franchisees—mainly international banks—who would sell it as part of their consulting services to multinational corporate clients. There were many unknowns about how companies might respond to computer technology for solving financial problems, which until then were analyzed by scribbling on the "back of an envelope," as several managers described their work. Yet we were confident we could convince them to opt for computer applications to make superior decisions.

Working with brilliant technology experts to create a computerized product was highly invigorating. Each of us operated from home with a "dumb" terminal connected to a shared mainframe computer through telephone lines. Often working past midnight, we exchanged ideas, created code, transferred files, and tested system components. I don't recall being exhausted at the end of a night's work—the thrill of innovation and creativity overtook us, and my mind overflowed with new ideas and solutions to the challenges we hadn't resolved.

I worked from home and cared for Ajit while Mariam pursued her MBA. With my one-year-old son nestled in my lap, I anxiously awaited calls from prospective clients I had contacted in advance. Each time the phone rang, I quickly placed Ajit on the floor, with cookies strewn about to distract him. Sometimes, his cry in the background gave away that my office was my home.

Nearing an initial version of the application, it was time to form a board of directors for MCM. We needed names prospective investors and clients would recognize, and I knew the first name I wanted.

"Bob, would you please consider serving on the board?"

His response was immediate. "I would be honored, Abraham."

I was elated. His full-throated support was humbling. From then on, Bob frequently visited MCM's office in our basement to attend company meetings.

Commercially usable personal computers wouldn't be introduced until the early 1980s. Until then, we were obliged to lease General Electric's time-share system, an expensive way to develop applications. To speed up the programming, we brought on two more part-timers, who were offered shares in MCM.

Business expenses piled up. Luckily, one of the corporate clients I had worked for at Chemical Bank hired me as a consultant. While this opportunity generated some income for a few months, more was needed. I paid bills with cash advances on multiple credit cards and a small loan from a local bank. After a few months, seeing that MCM hadn't generated any income and believing the business would fail, the bank loan officer insisted we repay the loan within three months. Desperate, I reached out to my parents for help.

Achachan said, "Monu, your cousin in Washington tells us you're having trouble, and this business of yours has little chance of success."

Annoyed, I tried to allay my father's fears and perhaps my own—I had many irons in the fire to bring in new business. While Achachan remained unconvinced, Ammachi enthusiastically supported me, providing much-needed optimism. As long as I could keep our programmers hopeful on the future of the company, I thought I could somehow get over the difficulties.

However, I knew that making MCM successful would be a huge challenge. We were breaking into a new field, where it was difficult to persuade companies to use computers for managing financial risk. Additionally, our competitors were some of the largest banks, and our extremely limited financial resources severely restricted our activities. And I knew being a foreigner of color was a barrier. We could succeed only with tremendous perseverance and with the value we provided our clients.

When the application's first version was ready for release after over two years of development, I approached Alan Teck and offered him first dibs on selling it to the bank's clients. He was taken aback. "This system is similar to what you created while working with us, Abraham," he said sternly. I explained that it was designed and coded from the start, but he declined.

However, The Hong Kong & Shanghai Bank licensed the application for its corporate clients, and soon after, Wells Fargo Bank and Continental Illinois Bank also became resellers under their brand names. A good portion of this revenue cleared our loan from the local bank and my credit card debts. We set aside the balance for future expenses.

Although MCM was making just enough to cover ongoing expenses, we needed more funds to undertake new initiatives. Our financial situation again grew dire in less than a year, with barely enough cash to cover just a few more months. Constantly worried about meeting next month's payroll, I thought of every possibility, including teaching part time at three nearby colleges.

It dawned on me that the business wasn't growing fast enough because the banks we had licensed struggled to explain how our system could address companies' specific concerns and complexities and sell it. Customers found our system too expensive because they had to pay substantial amounts to GE to rent computer time in addition to paying bank fees. As a result, clients were reluctant to renew their contracts after the initial year.

This realization led to my first major strategic business decision to terminate the licenses given to the banks and instead approach companies directly. Doing so presented a new consideration: hiring and training in-house marketing and customer support teams. I would have to involve myself directly with customers. Moreover, MCM would need sufficient cash to pay additional staff. With help from my parents and our limited resources, we ran the company for a while. I hoped that our fortunes would turn around soon.

I devoted myself full time to marketing. We hired our first salesman, a former senior officer at an international bank, and I traveled with him to meetings he arranged with prospects. Initially, to limit travel expenses, we approached potential clients within New York City.

I was conscious that my South Asian descent and accent gave

prospective clients pause. I didn't know anyone of Indian origin running a software business in the international financial arena. In meetings, prospective clients were more attentive to my white partner than me. This bothered me initially, but I recognized the need to establish my credibility. One friend encouraged me, saying, "Abraham, since you are starting from a low point in their esteem, you can only go up."

Although I was in my early thirties, I looked much younger. Heeding Ammachi's advice, I started wearing glasses with thick frames to appear more mature. But a company executive saw through my trick and asked, "Why are you wearing zero-power glasses?"

Embarrassed, I confessed, "I wanted to be sure you would take me seriously."

He burst out laughing.

The significant deafness in my left ear also affected my ability to confidently interact with others and spontaneously respond to their humor or counter their good-natured sarcastic remarks. In corporate meetings, I positioned myself on the left, so others were to my right. Addressing a large audience, I openly disclosed my handicap. "Please raise your hand before you ask me a question. I'm hard of hearing." Although self-limiting, I tried to not feel sorry for myself. I drew strength from the fact that my father had overcome his stutter and my mother her hearing loss to pursue successful careers.

• • •

It surprised me later when Alan Teck sought an association with MCM after leaving the bank to start a consulting firm. I was initially unsure of his participation, given his previous rejection of our system, but knew that he was knowledgeable and skilled in sales.

With his help, our marketing efforts soon yielded over two dozen corporate clients.

The introduction of microcomputers allowed us to shift application components from time-share, and in a few years, our entire system ran in a stand-alone PC environment. MCM's enterprise software cost the companies far more than their PC hardware, but time-sharing charges disappeared—a net saving of several thousand dollars annually. Having developed an innovative way to address financial problems using concepts and techniques previously unfamiliar to the market, I sparked interest among potential customers.

The early versions of microcomputers had severe limitations in hard disk space, memory, and processing power. Unable to quickly transfer files from one machine to another, I had to carry the bulky CPU unit on my shoulders from parking garages to prospective clients' offices for meetings and demonstrations. Once, on my way along Park Avenue in New York City, the machine got doused with water dropped by a window cleaner several stories above.

Thanks to our team's strong mathematical and computer skills, we were able to integrate complex pricing and valuations of financial instruments into our application. MCM kept up with the rapidly changing financial market and accounting rules and offered a complete array of interrelated applications under the Global Treasury Management System (GTM) brand name. In migrating from time-share, we had to develop our own superior user interface to the early versions of MS Windows and implement faster download capability, but after a while, personal computers grew powerful and carried features that enabled our system to operate properly on PCs.

Nonetheless, we steadily acquired new customers. Being known as an expert in the field, I earned their respect and appreciation from offering my in-person assistance. Enthused by the demand for our application, Bijoy and his team addressed the occasional technical problems. Vinita, who holds a PhD in economics and quantitative analysis from Columbia University, soon joined the company as a product manager, and I quickly trained her in her new field.

As our revenue soared, MCM outgrew its small office in Montclair, New Jersey, and we moved into a large office complex in nearby Fairfield. In 1982, Vivek, our second son, was born, and my improved financial ability enabled us to afford a house in North Caldwell.

Mariam took up a full-time job as an associate at Coopers & Lybrand, a major auditing firm. Her mother came over from India to help look after our boys, and when she returned to India, Ammachi and Achachan, who had by then retired from their teaching positions, moved in with us. We were thankful for all the support while juggling full-time jobs and parenting.

My hectic schedule didn't permit much family time. Sometimes, I would fly from New York to Los Angeles to attend a luncheon meeting, hop over to San Francisco for a dinner meeting, and fly back to New Jersey that night, only to leave early the following day. Mariam was frustrated when I couldn't make it to parent-teacher meetings and when the boys performed in plays and tournaments.

I tried my best to attend family get-togethers on weekends. I carved out time to coach the boys' soccer teams, and they excitedly sought my advice on strategies for their next match. If I got home before their bedtime, I would go over to their rooms to chat, hear their stories, and shower them with hugs and kisses.

When Ajit was in his early teens, he complained that some classmates called him derogatory names and excluded him from activities. As members of a minority in a predominantly white community, we

were afraid this would happen—there was no escaping racial prejudice. Mariam was upset and didn't know how to handle the situation.
My initial reaction was to report it to the principal, but after some
thought, I decided otherwise.

"Ignore their insults. Prove yourself by your performance. Don't
let it stop you from participating in school activities," I urged my
son. I was confident he could shoulder the prejudice by displaying
self-confidence and self-esteem. "Never retaliate with aggression."

Ajit probably felt we weren't empathetic enough because, not having grown up in America, we couldn't relate to his experience. Like
any first-generation immigrants, Mariam and I were learning how
best to help our children adjust and fit into America's social system.
However, we possessed the hunger to do well in our adopted country
and have our family accepted as its rightful citizens.

Years later, and harboring guilt from not being around as much
as I would have liked, I asked my sons whether they had missed my
presence growing up. Ajit replied, "Dad, we knew you would be there
if anything happened or we needed you badly." Vivek added, "We
used to hear your footsteps when you came home in the middle of
the night or early in the morning when you left. That was enough." To
hear that the boys were secure in my love for them was heartwarming.

By the early 1990s, MCM had become a market leader in treasury
risk management systems, capturing a significant share of the US
multinational corporate market. With our US operations running
well, I dispatched two of our most senior team members to London
to establish a European office. An excellent team of British and other
Europeans was quickly assembled. Within a year or so, MCM picked
up several customers, forcing Bank of America to discontinue its
product offering in this field.

Internally, we had grown from three full-timers to several dozen, including the systems developers who had been with us from the start. We maintained offices in New York, New Jersey, California, and London and had a representative in Brussels. Before long, MCM opened another attractive office on the thirty-fifth floor of One World Trade Center in New York City, overlooking the Hudson River and the Statue of Liberty.

One morning, Credit Suisse First Boston called and invited me to meet with William Schein, a partner and one of the managing directors. Bill, as he asked to be called, was interested in exploring the possibility of an association with MCM to offer consulting services to the bank's clients in the international financial arena. I wasn't sure how a small company like ours joining forces with a leading investment bank would benefit both parties, but I was interested in finding out.

I proposed four conditions. First and foremost, our company's name, MCM, should be part of the new business operation. Second, I would be the new entity's managing director and chief consultant. Third, I could avail myself of an office at the bank's Park Avenue building in New York City while keeping my MCM office at the World Trade Center. Finally, I would receive a six-figure salary and stock options I could exercise if I decided to terminate the relationship.

"Your request to include MCM's name beside the bank's is preposterous, Abraham. I doubt the bank will agree." Bill appeared flustered, probably because he didn't think we were big enough to make such demands.

As Bill had warned, of all my conditions, combining MCM's name with CS First Boston in naming the new business entity was the most problematic. It required approval from the top management of Credit Suisse in Switzerland. To my surprise and delight, the New York office got the green light in just two weeks. The new entity was named CS First Boston-MCM Consulting Company.

It was highly unusual in 1990 for someone of Indian origin to be in my position at a major investment bank. Soon after the deal was signed, I met with the bank's president, Archibald Cox Jr., son of the famed special prosecutor who had investigated the break-in and burglary of the Democratic Party offices in the Watergate building.

Bill and I walked into Mr. Cox's expansive and luxurious office. He politely invited us to sit on a large sofa and asked me his first question: "So this is a get-rich-quick scheme, right?"

I paused for a moment. "Yes, for you too," I replied with a mischievous smile.

He burst out laughing, and the chemistry between us turned positive with this opening. He winked at me a couple of times while addressing pointed questions to Bill about the newly formed department's operations.

A strong team, including two Ivy League graduates, was soon put together to start the bank's consulting work. For about five years, I traveled frequently with its officers to cities nationwide. Every other day, a limousine picked me up early from home and took me to the airport, where a junior bank officer handed over work papers and escorted me to the plane to join Bill. Over the next few years, we attracted nearly fifty Fortune 500 companies as our clients.

Hearing about me, the Church of Jesus Christ of Latter-day Saints (LDS Church) dispatched two senior officers from Salt Lake City to learn more and hire me as the church's international financial advisor. At the time, there likely weren't any others from outside the LDS Church privy to their confidential financial information. Over the next eight years, I earned enough trust and affection of senior church members to be honored at the sacred Salt Lake Temple and taken to the inner chamber where the "marriage sealing ceremony" for worthy members was held.

Among my notable consulting clients, I remember my ten years with Eastman Kodak from 1986 to 1996. As a leading multinational company doing business in practically every country, Kodak derived revenues in many currencies and expended considerable sums in each. I was hired as its financial advisor to help manage foreign exchange, debt, investment, and cash internationally.

When the Japanese yen's value dropped in currency markets, Kodak's competitive edge against Fujifilm weakened. I was asked to develop a financial strategy so Kodak products could be sold in yen at competitive prices in Japan while protecting the dollar value of its profits. I presented a foreign exchange strategy involving a combination of derivatives to the company's senior management, who accepted it and proceeded to execute hedges of over $200 million. Over the subsequent year, Kodak was able to partially offset its business losses in Japan with financial gains in its currency hedges, and I was amply rewarded.

• • •

Caught up in the excitement of consulting with major clients and generating money for the bank and myself, my accomplishments and recognition invigorated me. I had reached the peak of my professional career and was known as the leading expert in international treasury management. My family took trips to Europe, exposing Ajit and Vivek to other cultures. I was drawn to museums and ancient cathedrals, home to celebrated artists' exemplary paintings and sculptures.

We would occasionally go to Broadway plays and musicals like *Evita*, *Phantom of the Opera*, and *Cats*.

I took on outdoor adventures, like deep-sea fishing and fly-fishing, river rafting, and Jet Skiing on the ocean. I fondly recall one of my trips to Alaska to enjoy its wilderness in the summer. Wading waist-deep in the river, my friends and I walked upstream with the fly line, patiently enticing trout hiding behind stones. Catch-and-release—the practice of returning the fish alive back to the water after hooking it—taught me that the fun lay not simply in striving for and accomplishing what I set out to do but in giving something back.

With my newfound wealth came respect, especially from the local Indian community. At parties, people sought my company and friendship. Mariam and I were seen as a couple who had done well for themselves. But we were mindful not to let the family's wealth turn Ajit and Vivek arrogant. We didn't allow the boys to throw expensive birthday parties nor did we give them extravagant gifts on any occasion. "Don't show off. Be modest," we told them. If they ever acted arrogantly, I would firmly reprimand them, "Your behavior lacks humility. I will not accept this."

During the holiday season, I would ask them to consider forgoing snacks so they could donate to charities that saved children facing starvation in Ethiopia. The boys were glad to share, and I was happy they saw value in kindness and generosity.

I invested my savings in stocks and bought two beachfront condominiums on the Gulf Coast of Florida, one of which was a winter home for my parents in Marco Island, and a large luxury apartment in New Jersey. I acquired twenty-three acres of rolling grounds in a secluded area of Boonton Township, New Jersey, less than an hour from Manhattan, for building a seven-thousand-square-foot family house. Wanting to learn all about construction, I assumed the role of the general contractor and worked with an architect and subcontractors for each aspect of the building. It was an experience that offered a novel sense of creative freedom.

Once the building was completed, we hired a reputed landscape architect to design the lush gardens, a waterfall, a tennis court, a gunite swimming pool with a spa, and a volleyball court—all at different levels on the slope of a hill. Named after the nearby private road, Penny Lane had a distinctive beauty and a touch of my imagination for the house I wanted for my family.

Mariam and I enjoyed visiting nurseries to select different varieties of pine trees and exotic plants to create delightful gardens. I frequented antique shops and auctions to collect objets d'art for the house; Ammachi, too, purchased many items to decorate the house. My keen interest in marine life inspired me to create a sizable saltwater aquarium, covering much of the front wall of the entrance foyer, with exotic coral fish and live plants. I spent my evenings after work tending to the tank and admiring the colorful fish.

The house offered a separate section with a private entrance for my parents. I was gratified to take good care of them and give them company. I spent considerable time with them on days when I was home, discussing whatever concerned them.

Ammachi was delighted to have a music room with a piano and a *veena*—an Indian stringed instrument—and an art room in the basement. She spent a considerable part of the day there, working on her paintings of landscapes, birds, and animals, which she hung up all over the house.

Penny Lane also served as the gathering place for our extended family. Mariam and I didn't know who might visit my parents or stay over on any given night. Significant occasions like Thanksgiving, New Year's, Christmas, and birthdays were hosted at our place. Mariam was only too pleased to do much of the cooking; family members pitched in with their favorite dishes, and I served as the official taster and turkey carver.

My nieces and nephews stayed at Penny Lane during their summer vacations. The sound of children joyfully running about the house was an added pleasure, one their grandparents looked forward to. With great fondness, I would tell stories and make jokes to keep them entertained. Ammachi would set a schedule for them, detailing their activities from early morning until late evening, which included painting, clay sculpting, swimming, tennis, drama, piano, singing, and reading.

These pastimes kept the children busy and excited all day. Occasionally, they would treat a delighted audience of adults to their renditions of plays. After they retired to bed, my parents, siblings, and I would stay up, enjoying wine and talking late into the night. I only wished my paternal grandparents in Ayyampilly could have been with us.

The wealth I had acquired offered comforts I couldn't have imagined as a young boy in southern India. Our new home was a sweet reminder of our beloved Bella Vista. "You've done well for yourself, Abraham. This is fabulous," relatives and friends remarked. They saw Penny Lane as a reward for my professional accomplishments.

CHAPTER 11

A PROMISE TO KEEP

Fifteen years passed, and tension between Ammachi and Mariam gradually developed into disagreements on day-to-day matters, causing Ammachi to openly display unhappiness at how Mariam was running the home. For her part, Mariam felt she lacked the freedom to do things as she wished at home. I empathized with her desire to decorate the house how she preferred, invite the guests she wanted to entertain, and bring up the boys the way she thought best.

I reasoned, "Mariam should have the freedom to make her own choices, Ammachi. You must accept her ways." I wondered if Ammachi had forgotten how her mother-in-law had treated her during those summers at Ayyampilly.

I tried to appease Mariam: "You do what you want in the home, but don't be disrespectful to Ammachi." It was hard for her to understand that Ammachi belonged to a generation where a daughter-in-law lived under the dictates of her husband's mother in an extended family situation. Neither my mother nor my wife heeded my advice or requests. Mariam didn't hide her unhappiness, which annoyed Ammachi, and if I said anything supportive of Mariam, Ammachi would get upset with me. The disagreements between Ammachi and Mariam became far too frequent. Feeling helpless and exasperated, I told my siblings, "I am caught in the middle."

Even though we lived in America, Ammachi clung to Malayali traditions regarding family hierarchy and relationships. I was glad my children didn't have such a mindset given that they, unlike the first generation of immigrants, had lived their entire lives in America, absorbing its open-mindedness and personal freedom as their birthright.

My role as mediator was taking its toll, causing stress at home and work. Unhappiness hung heavily on me, and I worried how it was affecting our boys. Every evening when I returned from the office, I dreaded what might await me. I would go to the music room on the ground floor to be alone, something I did to reflect undisturbed. I finally made a decision I had never imagined making.

"Ammachi and Achachan, will you consider moving to a new place I have bought for you? This is the only way there will be peace in the family," I pleaded. My heart was heavy with guilt and sorrow. My parents were shocked into silence—nothing could have prepared them for such a request.

Ammachi stormed off to her bedroom. Her pride wouldn't allow her to argue or reason with her son who, according to her, was throwing her out of her home. Achachan, too, said nothing and followed her. I retreated to the study to reflect on what had happened and process my emotions. As heartbreaking as it was, I knew this compromise had to be made. My siblings were unhappy at this turn of events but understood the situation we were in. Some extended family members expressed their disapproval, and a few perceived me as arrogant and uncaring. I was emotionally devastated for years to come.

On the day my parents were to move out of Penny Lane, I drove them to their new home—a four-story waterfront condo with a private elevator by the Hudson River, overlooking the Manhattan skyline. Ammachi remained silent the whole drive. Whatever Achachan was feeling, he didn't show, probably for my sake. His sensitivity didn't console my troubled and guilt-stricken self.

I walked them around the beautifully furnished apartment and pointed out the World Trade Center and the Empire State Building from its top floor. "Ammachi, look, this is one of the best views of the Manhattan skyline," I explained. She still said nothing, stubbornly holding onto her long silence. My feigned cheery voice echoed oddly in the lovely apartment. I probably sounded like an insincere salesman.

I turned to my mother, took her hand, and said, "Ammachi, I'm sorry. I thought this was best for all of us." Nothing I could say or do could right this. My words sounded hollow to her ears; there could be no forgiveness for a beloved son who had betrayed her.

My siblings and I visited our parents weekly for the next eight years. At first, Mariam was nervous about accompanying me, knowing how upset Ammachi was with her, but she always came along. She would cook their favorite dishes on Saturday, enough for the entire week, and bring them over on Sunday.

Ammachi would speak poorly of Mariam to Ajit and Vivek. I advised the boys to understand her grief and not take sides. I knew how difficult it was for them to be caught between their mother and grandmother, two people they loved dearly. We were all hurting. Only time could ease Ammachi's resentment and heal us as a family.

• • •

Strangely, when I seemed to have it all—financial strength, privilege, and prestige—a persisting gloom overshadowed me. I couldn't focus at work, and I didn't enjoy attending social events as much anymore. Struggling to sleep, I would wake up by midnight and quietly slip out of bed and go to the music room. Sitting restlessly alone in the dark, I would yield to melancholy. The plaintive melody of Samuel Barber's "Adagio for Strings," which I often played, mirrored my troubled state.

Mariam would often find me staring blankly into space. Gently prying my fingers from my tense, clenched fists, she would ask, "What's happening to you, Aniyan? Tell me, please."

I tried to reassure her. "Everything's fine. I need some quiet time to think."

"You come home from work, but you're never here. Something is bugging you. Why can't you enjoy what we have?" she would ask in a helpless tone.

I tried to put her at ease, but my assurances fell short.

Other family members echoed the same concern and probably assumed that recent troubles on the home front were weighing me down or that I was going through a midlife crisis. Worried, Ammachi would ask whenever I visited her, "Monu, is anything bothering you? Why are you so down? Achachan and I have noticed this for a while now."

"Don't worry, Ammachi. I'm okay," I would reply, although my haggard face and dark under-eye circles said otherwise.

I couldn't disclose, even to my mother, that I was deeply discontented. I worried that others wouldn't understand that I was losing interest in wealth and material possessions and that I viewed my affluent lifestyle as self-indulgent. Moreover, the guilt I carried by separating my parents from Penny Lane left me empty. The joy of past accomplishments disappeared, and I needed a new purposeful challenge. It was, however, comforting that I had the flexibility to undertake what I might wish to do, as my boys didn't have to worry about the family's financial stability since Mariam and I had secured our children's futures through our professional success.

I was acutely aware that the promise I had made to myself to help those in need—a desire that had first come about in my days at Se La—remained unfulfilled. After work, I would retreat to my study for hours to consider several options to act on my original commitment. My thoughts wandered to people elsewhere who were suffering for a variety of reasons. Images of starvation in sub-Saharan Africa and India bothered me deeply, and I tried to determine why so much poverty existed in the world and what could be done.

Several articles and documentaries on widespread global hunger taught me that most poverty alleviation programs in less developed countries were built on feeding the masses, with foreign aid being the driver. Developmental standards like literacy and absolute poverty levels were poor yardsticks to gauge improvement in the condition of the poor. These countries relied on the World Bank, the United Nations, and their corrupt governments to improve their situation without adequate solutions to tackle the root causes of poverty.

I was convinced that abject poverty stemmed not from people failing to work hard but from a lack of opportunities and from the injustice perpetuated on the underclass for generations. It was unrealistic to expect high achievement from those who received only basic education through primary schooling.

In searching for stories of those who had successfully addressed large-scale poverty, I came across the work of M. S. Swaminathan.

He had introduced and developed high-yield varieties of wheat and rice to multiply crop output and address hunger, earning him the title of "Father of the Green Revolution in India." His work transformed India from having constant famine to having a food surplus within a short span.

The White Revolution followed this in India, pioneered by a close relative of mine, V. Kurian. He aimed to substantially increase the nation's milk supply through superior dairy farming. The massive cooperative movement he created in the villages started with three high-breed cows from Australia. He made me recognize the power of the individual and ideas as opposed to that of bureaucratic institutions. I was confident that I, too, could make an impact if I committed to it.

Aware of my passion for social work, a good family friend, Angeline, asked if I would consider sponsoring the private school education of five Black children who were attending a substandard public school in Newark, New Jersey. Their mothers were drug users in rehab with support from a Catholic missionary institution called LINK.

The prospect of seeing the children thrive in school excited me; after all, I owed much of my success in America to the opportunity Professor Hawkins had granted me. I readily agreed to pay the tuition fee and transfer the boys to private schools on the condition that their mothers would not go back to drug abuse. It was my naive attempt to bring stability into the children's lives, without which I felt their ability to concentrate on their studies would be hindered.

I recall taking the boys on a field trip to Wall Street, an experience I thought might inspire them to seek professional careers in business. Over time, I became frustrated by my inability to establish an emotional bond with the children. My contact with them was limited to just two meetings a year, and even when we did meet, it was in the presence of social workers, presumably for my legal protection. I wanted to involve myself in the children's upbringing and share a meaningful mentor–mentee relationship, which the system wouldn't permit.

Though I was disheartened, this philanthropic endeavor was eye-opening. It made me realize that I would draw great joy from participating in the children's daily lives, caring for their welfare, and aiding their progress at every step. It showed me that the best way to bring about a change in children like them was to run a residential school that offered quality education in a nurturing and stable environment.

· · ·

With a renewed purpose for my existence, enthusiasm thawed my depressed spirit. Now that I was successful financially, I could embark on what I had wanted to do all along. I couldn't wait any longer if I was to maintain the mental and physical energy to undertake demanding social ventures. At least before my fiftieth birthday, I wanted to establish a nonprofit organization to embark on my mission.

Feeling the urgency, I told Angeline, "I want to start a residential school where the need is greatest."

After careful thought, she said, "I urge you to establish your base in Bangalore, Abraham." She explained that this city, known as the Silicon Valley of India, offered opportunities to keep up with the developed world. Yet it had a disturbingly high poverty rate in its slums and the hundreds of neighboring villages surrounding it.

Of the 1.2 billion people then living in India, some 225 million were Dalits, meaning "broken people." Another 600 million were among the lower castes, classified by the government as Backward Classes and Most Backward Classes. The poorest stratum of society eked out their living at menial jobs considered too lowly or dirty for those in the upper castes. Present but invisible to the rest of Indian society, these poor folks were in the background, their plight an object of indifference.

India's caste system has existed since the seventh century CE. It came into being when societal conflicts created different classes of people assigned to different tasks. The theological justification of caste can be found in the Rig Veda around 1200 BCE. Over time, caste became legally entrenched, justifying itself as a part of daily life. Notions of "purity" and "pollution" governed the separation of the lowest castes from others above them.

Symbolic religious observances maintain caste status; certain rituals and prayers are known only to those in the upper castes. Differences between castes are assumed to be naturally ordained. Unlike race in America, where the physical difference between people is used to justify perpetuating injustice, caste depends upon imaginary differences and social or religious rules of separation.

India's central government passed two enactments to eradicate untouchability: the Civil Rights Acts of 1955 and the Scheduled Castes and Scheduled Tribes Act of 1989. In 1992, the government formed the National Commission for Scheduled Castes and Scheduled Tribes to protect the interests of Dalits and integrate them into mainstream society. The laws make the practice of untouchability a punishable offense for perpetrators, but they do not directly abolish untouchability. The constitution does not mention establishing a casteless society as a national goal.

Despite these steps, caste discrimination is prevalent in many parts of India. Members of the dominant and higher castes own more fertile land in the villages, with easy access to water. Lower caste men are exploited by upper castes, who appropriate their land (usually when they cannot repay high-interest loans), give them low wages, use them as bonded labor, and otherwise deny them fundamental human rights. In many schools in rural areas, Dalit children sit in a separate section of classrooms. When using public transportation, upper caste people often avoid seats near lower caste passengers. Prejudice might not be blatantly visible, but the underlaying attitude hasn't changed much over the years.

I was greatly offended by these degrading practices during my college years. I understood that the miserable condition of the poor was associated with their low social status. Government policies offering benefits and privileges to the deprived castes will not change the mindset of the upper castes; such change must stem from the accomplishments of those discriminated against. The path to social justice for the poor is through substantive economic opportunity for them—not by trying to persuade those who are privileged to treat all others fairly.

Extreme poverty and social discrimination have deprived lower caste families of the opportunity to properly raise their children and give them proper education to pursue professional careers. Without these privileges, the underclass will remain at the bottom indefinitely, with no possibility of attaining equality with mainstream society. Now that I was embarking on social work, it became my mission to do something about these issues, even if my efforts would be limited in scope. I wasn't interested in becoming an activist but rather a facilitator of economic opportunities for poor people.

In my opinion, empowering the poor from the bottom up is the right approach to breaking the shackles of the caste system. Hence, educating children of underprivileged communities would eventually give them financial power through well-paying jobs. With professional achievements leading to prosperity, they would overcome barriers and find acceptance in mainstream society as equals.

"When they do, they will carry many others with them, bringing forth a multiplicative impact," I told Angeline. The idea excited me, and I was ready to take it up as my life's mission.

. . .

The more I thought about it, the more convinced I became that Bangalore and its environs might be the perfect location for what I envisioned. I was familiar with its culture and societal ways and felt confident that the people I would serve would accept me.

Religious and lingual differences weren't my concerns; I was confident I could make friends with people of diverse sociocultural backgrounds and win them over with sincerity and honesty. My dual vantage point—the views of someone of Indian origin who had grown up in India but had spent much of his adult life abroad—could offer me a unique perspective.

I sought Bob's counsel on pursuing this new project. "I've decided on an action plan for my social endeavor," I told him "Establish an NGO, purchase land to build the school on, and recruit my core team."

"That would be remarkable, Abraham," he replied excitedly.

"I would like to create one hundred schools, a school or two in each state," I said, detailing my vision.

His confidence in me to undertake such an endeavor deeply encouraged me. Still, he worried about corruption and the official hurdles I would have to surmount to get things done.

As harsh as it might sound, I wasn't seeking anyone's consent. I presented the plan to my family one weekend as a fait accompli. My interest in social work didn't surprise them, as I had spoken about it often in the past. But no one expected me to jump into a new, quixotic venture at the height of a thriving business career.

"I'm leaving for India in two months. Angeline is returning to Bangalore, and she has offered to help me establish a foundation," I said.

"How long will you be gone?" Mariam asked in an anxious tone.

"Two to three months this time."

"How frequently?"

"I don't know, Mariam. There's so much to be done. I'll know more after I get there." I was deliberately brief in my replies, unfairly so, to avoid facing her apprehension.

"What about our sons? You'll be away from them," she continued. Ajit was twenty and in college, and Vivek was twelve. I, too, had concerns regarding my absence's impact on our boys. I hoped that someday they would understand why I had pursued this path and that they would embrace the mission as their own.

"I'm always there for them, Mariam. I'm just a phone call away," I replied firmly, hiding my sadness. "Moreover, you three can visit me during vacations." But I knew it would be hard for Mariam and the boys to live without my daily presence.

"But why India? Nothing is easy there," Achachan cautioned.

I nodded. "I'll operate independently of the government, so I'll be free to run the school the way I want."

Ammachi hadn't seen me this happy in a long time. "Aniyan, if this is what you want to do, go ahead."

There was much discussion in the family, as it entailed many unknowns. Lekha readily offered to assist in creating a school policy and procedure manual. Having earned a PhD in education administration, she was well suited for the task and was excited by my idea.

I arranged for MCM to operate without my daily oversight for three months. The top three managers, including Vinita, were assigned major managerial roles. Bob visited me at Penny Lane to offer guidance about protecting my family's interests in MCM and document my will if something was to happen.

On the day of my departure, Vinita hugged me and said with concern, "Kochetta, I hope you find what you are searching for."

PART III

CHAPTER 12

A HAVEN OF PEACE

IN EARLY FEBRUARY 1995, Vivek and I arrived in India. We traversed the country, from the bustling cities of Mumbai and Delhi to the cultural hub of Chennai and, finally, my hometown, Trivandrum. Vivek's first impressions bewildered him; his understanding of India was primarily shaped by the vivid descriptions of its physical beauty and the lives of its most remarkable souls, from Buddha and Gandhi to Tagore and Vivekananda. Now he was seeing an India quite different.

I wanted Vivek to develop a deep appreciation for India's rich cultural heritage—its poetry, music, visual art, architecture, philosophy, and religion—which shaped the temperament of its people over thousands of years and demonstrated their remarkable resilience. Despite foreign invasions and natural disasters throughout India's expansive history, the spirit of the country's people remains unyielding.

We visited relatives who extended the warm hospitality I had promised Vivek he would receive. After years of absence, my sudden appearance surprised them, and they were pleased to meet my son. Having heard about me from my parents, they knew I had a successful business in America and that things had worked out well for me.

So much had changed since I had last seen them years ago. My memory of them as healthy and energetic was different from now seeing them old and frail, which saddened and frightened me. My paternal grandparents were no longer alive, so we didn't go to Ayyampilly. I took Vivek to my late maternal grandfather's house in Trivandrum, where I had spent wonderful childhood years.

At last, we arrived at our ultimate destination, Bangalore. Tempted to enjoy the luxuries of modern-day India, we decided to stay at the Taj West End, one of the few five-star hotels in the city at the time. Globalization and a robust technological revolution had unleashed a wave of newfound prosperity in the country since it liberalized its economic policies in 1991.

Driving around the city, I noticed bustling, busy streets, fancy textile and jewelry shops, towering multistory office buildings, gated apartment complexes, and foreign cars. Motorbikes, bicycles, buses, trucks, and bullock carts flooded the narrow, tarred roads strewn with large potholes, presenting a complex picture of city life.

Amid the display of wealth lay the distinct face of poverty: Daily wage earners and migrant workers flocked to the city for jobs in factories and construction sites; desperate street vendors sold flowers, toys, and fried snacks in the tropical sun; beggars pleaded with passersby amid traffic jams; and the urban poor lived in tarpaulin sheds in slums beside large garbage dumps and reeking open sewers. The squalor-filled existence of people with low incomes juxtaposed with those reaping the fruits of economic progress in a populous country of over one billion people was jarringly unnerving. It became clear to me that wealth and income gaps between the haves and have-nots had already widened substantially.

After Vivek returned to the United States to resume his studies, I joined Angeline to start my work. She arranged a breakfast meeting at the hotel to introduce me to prospective board members for a soon-to-be-formed charitable trust. Most of them held prominent positions in business or government. I didn't know any of them except Elizabeth Jacob, a childhood friend from Kerala. Everyone was cordial and curious about my background, but unreserved objections arose when I shared my interest in starting a private boarding school of excellence for children from socially deprived backgrounds.

"What I plan to embark on is an attempt to bring about major transformation within one generation," I continued animatedly, hoping my vision would inspire them. "With proper upbringing and excellent education, these children will overcome their economic disadvantage and inferiority. They and others to follow need not suffer what their ancestors endured for fifteen hundred years. With financial progress, their communities will prevail over their low social status and caste prejudices."

It was too much to grasp in succession. No one seemed to agree, except for Angeline, Elizabeth, and a renowned pediatric neurologist named Dr. Mahadeviah.

"Why do you need a residential school? It's very difficult to manage. Instead, you can fund government day schools that serve thousands of children," one said.

"You're not going to get the results you're seeking with children from uneducated families," expressed another.

"Your mission is going to fail miserably. You'll be wasting money on children who don't have role models to follow," a third potential board member joined in.

The most discouraging comment was "Children from poor homes

don't have the mental capacity to learn well and succeed. They don't need the comforts you plan to offer them, like a pretty garden, modern classrooms, and comfortable dorms. If you just rent a suitable building, you can have many children come to study there in the daytime and return home after school."

Their objections took me aback. Well-educated people were affirming India's entrenched social prejudices of centuries past. They were not seriously disturbed by the inequality between India's wealthy and those left behind. They didn't see the importance of advancing the human potential of poor people through excellent education, leading to their contribution to the country.

"There is no data to support your claim that these children can't overcome their disadvantages and achieve success, so you can't possibly know the outcome. No one has tried this approach. I believe that nurture is just as powerful, if not more, than nature," I responded with conviction, trying hard to withhold my irritation.

"Abraham believes that if we raise children from poor homes properly and provide them with an exceptional education in a safe, supportive environment, they can do just as well as their affluent peers," Angeline added.

"Look, I don't deny that developmental problems caused by early life stress like malnutrition will still exist. If we accept children at a young age, say three-and-a-half or four, we might overcome or reverse the effects of cognitive deficiencies or traumas." Despite my arguments, I saw no sign of having convinced anyone, but they were attentive, so I continued.

"Further, I don't believe academic performance alone dictates their future accomplishments. Children will flourish if we bring them up to be well-rounded individuals. The financial impact of their success on surrounding communities and families will be exponentially greater."

Were my expectations of the children too far-fetched? The board members continued to argue—I hadn't persuaded anyone.

"I believe the results will be predicated on the children's upbringing and the program's quality, so I propose we move forward," I said emphatically, hoping to conclude the argument.

The discussion then turned to potential bureaucratic hurdles. I explained that I would run the school as a private organization and not seek financial assistance from the government. Again, my insistence on not engaging the government was met with concern. They reminded me that social work in India involved government participation, oversight, and financial support.

One member pointed out that government officials and labor unions would object if we terminated the employment of any full-time staff member. "Employee unions in India are powerful enough to bring down an organization," he warned. No one agreed with my views on strict hiring and firing practices: Hire based on merit and fire for poor performance. The team saw me as a hard-nosed businessman.

On this and several other issues, I couldn't reach a consensus from the board, nor was I willing to relent on my operating principles. It was time for everyone to focus instead on how to accomplish my vision.

When another obstacle was raised, Elizabeth jumped in and said, "Make it happen," gesturing to me. The phrase had become my mantra. Her good-humored remark broke the tension and gave us all a good laugh.

"It's your money and your idea. We will not stand in your way. But remember, Abraham, you're in India, not America," one of them advised.

Despite their lack of enthusiasm, the prospective board members agreed to lend their support, which reassured me. It was their moral rather than financial assistance that I had been seeking all along—boots on the ground with influence in the local area, in case we encountered trouble.

The next order of business was selecting a name for the school. Inspired by my maternal grandfather's house, *Shanthi Niketan*, I chose *Shanti Bhavan*, meaning "haven of peace." For the first time, everyone unanimously approved my suggestion.

I clarified that the school would be secular in all respects—I didn't want it to be mistaken for a Christian institution. The board members wanted the foundation to be named after the person who conceived the idea and would fund it, at least in its initial years. That's how our NGO officially became The George Foundation.

Following the meeting, at parties with the affluent society in Bangalore, guests approached me about the project and offered advice. Most reactions echoed the initial sentiments of the board members. My decision to return to India to work in the social arena appeared irrational to some. Given their strong views, I didn't reveal my desire to transform the social status of the Dalits by establishing many Shanti Bhavans all over the country.

I grew tired of arguing with them. "Listen, this is my mousetrap, and this is how I wish to catch mice," I would occasionally reply in exasperation. I was consumed by the excitement of what I was about to undertake, and no objection from others would stop me from moving forward. My mission was set long ago, and plans were made after much consideration, and I was determined to prove them wrong.

One morning, I was surprised by an uninvited guest at the hotel. Since I didn't have a meeting or appointment for the day, I figured word had spread about the school. Entering the lobby, I met a middle-aged gentleman traditionally dressed in South Indian style—a shirt and a *lungi*, a cotton garment tied around the waist. We sat down, and I ordered tea.

Without introducing himself, he said, "Mr. George, I heard you have come here to start a school for the poor."

"Yes." I assumed he had learned about my plans from the board members.

"You're nothing but a hypocrite. You stay in such a posh hotel and claim you have come to help our poor people!"

I was stunned. Irked at having a stranger question my sincerity, I cut him short. "I don't need to explain or justify why I'm staying here."

"You should live modestly if you are honest," he replied, gesturing to the luxurious surroundings.

I countered, "I want to be comfortable as well as care for poor people. I can do both." I saw no conflict in enjoying the new India while undertaking social work.

Livid, he walked out.

I calmed down and thought about what had just happened. Perhaps he found my demeanor to be that of an arrogant foreign businessman. Most people didn't seem to trust anyone claiming to help the poor, and I was no exception. This was the first of several mistrusts I would face as a philanthropist in the coming years.

· · ·

I set out to find suitable land to build the school outside Bangalore in a rural community. This task wasn't something the new board members could manage or had time for. As I drove farther from the city, traces of the burgeoning wealth and prosperity turned into scenes of thatched huts, small shops, and run-down government schools. Children ran barefoot, men and women worked in *ragi* fields, groups of older men sat under banyan trees smoking *bedis* or small hand-rolled cigars, and women carried plastic cans on their heads to fetch water from the lake or gathered in groups to wash clothes by the canal.

Some people have a nostalgic view of rural India. Villages are peaceful havens where people live simple lives, where the air is pure, and the land is green as far as the eye can see. Some of those images are indeed true, but the cruel realities of the day-to-day lives of the poor are also real. A great majority of the country's 800 million rural people live in poverty, constrained by their limited skills and education. The rural populations are mere spectators and marginal beneficiaries of the newfound wealth in the cities.

My land search over the next month yielded no results. The leads received from the board members hadn't materialized either, and time was running out. Disappointed, I wondered what to do.

On the last day of my brief trip to India, a stranger appeared at my door unannounced. Was it another disgruntled person who wanted to rebuke me? He introduced himself as Jude Devdas and said, "Sir, I learned about you and the project from one of the board members. I want to be involved."

I soon discovered that Jude came from a family that had been in deep-sea tuna fishing with Japanese crews for months. I understood he was a doer, with a natural taste for adventure. His firm voice, charming smile, and pleasant demeanor impressed me. For a fee or employment with the foundation, Jude offered to find land for the school.

I asked him to write me and suggest sites.

"Dr. George, I will get going on this immediately."

True to his word, Jude frequently faxed me maps, drawings, and photos of potential properties. He narrowed his selections to a piece of attractive land that met my main criteria: rolling rather than flat terrain and a fair distance from noisy, congested roads. After further investigation, he stopped pursuing this property, concluding that the landowner didn't have sufficient documentation to prove he owned it. I was grateful that Jude didn't try to persuade me to purchase something that could have resulted in financial loss and disputes. His honesty solidified my confidence in offering him a senior manager's job with The George Foundation.

CHAPTER 13

A PLACE OF OUR OWN

U PON RETURNING TO INDIA on my next trip three months later, Jude showed me other options, but none fit the bill. Resuming the hunt myself, I drove to the neighboring state of Tamil Nadu one rainy morning, accompanied by a broker who understood my desire to set up a school in a poverty-stricken area. He asked whether I would consider his ancestral village, Baliganapalli, nearly two hours from Bangalore, in the Dharmapuri District of Tamil Nadu.

Describing the village, he emphasized, "Sir, people there are impoverished. Female infanticide and child marriage are still widely prevalent." I knew of these cruel traditions from childhood; they had long existed, even in Kerala. Poor families who couldn't afford a dowry for their daughters looked upon the birth of a female child as a curse.

He told me that the upper castes oppressed the lowest castes in this village and sixteen neighboring ones. Lower caste colonies were established where the wind would not blow toward the upper caste dwellings and contaminate them. The lower castes could not draw water from higher caste wells, touch food vessels used by upper castes, or pray in higher caste temples. They were barred from the prominent part of every village and relegated to menial and degrading tasks such as clearing waste and collecting recyclable items from garbage heaps. They were forbidden to bury their dead anywhere near the village for fear that their "ghosts" would harm the higher caste people.

I replied, "Let's go see it."

We drove along unpaved, bumpy rural roads to reach the location. Pointing across a vast, beautiful lake bordering a village entrance, the broker said, "There are close to thirty acres for sale over there. We'll have to walk along the cart track to get to it, though." The narrow cart track along the lake shore was partly submerged. Undeterred, we rolled up our trousers and waded for some distance before coming upon a couple of *nallas*, or ravines, and then set foot on raised land that didn't look like it had ever been touched.

"Be careful of snakes and scorpions, sir!" the broker shouted as I clambered up a large boulder on the property's highest point. I surveyed the terrain and took in its raw beauty. An endless line of eucalyptus trees bordered the rolling grounds covered with dry shrubs, cacti, thorny bushes, anthills, and massive rock formations. The surrounding lake was bursting with life, attracting beautiful migratory birds. The setting was serene and splendid. *How wonderful this deserted terrain will look when the campus is built,* I thought. The land beckoned me, and I knew this was where Shanti Bhavan would be.

Overcome with excitement, I asked to meet the landowner, and the broker escorted me to the nearest village. We arrived at a large, single-story traditional house with a tiled roof. An older man, probably in his late fifties, was resting on a wooden recliner on the front veranda, chewing tobacco and talking to two men in their early twenties. As we approached, all three turned in our direction with surprise. I greeted them with the traditional *namaste*.

"This is Gowda, the head of the village, and his two sons," the broker said, introducing the older man. *Gowda* was the local term for landlords who belonged to the upper caste. He pointed to me, "This 'sir' has come from America. He wants to buy your land on the other side of the lake to build a school for poor children." Gowda's interest was piqued, and he gestured to his sons to spread a mat. Rising from his recliner, he joined us on the floor. None knew English, and I couldn't speak their language, so the broker translated.

Without consulting his sons, who were listening attentively, Gowda said, "I'd be blessed for selling my land for such a worthy project." His sons didn't object. Gowda assured me of the lowest price, yet his offer was the going rate the broker had mentioned to me. We haggled over the price and finally settled.

I was pleased to quickly conclude the terms but insisted that Gowda arrange a meeting with the heads of the surrounding villages. I wanted to inform them of my intentions and obtain their approval. Without it, I foresaw objections and troubles. He readily obliged, and Jude met with them a few days later. Speaking on my behalf, he emphasized that we would buy the land only if they permitted a school for poor children.

Jude listed our terms in quick succession in the local language of Kannada: "This school will be private. There will be no government involvement, funds, or quotas. All employment will be at the discretion of the school management. No one can dictate which child will be admitted. Children only from the poorest families will be chosen."

One of them interrupted, "Is my child qualified? I only have two acres of land."

Jude smiled and replied, "That's not poor enough."

Hoping they would have employment opportunities or other benefits from the school, the village heads agreed to our terms and offered their assistance. Gowda and Jude were relieved. The village priest was summoned, and a brief *puja*, or religious ceremony, was held on the land. "It's auspicious to get God's blessings for a good venture like this," Gowda advised Jude. We offered fruits and sweets to the local shrine and all those present.

With the land now publicly marked as ours, Jude worked through all the official formalities and paperwork, and within a month, the property was registered in the foundation's name. The board members were eager to see the land, but they were shocked at how far they had to drive from the city on muddy roads with huge potholes. Adding to their apprehension, Jude warned them upon arrival, "There are snakes and scorpions here. Be careful while walking around!"

Horrified, board members glanced at the site, proceeding cautiously and eager to leave. One remarked, "There's nothing much to see here besides shrubs and large boulders." It was hard for anyone to visualize this harsh, rugged land as habitable and attractive.

Later, I received a scathing note. "This is a horrible selection!" the board members wrote, citing every deficiency. They complained about the long and challenging commute and the lack of electricity, telephone access, and public water supply.

I patiently read their complaints and listed solution after solution in my reply:

"We're already working on proper road access."

"We'll install solar panels for electricity."

"We'll find high points where we can get wireless signals."

"We'll drill wells for water."

I urged them to understand that the rural location and the beautiful grounds were more important than the practical infrastructure problems. The school being for children from deprived families, it was only appropriate we selected land in one of the state's poorest districts.

• • •

Having acquired the property, the pull to submerge myself intensified. I couldn't simultaneously run MCM and undertake a novel project, as both required my utmost dedication and commitment. After considerable thought, I decided to sell my company and commit my time to the school.

Mariam exclaimed, "Why do you want to sell your company that is doing so well? You wake up with a new idea every morning! I hope you know what you're doing, Aniyan." Her fear and annoyance were understandable because it was becoming hard for her to keep up with what she saw as my reckless decision-making.

I informed the senior heads at MCM, "I need to devote my time to the new school I'm starting in India. We will have to sell our company." They expressed serious reservations about my withdrawal from the business without prior planning. "What would happen to the employees if the company is sold?" was a common question. Vinita didn't raise any concerns but appeared worried. I assured them that the buyer would want to retain all its employees, as the company was thinly staffed, so their jobs were safe. Upon sale, I expected a smooth transition to new management, and I would remain with the company for some time to ensure that.

Over the next few months, I worked with my team to plan the sale and manage the transition process. I relied on Vinita to continue

MCM's product development and customer support activities until the business was sold.

At the same time, Lekha and I met weekly to work on a school policy manual. We found limited literature on remedial education for children from impoverished homes in India, especially those from the social underclass. We interviewed psychologists and academicians who worked with marginalized inner-city children in the United States and others of Indian origin. Our findings were further supplemented by our own experiences of growing up in India.

The question arose of whether Shanti Bhavan should be exclusively an all-girls school. After some thought, I decided that a coed school would enable boys and girls to grow up together from a young age and learn to treat each other respectfully. For our first academic year, we would recruit twelve boys and twelve girls each for preschool and kindergarten. The selection process would involve a three-pronged approach that combined the skills of a social worker, a clinical psychologist, and a pediatrician. The social worker would initially screen families through interviews and home visits to determine whether they were below the poverty level, which in 1995 was less than one dollar a day.

To avoid any actual or perceived conflict of interest, I decided not to take up any business opportunity in India. Aware of the human tendency to seek recognition or reward, I endeavored to guard myself against such self-gratification, which could distract me and alter the purpose of our work. I would not allow portraits of me displayed anywhere on campus or participate in ceremonies intended to honor me.

We would not seek government funds to carry out our humanitarian activities, as that would impinge on our autonomy. Most people I spoke to considered this an impossible proposition, as the government remained an integral part of every social venture in India at the time.

Besides emphasizing intellectual accomplishments and leadership qualities, Shanti Bhavan would foster humane values. To that end, we decided on some core principles. For a start, the foundation's management and staff would adhere to universal values like honesty, personal integrity, inclusiveness, equality, and openness.

The staff would treat the children with respect and affection. The children's self-esteem, dignity, and sense of security should never be compromised. For instance, the children would be addressed only by their names or endearingly. Further, occasional hugs of younger children were the only physical touch allowed; spanking, slapping, and other corporal punishment were strictly prohibited.

To create a respectful culture, words describing the actions and beliefs of staff must align with the values we wanted our children to embrace. For example, doing our *duty* to others or meeting our human obligation can't be called a *sacrifice*. In this context, *generosity* is an essential part of this duty. Similarly, acknowledgment or appreciation is preferable to *gratitude*, which sometimes is mistaken for subservience.

Service would replace *charity* to avoid the impression of granting a favor. It was understood that acting on compassion toward others' suffering is the consequential form of empathy. Service rendered is not a favor we do; there shouldn't be an expectation of anything in return. Some refer to it as "God's work" and a person's essential duty, which is core to the Indian concept of *dharma*.

The word *foreigner* would not be used because it separates us from others; instead, mention the place they come from. We would encourage the staff and children to live by these and other distinguishing expressions so that it would become integral to the school's culture.

For these terms to become a part of the school's ethos, we would encourage the staff and children to speak and live by them daily. The rightful way, I concluded, was to be free of prejudices and embrace our differences.

We devised a one-child-per-family rule, as our limited resources prevented us from taking more from the same home. I was convinced that an empowered, prosperous individual would be able to care for their entire family and serve as a catalyst for change in their larger community. It would also enable us to expand and spread the benefits offered to a growing number of families. This policy evoked considerable criticism by people who felt strongly that we would be dividing up families. "You can't play God," Mariam warned.

While searching for a school principal, I met Lalita Law, a middle-aged woman married to an army officer, at a party in Bangalore. She was teaching middle grades at an international school in the city. She enthusiastically expressed her desire to work at Shanti Bhavan. Her command of English was one of her major strengths, and I thought she could help develop strong English-speaking and -writing skills in the children. After a second round of interviews, I offered Lalita a senior position as head of academic programs and residential care, and she was thrilled to join the team.

• • •

With construction in full swing, the laborers stayed overnight in makeshift tents, and I took an apartment in the city and traveled daily to oversee the work. Jude enlisted the services of a young man named Frank as his assistant, and together, they followed my instructions even when I was absent.

The first task was to drill ground wells and connect pipes to supply clean water to the temporary residences and kitchen. Electric power lines had to be laid, but this was challenging because the campus was a mile from the main road. The electricity department wouldn't erect electric poles and a transformer without extracting money from us. When the connection was made to the grid, voltage fluctuated, and unexpected blackouts and brownouts were frequent. Jude remarked, "We get electricity, but no power." With inadequate public electric, we considered alternatives such as diesel generators and wind power.

Finally, we determined solar energy was the most reliable option, though solar panels and batteries were expensive and less efficient than they are today. Installation expertise was scarce, as few facilities in India used solar energy. I was told it would take eight to ten years to recover the initial capital investment. Eventually, solar panels were installed to light dormitories, classrooms, and streetlights along walkways throughout the campus. Overhead tanks on every residential building were connected directly to solar panels to provide hot water for bathing. Pumps for shallow wells and water storage sumps ran on solar power.

As one of the largest solar installations in a school in the world at the time, our campus drew the attention of a British television network. The British Petroleum Company, from which we purchased the solar panels, presented a film on our use of solar energy at an industrial exhibit held at the 1998 G8 Summit in Birmingham, England, attended by US President Clinton and Russian President Yeltsin.

Monsoon showers were a mixed blessing: They provided respite from the sweltering heat but halted work for days. Given the rolling terrain with steep slopes and large protruding rocks, considerable earth blasting and removal were required. There was no shortage of adventures, though; the bulldozer driver leveling the ground once saw cobras slither out of an anthill, and he leaped out of the vehicle and fled. Despite assuring him that Frank had chased away the snakes, it took Jude some effort to convince him to return to work.

As I walked the grounds with Jude, Frank, the surveyor, and the architect, we worked out the locations of the living quarters, dining hall and kitchen, playgrounds, and school building. Jude and Frank translated what I said into Kannada or Tamil for the rest of the construction team.

Dorms would have two wings to house twelve boys and twelve girls separately, a playroom, a television lounge, an isolation room to quarantine sick children, and private rooms for three residential caregivers and a supervisor. Every dorm exterior was painted in bright colors that children like. Designed like my early childhood home in Kerala, every building would have a central, grassy courtyard that opened to the sky to let in fresh air, sunlight, and rain. The dorms would be spacious and have high ceilings and clay tile roofs to keep the building cool in the summer; large windows on both sides would ventilate rooms.

The expansive, two-story school building would include an auditorium, administrative offices, two lower- and upper-grade libraries, computer labs, an art room, a music room, a storage space for supplies, and a medical room. I arranged for a Steinway piano to be shipped from the US. Like the dorms, each classroom would have high ceilings and windows on two sides for cross-ventilation. The central courtyard and assembly hall would offer plenty of space for everyone to gather for school festivities.

The staff would live on campus, so quarters for the teachers and the support team of cooks, security staff, and administrators would be provided. A modern kitchen and a large dining hall, mostly open on three sides, would offer a relaxing environment. I was confident that the children and staff would find the arrangements comfortable.

Besides overseeing the construction, I met with Jude and Lalita at my residence in Bangalore to plan and discuss the progress. We scouted for construction materials, like tiles and paint, and conducted interviews with prospective teachers and residential caregivers. Personal prejudices against looking after children from lower castes made it difficult to find willing and qualified caregivers, so we approached convents and shelters for abandoned women from the same communities as the children. We held a six-month boot camp to train our initial team of teachers, caregivers, and administrators, and familiarized them with our mission, practices, and expectations.

I returned to the States and began winding down my business activities outside of MCM, the first being my partnership with CS First Boston. Bill Scheen was shocked when I disclosed my plans. "Abraham, why do you want to destroy a successful business?" he asked, unable to understand why anyone would suddenly leave an exciting career for another path that offered no monetary reward. Bill feared our consulting activity might not stay afloat without me, but I assured him of a smooth transition.

In short order, I ended my other business associations—my consulting relationships with companies like Eastman Kodak, General Electric, and, most importantly, the LDS Church. I explained that I would not be able to perform an adequate job for them while being absent for months in a remote Indian village. As a token of appreciation, the LDS Church generously offered to ship forty-foot cargo containers laden with clothes, blankets, furniture, and food items for the school twice or thrice a year. Apart from professional relationships, I had become friends with the managers I worked with in these companies, and they were disappointed. Leaving behind my career and all that I had accomplished professionally was heart-wrenching.

The excitement and anxiety of establishing a new institution consumed me. All I thought about was the work ahead. I stayed up late reviewing drafts of the policy manual and making long calls to Jude and Lalita for daily updates. What Ammachi had once said to me constantly replayed in my mind: "Aniyan, this isn't something you can back out of. It isn't like your company. You'll be responsible for young lives."

I was determined that Shanti Bhavan would be one of the best schools in India, a unique educational model for poverty alleviation no one else had yet attempted. I visualized the school as a paradise where children could grow up with dignity and enjoy the same opportunities as their peers from wealthy homes. Most importantly, beyond a good education, every child would have the intangibles they needed most: love, care, security, and a happy, carefree childhood. Through their success, they would one day attain equality for themselves and their families.

CHAPTER 14

TREKKING THROUGH UNFAMILIAR TERRAIN

T HE SEARCH FOR CHILDREN for admission to Shanti Bhavan started in earnest. The recruitment team comprised Lalita Law, the principal; Dr. Maya Mascarenhas, the pediatrician; Dr. S. Venkatesh, the clinical psychologist; and A. Christopher, the social worker. We also enlisted two experienced social workers, a psychologist, and a professor specializing in early childhood education from Canada and the US. They visited villages, slums, and orphanages in Tamil Nadu and the neighboring Karnataka and Andhra Pradesh States for eligible children. I joined our team occasionally to witness the admission process.

Lalita updated me by telephone on the day's work, detailing the villages, their living conditions, and families' reactions. Most homes they visited were makeshift shelters or one-room huts with thatched roofs and no electricity or nearby water supply. The families we finally considered were surviving on little food and scraps of clothing, barely getting by as menial laborers. Most lived amid crime and faced social prejudice from the upper castes. During the visits, our team faced hostility from village heads who spread rumors to scare families away.

"We heard that the foreigner starting the school is planning to take poor people's children to America for bad purposes. We'd rather beg to feed our children than give them to you" was a remark we heard more than once.

"Why would anyone provide anything free for the poor?" some families asked. "Nobody brings up another's child for fourteen years for nothing."

Poor people had good reason to distrust strangers, especially those who offered benevolence without any strings attached. They didn't nurture hope for their future and distrusted help from others. Our team tried to allay their fears. "Dr. George is a businessman from America who has money and wants to help poor people's children."

On one occasion, our team scheduled a follow-up to screen the families, but they were confronted by angry village leaders instead.

"Where are the children?" Christopher, the social worker, asked.

"There are no children for your school here," a village leader responded curtly.

"But we saw five children here last time! Their mothers permitted us to interview them. I've brought our doctors to see them today," Christopher replied.

"You people want to convert our village to Christianity," the village leader accused.

The foundation's name might have aroused some concern about our intention. The team returned disappointed, without interviewing any children that day.

Fortunately, some in other villages took a chance. They were among the poorest, without even one square meal a day, and wanted their son or daughter to have a better life. Our clinical psychologist administered simple tests to ascertain the cognitive ability of each child. The pediatrician examined each child to rule out severe disabilities requiring resources Shanti Bhavan couldn't offer.

Determining a child's age was tricky. Some lacked birth certificates, and parents couldn't remember their child's date of birth. A few had no official name and were called only by pet names. Our pediatrician had to assign a date of birth and a name for the records.

One day, I received a frantic call from Lalita. It was about Vijay, a five-year-old child who had already been selected for admission to preschool. He and his mother were nowhere to be found when our team returned for a second home visit to finalize the admission. A villager reluctantly directed Lalita to the nearby Victoria Hospital.

To our horror, we found the little boy there, recovering from second-degree burns. A group of men had come to the village and promised Vijay's mother employment in the Middle East at high wages. A poor single woman, she readily agreed and went with them to the nearby town, supposedly to complete paperwork, only to be gang-raped for three days before they dumped her at the village border.

Back in her village, Vijay's mother was ostracized by her neighbors and the village heads, claiming that the "wanton woman" had brought it on herself. Unable to bear the shunning, she doused herself with kerosene and set herself ablaze. Seeing his mother aflame, Vijay tried to smother the fire with his bare hands. She died, and he was left severely scarred physically and emotionally.

"It will take many years and one or two plastic surgeries to regain the proper use of his hands," Lalita informed me.

I was saddened to hear about this terrible incident and worried about the trauma Vijay might endure. Thoughtfully weighing the situation, I said, "Even though our policy doesn't allow taking in children with serious disabilities, it's not fair to reject a child for no fault of his own when we had already granted him admission." In dealing with children with complex family circumstances, our rules had to accommodate special situations. People in helpless situations suffer unpredictable consequences out of their control.

• • •

After an arduous selection process, twenty-four boys and girls, each between the ages of three-and-a-half and five-and-a-half, were accepted for admission to preschool and kindergarten. We had planned the opening for October 1997, but construction of essential buildings wasn't complete. Postponing the start wasn't an option because the parents might lose confidence in us. If we could provide clean drinking water and working toilets, I insisted, we could bring the children in as planned. Jude and Lalita didn't object.

On the eve of Shanti Bhavan's opening, the managers gathered for dinner in a large tent with a wood-fired cooking furnace. The cooks moved in and out, serving hot rice and a watery lentil dish. Jude, Lalita, and I huddled near each other, discussing the next morning's big event.

"Do you think we are ready?" I asked, smiling to mask my nervousness.

"Yes! We will have great fun tomorrow," Jude replied with a chuckle. His optimism and drive made it that much easier to overcome challenges.

We sat in silence for a few minutes, lost in our thoughts. I was particularly distracted, having concluded the sale of MCM to

SunGard just a few days earlier, and many issues still remained. I had stayed up all night reviewing hundreds of pages of documents faxed by our US lawyers and accountants that required my signature. Having worked diligently for over two decades to build the company, my parting from MCM was heavy. It was painful not being able to say goodbye in person.

I agreed to serve SunGard as a vice-chairman of the newly formed division to smooth the transition and maintain continuity in relationships with employees and customers. A major chapter of my life had ended; now, Shanti Bhavan was my future.

I reached for my steel tumbler, poured water into it, and raised it in a toast: "This is the beginning of a memorable journey for all of us." Jude and Lalita joined in.

• • •

The children and their parents trickled in during the day. Some took buses from faraway villages and towns, traveling the entire night. We arranged to pick up the rest from their villages, as public transport to the campus was limited.

The families were treated to a delightful breakfast consisting of a regional favorite, *masala dosa*—a traditional Indian pancake folded in half and filled with spiced potato and onions. A campus tour followed. The little boys and girls appeared fascinated, their large dark eyes displaying excitement and confusion. Venturing into a distant, unfamiliar place, they tried to make sense of their strange new surroundings.

The head matron requested that parents not linger over goodbyes, which could make the separation harder. "When will I see my child again?" almost every parent asked, and the matron reassuringly replied, "Please give us the next three months to settle the children into their new life here. You can visit them after that."

When the parents prepared to leave, the children clung to them and wept as the housemothers tried to distract them with toys. Some ran out of the dorm, begging their parents to take them. The house-mothers chased after them, saying, "Your mom and dad will be back soon. I promise." They tried their best to calm the uncontrollable ones as they responded by biting and hitting. Not too long after the parents left, the children's attention drifted to play and food, and everyone calmed down.

In the subsequent months, our goal was to help the children adjust to their new surroundings and gently ease them into a struc-tured daily routine. The caregivers attended to the children's hygiene by examining their hair for lice and disinfecting their clothes and belongings for fear of transmitting disease. Most of them had unruly, long hair that needed a haircut. Dr. Maya oversaw vaccinations against common childhood illnesses. Deworming tablets and multi-vitamins were administered. Those who needed medical attention for infections and skin conditions like scabies were taken to the medical center in the nearest town.

Each child was given new clothing, toiletries, indoor and out-door footwear, and assigned beds with clean sheets, blankets, and a doll. Most had never used toilets, slept on beds, sat on chairs, worn footwear, eaten a square meal in a day, or played with toys—things most of us take for granted. The children were bathed every evening in running water from taps—an exciting new experience.

Breakfast, midmorning snacks, lunch, afternoon snacks, and din-ner were served warm in the dorms, as the dining hall was not yet ready. The children were excited to try cocoa and eat new foods like spaghetti. Everyone had a modest lifestyle at school: suitable residential accommodation, tasty and nutritious meals, proper clothing, medical care, music lessons, and fun playtimes. Exhausted from a full day of fun, the children often fell asleep soon after dinner.

One week in, I met with the children as a group for the first time. The matron introduced me to them in Tamil, saying, "This is Dr. George. He built this school." Upon hearing the word *doctor*, one child asked in a fearful voice, "Is he going to give me an injection?"

I eased his worry by handing him my sunglasses, which fascinated him. Others fought to try them on. A few tugged at my hand, hoping to draw my attention, while tiny fingers probed my pockets for sweets. It was utter chaos but a novel and welcome experience. Even though none of them spoke English, I found ways to communicate through smiles, hand gestures, and mimicry.

On weekends, the caregivers took the children on nature walks to the banks of the lake. They returned with smooth pebbles, colorful leaves, wildflowers, and the feathers of herons, woodpeckers, and kingfishers, which they proudly showed me when I visited them in their dorms.

As my constant presence boosted staff morale, I stayed in the partially built guest quarters on the school premises. Looking out through the window, I could see the vastness of the forest, dense with eucalyptus trees on rocky grounds. As night fell, the shadows brought forth by moonlight and the howling of jackals gave me an eerie feeling. I felt alone on the campus, disconnected from the rest of the world, without the company of anyone I knew well enough to really trust. The single room I stayed in would be my comfortable home for the next twenty-five years.

Each day, Jude, Lalita, and I met with staff members to give them attention and show appreciation. Early every morning, I would walk along the pavers leading to the school plaza and spend time with children in the preschool dormitory. One morning, staff informed me that Vijay had screamed at seeing the rows of beds, as it reminded him of the hospital. Recognizing that the child was affected by PTSD, I advised the caregivers to be especially attentive and reassure him that he was safe.

As promised, the parents returned to campus after three months. It was an emotional event, as mothers and fathers expressed delight and shock at seeing how smart their sons and daughters looked. Seeing the children with full cheeks, kempt hair, new clothes, and a twinkle in their eyes, some parents had difficulty identifying their own. Hearing the happy chatter of their children and the details of their life at school was a much-needed comfort for them.

After lunch, my team and I gathered to address the parents as a group for the first time. The fathers and mothers immediately rose from their seats respectfully and greeted me with a *namaste*. "Sit. Please sit," I urged them, embarrassed. They remained standing until Jude, Lalita, and I were seated.

I scanned the room, smiling as I made eye contact. Most in the group were probably in their mid-twenties. The women were dressed in colorful saris, with flowers in their hair, and some had stained teeth from chewing *paan*. Several siblings of our children, not much older than their brothers or sisters who had joined the school, sat by their mothers or fathers, curiously watching me. I waved to them, wanting to put them at ease. They smiled back shyly. A young mother with burn marks on her face and neck caught my attention, and Jude later explained that her drunken husband had tried to set her ablaze years ago.

"I'm happy to see all of you. My name is Dr. George, and I am from America. I was born in India and went to America to study and work. I have a wife and two sons," I said in English, and two staff members translated it into Kannada and Tamil. The parents listened attentively.

"I returned to India to start a school for children from poor homes. I want to give them a chance to get a good education and live a good life. It bothers me that thousands of children continue to live in difficult conditions and don't have the same opportunities that my two sons have had," I continued.

Heads nodded, and I saw some understanding smiles. Encouraged, I added, "People like you haven't had the opportunity to overcome poverty. You have been poor since birth, and your ancestors were poor for generations. With education, your children will get well-paying jobs, and they will help you break out of poverty."

I paused, seeing a hand go up.

A young father said, "Sir, you are our god."

Embarrassed but touched, I replied, "I am no god. I am an ordinary man who wants to help."

"Sir, in our village, some people say you will kill our children, take their kidneys and eyes, and sell them in America. We are afraid," a loud male voice interjected.

A few heads nodded in collective assent.

"I will not take your children's kidneys or eyes. I will give them my heart." I saw some smiles but knew it would take some time to convince families. I expected these questions and was glad the crowd felt comfortable expressing their doubts. It was apparent they were still unsure of my motives. Their lack of trust in me didn't offend me—I was a stranger.

"Are you getting any assistance from the government?" another father asked.

"I haven't accepted any financial assistance from the government, nor do I plan to," I answered.

The crowd was confused. They couldn't understand where the money was coming from. They were accustomed to receiving concessions and food subsidies from the government, and it was difficult to grasp why anyone would reject government assistance.

I appealed to their good sense not to pull their children out of school in later years and force them to work or marry the girls off early. "I promise you that someday your children will improve your lives," I said confidently.

The meeting concluded with our assuring the parents that they would get to see their children every three months and take them home twice a year over winter and summer breaks. The parents were overjoyed and left comforted, and I was moved by the human drama that had played out that day. It was my first encounter with the parents, but a good start, and I could build on their trust to gain their future cooperation.

CHAPTER 15

A NEW DAWN

WITH THE INAUGURATION OF SHANTI BHAVAN barely
two months away, Jude and his crew worked feverishly to prepare the campus. With the help of a landscape architect, we designed
and laid out the gardens, walkways, and play areas. Considerable
earth was moved to level the grounds for a large soccer field and a
children's park.

Lalita ambitiously taught the children the English lyrics of the
school song. I wasn't sure they could learn it in time to perform on
the inaugural night, but we thought it would be fun for them to try it.

I made a quick trip to Delhi to invite the then president of India,
R. K. Narayanan, to be the chief guest of honor. He was known to our
family from his early years when he lived and studied in Kerala. He
was from the Dalit community but overcame discrimination through
education and rose to national prominence. His attendance would be
especially relevant and inspiring.

President Narayanan received me warmly at his official residence,
Rashtrapati Bhavan, a palatial structure with over three hundred acres
of stunningly beautiful gardens. He graciously agreed to consider my

request, and I left hopeful. Unfortunately, his office sent his regrets two weeks before the event, leaving precious little time to find a notable replacement.

I hurried to Calcutta to visit Sister Nirmala, who had succeeded Mother Teresa as the head of the Missionaries of Charity. She, too, could not attend but offered us her best wishes. Time was running out, and so were the options for a suitable chief guest.

I was reluctant to invite a local politician to preside over the inauguration ceremony for fear of unwanted demands in the future and any perception of political affiliation. Achachan suggested I call upon Fatima Beevi, the current governor of Tamil Nadu State. She had been his student at Trivandrum Law College over forty years ago.

I made a third trip, this time to Chennai. The governor accepted my invitation out of respect for my father. I was glad to have the problem solved but would soon discover how unhappy and slighted she felt about being third in line.

My parents, Mariam, Ajit, Vivek, my siblings and their spouses and children, and extended family members arrived from the US. I was disappointed that Bob Hawkins couldn't make it because of his teaching responsibilities. I arranged to have my family stay in the newly built staff quarters on the school grounds. They were eager to see how far the construction had progressed and how well the children and staff were doing.

My family toured the campus, curiously inspecting the newly constructed dormitories brightly painted in multiple colors and spread out in a semicircle, the large open dining hall that could seat about three hundred, and the main school building with a spacious auditorium. A statue of four dolphins rose from the center of a small pool, its water reflecting the morning light.

"How beautiful, Aniyan!" Mariam exclaimed, eagerly taking in the sights. Like her, my parents were thrilled. "This is amazing. Quite an accomplishment in just two years," Ammachi said. It was very satisfying to see that my family was pleased.

Though unfinished by the morning of the inaugural event, the campus looked splendid, with lush lawns, gardens, manicured hedges, and meandering cobblestone walkways connecting every building. Shade and ornamental trees were planted along borders and rocky areas.

"Jude! You've worked an absolute miracle here!" I said, patting him on his shoulder. I marveled at his ingenuity in digging up mature trees from the neighboring land, with the owner's permission, and transplanting them on our grounds. The soil's high clay content made it difficult for plants to take root and grow, so he hired a crew to import large quantities of sandier soil from lake beds and ravines to mix with the native clay.

"A dozen of our staff helped me," Jude explained, his face beaming at the compliment and sharing the credit with his colleagues for a job well done. He had assumed responsibility for infrastructure development, maintenance, and all administrative functions, and saw that everything went right.

The children gathered for photographs with us outside the school building, in front of the black granite slab engraved with the school's mission statement, the list of board members, and a quote I had penned: "Dream of a world only your heart can build, act with courage and love, and never ask why."

Guests, board members, village leaders, and journalists had trickled in by early afternoon. Governor Fathima Beevi arrived with more pomp than was warranted. Her entourage included a motorcade of government officials and a police force of more than one hundred officers and constables. Shouldering rifles, they were an intimidating presence.

There was no expression of familiarity or friendliness on the governor's face as I greeted her. She didn't inquire about the event, the children, or my father. Despite my efforts to converse politely, she remained cold and aloof and stiffly followed her assistant straight toward the area for dignitaries.

The sub-collector, the senior-most bureaucrat in a subdistrict, wasn't easy to deal with either. She asked to be seated on stage with the governor and other dignitaries, as did the deputy inspector general of police. The stage was already crowded with more than half a dozen important guests, including the chairs of three major banks, the district collector, and his personal assistant standing behind his chair.

"Please be seated next to my father in the front row," I politely requested of the sub-collector and the deputy inspector general. They gave me annoyed looks and grudgingly agreed.

The much-anticipated ceremony commenced with the traditional lighting of the lamp. Lekha took pride in being the emcee and thanked those gathered for their presence. When it was my turn, I approached the podium with a smile to give the founder's address. It was a surreal moment, a culmination of years of envisioning a mission for social change and the start of a new journey. I was living the dream I had carried for so long in my heart.

I began by describing the school's mission: "The cycle of poverty that has trapped millions of families for generations can be broken by the impact of quality education and proper upbringing of their children. This is what we aim to begin here." Addressing a skeptical crowd, I felt pressure to communicate my vision effectively.

"The children of Shanti Bhavan, regardless of their backgrounds, shall one day be exemplars of achievement and inspiration for others. This school will produce some of society's brightest and best future leaders. That is my hope. They will be ready not just for India but for the world market. They could be employed by IBM India; they could be employed by IBM New York. It doesn't matter where they go for their jobs," I prophesied. Energized by hopes for the future, my loud and passionate voice reverberated through the hall.

"Shanti Bhavan is our first institution. We plan to establish many more, maybe in Karnataka, Andhra, and other states." I wanted everyone to imagine what India would be like if only we could unleash the untapped potential of the poor through one hundred schools like Shanti Bhavan.

Following my speech and remarks by the dignitaries, our precious preschoolers and kindergartners came on stage. They looked dazed at being in the spotlight, but much to everyone's delight, they sprang up, performed a traditional folk dance, and sang the school song. I was thrilled. Their young mothers and fathers applauded joyously at seeing their little ones so confident and singing in English.

The ceremony ended with a recording of Andrea Bocelli and Sarah Brightman singing "Time to Say Goodbye"—an appropriate duet to disperse the audience and signal dinner. The crowd stepped outside into the fresh night air and strolled under solar lights illuminating the pathways and grounds. Walking beside my parents, I sighed at having concluded a beautiful function.

"It was lovely, Monu," Ammachi remarked.

Achachan added, "We are delighted."

My parents' enthusiasm was comforting.

"Dad, can we stay back and help out here for a few days before returning to the US?" Vivek and his cousins asked.

"Of course! It would be nice to have you as the first set of volunteers," I replied excitedly.

At dinner, one of Mariam's elderly cousins asked, "Aniyan, how do you plan to fund this massive project through the years?"

Having cut off sources that generated much of my income, I relied on my real estate and stock market investments. I had invested heavily in beachfront properties, believing there were only limited waterfront sites, and I couldn't go wrong with them. I had concluded that technology was the future and that stock investment in it wouldn't be risky.

"I have personal investments in place and the proceeds from the sale of MCM. We estimate an operating cost of $350,000 to run Shanti Bhavan this year, then a few thousand dollars more in subsequent years. I'm confident we can handle it," I replied without hesitation.

As we headed over to see off the guests, Governor Fathima Beevi curtly asked Jude, "Have my policemen been fed?"

"Yes, madam," he replied politely.

But feeding so many unexpected people had caused a shortage, and we had to hurriedly cook for our resident staff, who graciously settled for a skimpy meal on a night meant to celebrate their hard work and accomplishments.

The parents, dazzled by the evening's overwhelming experience, boarded the buses we had arranged to take them back to their villages. I wondered what thoughts passed through their minds. As I watched them leave, it suddenly struck me: *My God! The children are mine now.* Their parents had left them in my care, trusting that I would look after them and do my best for every child as I had promised. The weight of my new path and its colossal responsibilities finally sank in.

I wondered what kind of relationship I would have with the children in the long term. I didn't want it to be impersonal, as it was with the boys from LINK, nor did I want them to see me as an omnipotent authority.

I worried about my family. Was I selfish in pursuing my dreams despite the loneliness for Mariam? She was enduring my long absences, and returning from work every night to a dark, empty house. I fought off the guilt, telling myself that this work was something I felt morally compelled to undertake. There was no turning back from this.

• • •

Shanti Bhavan's inaugural festivities raised staff morale and reinforced our stated mission. Although we won new admirers and friends on its inauguration day, we also made enemies. Perhaps feeling snubbed for not being treated with more deference, the sub-collector claimed that our boundary fencing encroached on public land by a few feet. She dispatched officials to tear it down and arranged to destroy the lakeside access road built at our own expense. I filed a writ petition in the state High Court requiring the sub-collector to show cause, but she backed down and asked us to withdraw the case.

Other troubles followed, with village heads unhappy that we were offering an excellent education to children from poor families who might one day hold high positions and disrupt the social status quo. "If everyone in our village gets educated, who will work in the fields?" one landlord protested.

In another instance, a state legislator asked us to admit a child he had recommended, though the child didn't meet our selection criteria. He solicited the support of the *panchayat*, the local village council, which insisted that we alter our admission rules and set quotas for each of the seventeen neighboring villages. We refused.

NGOs usually relied on government financial assistance for their humanitarian projects. But since we didn't accept public funding, officials wielded little power over us, which annoyed them and fueled their resentment. As a result, the school received little to no cooperation from officials on our requests to improve public services such as electricity, telephones, and roads.

We quickly devised solutions: solar for electricity, bore wells for water, and cell phones instead of landlines. After waiting three years to improve the road connecting our campus to the public highway, we paid a substantial sum to the panchayat to lay four kilometers of gravel and asphalt on the existing mud road.

Achachan had once told me, "Anything in India is possible for a price." Now I found the corollary was also true: Nothing is possible without paying a price. If it was not for my gain but for the greater common good, I justified my improper action by making an ethical distinction.

Government corruption was a hurdle we faced on multiple fronts. For instance, customs agents at Chennai Port impounded a precious wheat powder cargo the LDS Church had sent us and insisted on testing its quality. Lab results found traces of alcohol, but it was natural for the powder to ferment slightly during long sea transport, and it certainly didn't pose any danger. Sure enough, the customs officer privately informed Jude that his department could be persuaded to release it if we paid a bribe—a shockingly hefty sum.

"We need this wheat powder to make chapatti for the poor children at our school," Jude pleaded. "It can last an entire year."

"We, too, are poor," the officer retorted.

Jude immediately notified me. I suspected they would sell the wheat and keep the proceeds for themselves if we didn't clear customs. "If it is not fit for anyone to eat, I guess we have no choice but to burn it," I said, outraged.

In retrospect, I should have vigorously negotiated a "reasonable" bribe. I was perhaps too self-righteous, costing the children an essential item in their daily meals. Similar unpleasant experiences and ethical dilemmas were to mark the coming years. I would learn to temper my ways for the greater good.

CHAPTER 16

A BREATH OF CLEAN AIR

I T WAS 1997. BY THE END OF A DAY spent in Bangalore, my eyes stung and had turned watery, my breathing was raspy and shallow, and a black substance coated my hair—all of which I attributed to pollution. Rapid urbanization left its ugly imprint everywhere—dust-coated trees, dried-up lakes, sweltering heat waves, waste-cluttered roadsides, suffocating traffic, and buildings encroaching onto grasslands. Bangalore, famously known as the Garden City of South India for its beautiful parks and lakes, was failing to live up to its name.

Unsurprisingly, vehicles in India ran on leaded gas and diesel. Their emissions spewed lead into the air, putting urban children at risk of lead poisoning. Moreover, vehicles lacked catalytic converters to clean their exhaust of other harmful discharges. The poor were disproportionately at risk, as they lived near factories, congested roadways, and hazardous waste sites. They suffered from a myriad of health disparities, such as asthma and lead poisoning.

I learned that elevated levels of lead in blood impair children's brain development, especially when compounded by the adverse effects of nutritional deficiencies. By my initial unscientific estimates, lead poisoning might have already harmed no fewer than one hundred million children in India's cities. It was alarming to discover that lead had entered the food chain. A study of vegetables grown near Delhi showed dangerously high lead levels in spinach, but no environmental laws addressed soil contamination by lead particles.

Many families used lead-coated cookware and utensils in their homes. Other sources were lead smelters, leaded water pipes, Ayurvedic or herbal medicine that used lead as an additive, paints, toys, pencils and, most prominently, the cottage industry engaged in recycling batteries to extract lead plates. Unless such sources and pathways of lead poisoning were prevented, I feared the country would be faced with a significant health crisis.

Most developed countries had already taken measures to prevent lead poisoning. America introduced unleaded gasoline in the 1970s and wholly phased out leaded gasoline by 1996. Similarly, China began its phaseout in 1995 and fully eliminated it by 2000. My inquiry with the Karnataka State Pollution Control Board in Bangalore revealed no immediate plans to deal with lead or carbon monoxide in vehicular exhaust.

"This complacency is troubling. We must do something, Jude," I said, concerned.

"We should, but the government's priority is to address poverty and illiteracy. Nobody understands how serious pollution is, Dr. George," Jude replied, echoing my worry.

I was glad he saw the urgency. Even though environmental health issues were beyond the scope of my original mission, given the gravity of this problem and the vulnerability of the poor, I decided to alert policymakers to act.

Back in the US, I inquired with the New York City Department of Environmental Protection about how to reduce lead poisoning. They introduced me to Steve Null, a crusader for a lead-free environment and head of a nonprofit organization called Friends of Lead Free Children. Steve was helping the Dominican Republic clean up its lead smelters and testing the blood-lead levels of workers in the battery-recycling industry. His energy and commitment were contagious, and I was excited to partner with him.

Steve introduced me to ESA Inc., a leading manufacturer of lead testing equipment. ESA offered us its testing machines, reagents, calibrators, and other supplies at steep discounts. I visited the Centers for Disease Control and Prevention (CDC) in Atlanta and met with the environmental risk assessment team headed by Dr. Henry Falk, director of the National Center for Environmental Health and a highly regarded physician with a successful public health career. Dr. Falk supported my testing plans for India and even provided the CDC's screening protocols and trained me to conduct testing.

We launched Project Lead-Free, a pioneering nationwide initiative to address the health crisis affecting hundreds of millions of urban children and adults. To confirm that the screening devices and supplies purchased from ESA wouldn't be subject to customs duties upon arrival at Chennai Port, Steve and I met with the Consulate General of India, New York, with whom I was already acquainted. I requested his support by contacting the Trade Ministry in Delhi so we could import our equipment duty-free.

He responded, "Mr. George, I am unaware that lead poisoning is a pressing issue for India now." I tried hard to explain the long-term consequences for the nation if India failed to act. Not giving much credence to my words, he dismissed me as an alarmist.

On our way out of his office, an agitated Steve turned around and said, "Mark this day."

I thought India's ambassador to the United States in Washington, DC, would be more receptive. Sadly, he held the same sentiment: "India has more critical problems to focus on, like providing clean running water and fighting poverty. Why don't you use your money for one of those issues instead of this lead thing?"

We were disappointed by the officials' patronizing attitudes.

"It looks like we're on our own, Abraham," Steve remarked.

I entrusted Jude with receiving delivery of the shipped testing equipment. I instructed, "See if we can persuade the customs to give us a duty waiver for the import." A week later, Jude got back to me with bad news: "The customs officials denied our request. They don't have the authority to grant the waiver." Disgusted, I paid the duty in full.

I saw the importance of someone with national repute to champion our cause and lead a significant blood-lead-screening effort. The George Foundation's board suggested I contact Admiral O. S. Dawson, retired Chief of the Naval Staff of India. He enthusiastically agreed to lead the project and relentlessly campaigned for the government's nonfinancial support for our efforts. He repeatedly contacted cabinet ministers and senior bureaucrats of the central government and heads of several agencies responsible for overseeing industries like petroleum, paint, smelters, and consumer protection to appraise them of the dangers of lead. Research papers and case studies held in the US and elsewhere were presented to convince them to address the crisis. We met with several senior officials, including the Central Minister for the Environment, to apprise them and seek their support. We were surprised that they were either unaware of the harm caused by lead in the environment or ignorant of the urgency. Worst of all, the Pollution Control Board at both state and central levels were lax in enforcing safeguards.

Seven hospitals in the Bangalore area agreed to test blood samples, with parental consent, from children who came to their outpatient and emergency departments. Dr. Thuppil Venkatesh, head of the Biochemistry Department at St. John's Medical College Hospital, Bangalore, oversaw these screening efforts.

Dr. Maya from Shanti Bhavan's medical team and over a dozen locally recruited social workers joined the team. The parents were motivated when informed of our willingness to share the results of their children's tests. This revealed that the public would gladly participate if we explained the benefits.

Lead-polluted air from vehicle exhaust was the most dominant pathway, but there were other significant sources. One father brought his two young children to the hospital, complaining of their progressive inattentiveness and hearing loss. Their blood samples contained elevated levels of lead, well above fifty micrograms per deciliter. Further investigation revealed that the father worked all day scraping and painting houses. He came home in lead-coated clothes and greeted his little children with hugs, unwittingly exposing them to lead dust. Similar cases were noticed among the children of traffic policemen who spent their workdays amid exhaust fumes.

In another instance, an affluent mother complained that her child exhibited severe developmental delays. Tests found that the child's blood-lead level was extremely high, at over sixty micrograms per deciliter. Our follow-up discussions uncovered that she was using lead-coated ceramic pots to serve meals. Having learned about this danger, I traveled to Salem, Tamil Nadu's famous steel fabricating city, to purchase authentic, thick, stainless-steel cookware for Shanti Bhavan's kitchen instead of the toxin-coated cookware sold by local shops.

By the end of the first year of testing, our screening expanded to major cities—Madras, Bombay, Delhi, Calcutta, and Hyderabad. We partnered with the prestigious All India Institute of Medical Sciences in New Delhi for an additional testing center. Screening continued for six months at each center, and test results were periodically reported to us.

To supplement random lead screening at the hospitals, our staff traveled in a mobile unit to assess workers at various locations, including construction and industrial sites. We would stop at traffic intersections to collect blood samples from traffic cops. They cooperated when we told them of the dangers of breathing polluted air, and we promised to share the results with them.

We took the mobile unit to urban slums where women were removing lead plates from used vehicle batteries, an occupation they had had for years, putting themselves at grave risk. We visited factories that used lead soldering, where the employees were either not supplied with face masks and gloves or weren't using them. When we asked why not, a worker softly replied, "The gear is too uncomfortable to wear all day. The management doesn't insist on it."

By the end of 1998, we had collected and analyzed twenty-two thousand blood samples, eighteen thousand of which were from children. The samples included hundreds of pregnant women and workers in hazardous industries. The CDC declared it the largest blood-lead screening conducted anywhere.

Aware that most developing countries hadn't yet implemented

lead poisoning prevention measures, including unleaded gasoline, I invited environmentalists, subject-matter experts, and government officials from several countries to our upcoming international conference. We wanted them to gather under one roof and propose practical measures that developing countries could implement, even with limited financial resources.

We approached the World Health Organization (WHO), the United States Environmental Protection Agency (EPA), and the World Bank, among others, for their financial and managerial support. Twenty-four governments of developing countries and well-known scientists accepted our invitation. Several environmental organizations and health-related research institutions in India and abroad agreed to participate. Even more encouraging was that Bharat Petroleum, Hindustan Petroleum, and Indian Oil—India's top three oil companies, the major polluters—were willing to send senior executives.

· · ·

February 8, 1999, the conference's opening day, finally arrived. Over four hundred scientists, academics, senior government officials, and representatives of major international institutions signed up to attend the three-day event. Seven floors at the magnificent Ashoka Hotel in Bangalore were booked for participants; all banquet halls and conference rooms were assigned for holding panel sessions.

Following the introductory formalities, I delivered the keynote address, summarizing the results of our two-year lead-screening initiative. Steve and I had kept our findings confidential until the conference because we wanted to kick off the event with news that would jolt the participants into action.

"In India, there are more than two hundred million children below the age of twelve living in urban areas, and it is shocking to imagine that half of them have already been poisoned by lead," I said, pausing to gauge the audience's reaction.

"For every ten micrograms per deciliter increase in lead levels in the blood, there is an approximate loss of 5 to 6 percent in IQ levels. If lead levels are not held in check, it could result in significant loss of intelligence among the population," I continued. Almost 50 percent of the children in the seven cities we screened had shown blood-lead levels over five micrograms per deciliter, the permissible upper limit set by the CDC. In 2017, this threshold would be lowered to zero; no blood-lead level in children is considered safe.

"Our estimate of those affected by elevated lead levels among people living in urban areas is no fewer than two to three hundred million adults and children combined," I announced. This came as a complete surprise to the attendees. Lead poisoning was causing neurological damage from decreased IQ and attention span, along with other developmental problems such as delays in motor skills and communication. Looking at the issue of falling IQ levels from another angle, I continued, "If children lose IQ, what is the loss to the nation? We are creating a future labor force that functions at lower intellectual levels."

Some alarmed representatives from various countries approached me at tea and lunch breaks to express their concerns. Having outlined the scope of the problem, discussions turned to prevention and treatment. Undoubtedly, the best way to prevent lead poisoning was to eliminate the pathways of lead by removing it from gasoline and paint, using unleaded cookware, establishing proper safeguards in smelters, cleaning up industrial waste sites, and ensuring worker safety in factories that soldered with lead.

Dr. Henry Falk's presentation discussed treating very high levels of lead poisoning in children. He shared that in blood-lead levels exceeding thirty micrograms per deciliter, it might be beneficial to remove lead through blood chelation therapy. However, this method risked losing vital minerals such as iron, zinc, and magnesium from the blood, requiring patients to receive costly infusions.

In addition, lead dislodged by a chelating agent could be carried to the brain and accumulate. Removing lead from the neurological system was difficult; permanent damage might have already occurred. In short, there was no cohesive, satisfactory treatment for lead poisoning.

Those responsible for developing policies on lead poisoning prevention and treatment programs in several countries were more interested in finding preventive measures. Participants discussed source elimination, pathway identification, early detection, and treatment protocols. They were keen to learn about blood screening, environmental monitoring, and low-cost prevention methods that poorer countries could feasibly adopt. Our goal was to formulate policy recommendations that developing countries could economically implement to prevent and treat lead poisoning.

For prevention efforts to succeed, governments needed laws and regulations that the private sector would uphold. Educating ordinary citizens about lead poisoning and its prevention was of paramount importance to a successful public health campaign.

To our pleasant surprise, at the end of the conference, top executives of the three Indian oil companies pledged that their refineries would start offering unleaded gasoline within the next eighteen months. We were surprised by this announcement and didn't know whether they were reacting to the constant barrage of letters and scientific material we had sent to them over the past two years.

The excitement in the room was exhilarating. "This is the most rewarding news," participants said at the outdoor parting dinner. Everyone knew that this decision by the oil companies would substantially reduce airborne lead in a short time. I couldn't have been happier. Our persistent effort yielded a most unexpected reward bigger than what we had anticipated.

The press covered the event well on the front pages of newspapers and on television. Nationwide, articles appeared on lead poisoning cases and their sources. I received inquiries from scientists in different countries who wanted to know how to prevent lead poisoning in their specific surroundings. Most officials and institutions admitted they knew little about the problem and were eager to learn more.

As a first step toward implementing policies, the entire proceedings of the three-day event were compiled into a book and published within six months of the conference. I drafted a six-page white paper on policy recommendations for developing countries on prevention, screening, and treatment. We sent the draft to senior officials from the World Bank, WHO, US EPA, ICMR (Indian Council of Medical Research), and CDC who had attended the conference. We revised the document many times and obtained consent from all signatories. By the end of 1999, a coherent action plan was agreed upon by all key participants—a miraculous accomplishment.

The World Bank sent this paper and the book on the proceedings to the governments of developing countries to formulate their own policies and action steps. Most governments responded positively to our recommendations and appointed task forces and committees. The CDC informed me that some countries followed suit by taking stringent measures to prevent lead poisoning.

In 2000, we wrote to several government agencies and ministries in India to increase awareness on lead poisoning. The Central Ministry for Environment in New Delhi invited me to join a national committee to make regulatory recommendations. This committee met under the auspices of the Central Pollution Control Board and approved most of our action plan's recommendations.

By June 2000, gas stations in major cities began offering unleaded gasoline at their pumps. Within three years, India's gasoline supply would consist entirely of unleaded petrol and diesel—a rewarding major outcome I hadn't anticipated would happen so quickly.

My next goal was to prevent pathways other than vehicular emissions. Under Dr. Venkatesh's leadership, the National Referral Centre for Lead Poisoning Prevention in India (NRCLPI) was established at St. John's Medical College Hospital, and our foundation provided the initial funding. In subsequent years, NRCLPI served as the country's central agency for guidance on prevention, blood testing, and awareness campaigns. We encouraged the Central Pollution Control Board to inspect smelter and battery-recycling operations and to ensure worker safety in factories. Researchers around the country investigated sources of lead poisoning and published their findings.

Having accomplished the initial goal of halting lead pollution from vehicular exhaust emissions and paint in India, I entrusted subsequent efforts to Dr. Venkatesh, who continued the mission with zeal and commitment. Hospitals consulted NRCLPI on lead poisoning cases, and blood samples were sent to us from different parts of the country for testing.

Now that leaded gasoline was being phased out, NRCLPI turned its attention to lead in paint. Paint manufacturers could have been more responsive initially, but they, too, came around in a couple of years. The NRCLPI then focused on informing the general population about safeguards in the use of paint, cookware, and toys, as well as persuading companies to clean up contaminated areas.

Thousands of lead smelters and lead-based industries across India still continued to operate without environmental controls or inspections, contaminating surrounding neighborhoods and exposing millions of children and adults to its dangers. Only a limited number of companies using lead in their manufacturing offered adequate safeguards against lead poisoning in their workplaces. Despite all the fanfare and promises, it soon became apparent that, in addition to offering unleaded gasoline, more commitment by the Central Pollution Control Board was needed to ensure proper regulatory enforcement and to clean up contaminated soil. Other than alerting the Pollution Control Board, these concerns were beyond my capacity to address.

I read an article hypothesizing that lead poisoning might have caused the fall of the Roman Empire. However, it is unclear whether there were sufficient pathways for lead contamination to occur on a significant scale back then. Experts are studying archaeological evidence to determine whether leaded plumbing systems caused poisoning. Modern living has many more potential lead sources than what might have existed then, making it imperative to undertake adequate preventive measures urgently to avoid direct human contact with lead.

I was grateful that my financial strength enabled me to undertake such a massive endeavor. Our accomplishments as an NGO in addressing a major national health threat renewed my confidence in embarking on other social endeavors in India, especially those affecting rural communities for which I have a particular affinity.

CHAPTER 17

THE WOMEN OF RURAL INDIA

SHANTI BHAVAN COULDN'T REMAIN an island of relative prosperity amid poor villages. The welfare of the villagers and our peaceful coexistence with them were closely linked. Indifference toward the villagers' needs would fuel resentment over time.

We prioritized our effort to win the support of the communities served. To meet the people's spiritual needs, our foundation built two small temples in nearby villages for those who did not have places of worship and repaired an old traditional chariot used for religious processions that had been lying idle for over twenty years. Concurrently, we identified and undertook several educational and health-care initiatives to assist them.

During frequent visits to neighboring villages, I reached out to village elders, school principals, and local leaders—anyone willing to give me a revealing account of their difficulties. Weary of corrupt officials and external interference, we directly distributed books, clothes, school bags, and secondhand computers to local students. In addition, we repaired broken-down school toilets to prevent female students from returning home during school time or walking long distances to the fields. To overcome water shortages in two villages, bore wells were drilled and pipes were laid to reach the poorer sections, and proper drainages were dug to avoid wastewater stagnation.

Village women, especially those who were poor, were my window into rural India and its myriad problems. They were illiterate and earned their living as laborers in landlords' fields. Those belonging to the Dalit caste led a life of economic deprivation, with no opportunity to overcome inequality. They were forced to send their children as indentured laborers for landlords to whom they owed money. Female infanticide was a tragic phenomenon among rural families where women were ostracized for giving birth to daughters.

On one occasion, a social worker named Nagaraj arranged a meeting at a village with a group of single women aged twenty to forty. The village elder proudly presented his daughter, Banu, as our translator between Kannada and English. The assembled group was submissive but cooperative—a natural predisposition for rural women being interviewed by a man presumed to be in authority.

Noticing that the group was uncomfortable with the panchayat head's presence, I politely asked him to wait outside. He grudgingly obliged. I turned to the women. "As you might already know, I head Shanti Bhavan, a school that brings up children from poor homes like yours. I want to learn more about your lives, so I might be able to help." With friendly and relaxed gestures, I put the women at ease.

Although shy at first, Manju, the youngest, began. "I married a local boy I was in love with at fourteen. He turned out to be an alcoholic and beat me. After a few years, he left me for another woman."

She struggled to hold back tears. "I married again. My second husband left me after a year. My son and I now live with my parents and younger brother."

"Do you have any difficulty staying with your parents?" I asked.

"I am a burden to them. They would like me to move out, but I can't live in the village alone," she said. "I work six days a week as a bonded field laborer because my parents borrowed money from the landlord and haven't repaid it." With whatever little she made, she was looking after her parents, grandparents, and in-laws. I was moved by her sensitivity and respect for her elders.

When I asked her about her prospects, she answered in a subdued, fatalistic tone, "I have nothing to look forward to, no hope. I will be content if my family treats me well, but they don't, even though I am working to pay off their debts and care for them."

"What is your biggest need?" I probed.

"Shelter. A home," she replied without a thought. "I am afraid there will be no one to look after my son if anything happens to me." It was terribly sad that at the tender age of twenty she was already thinking about her death.

It was Roopa's turn. "After nine years of marriage, my husband died. Our son is now twelve years old. He doesn't attend school because I can't afford to buy him books and uniform."

"What does he do now?" I asked.

"He works as a servant in a rich man's house. I don't mind my son staying at the landlord's home and working late into the night. At least he gets some food to eat." She had accepted her son's status as a bonded laborer in exchange for receiving meals.

Later that day, I was introduced to an elderly woman from the Dalit caste. I inquired how she felt about being classified as a lower caste. "My parents and grandparents were Dalits. Who am I to question it?" she replied. I had expected her to be troubled by her inferior position, but centuries of upper-class oppression had resigned her and others like her to accept things as they always had been and always would be.

The submissive fatalism of the Dalits was exploited and reinforced by the landlords. They were conditioned to believe that fate or God's will predestined their caste and societal status. To break from the status quo intellectually, they would need to reject this social arrangement that trapped and oppressed them. Could a shift in their belief be possible?

The truth I discovered about their lives couldn't be erased from my thoughts. "Why are they destined to suffer for no fault of theirs?" I asked myself. There was no end to their miserable predicament. But I couldn't possibly fathom their mental anguish without having experienced it. They had let me into their personal lives, trusting that I would be sensitive to their human condition. I couldn't be indifferent to their suffering and walk away without reassuring them of some assistance, although my capacity to help all of them had limitations.

We initiated a savings plan, and Roopa, who already had some scant savings, chose to participate. She would contribute three hundred rupees—less than five dollars monthly—and the foundation would match it. We negotiated a ten-year deposit scheme with a bank at its best interest rate. At the end of ten years, Roopa would receive one hundred thousand rupees, which is roughly fifteen hundred dollars. She would have contributed about one-third of that amount by then, and the balance would come from the foundation and the earned interest.

On another village visit, I ran into Lakshmamma, a middle-aged woman with three children. "A few years ago, my unmarried teenage daughter got pregnant. Since we couldn't afford the expensive treatment, we went to a village doctor. He botched the abortion," she said, tearing up.

"My daughter was bleeding profusely, so I took her to a nearby private hospital. The physician there refused to do the procedure for free. He wanted me to pay a discounted fee of four thousand rupees." A fee of that size—roughly one hundred US dollars—was impossible for a woman who earned a meager income as a laborer.

"I had very little savings, and time was running out," she said. "I had no choice but to turn to a local lender who arranged a loan in less than two hours. I agreed to repay two hundred rupees in interest and two hundred in principle each month for twenty months."

Lakshmamma had sealed this deal with her thumbprint on a two-line promissory note. The surgery had gone well, and her daughter had recovered. But the high interest was not something she could readily meet.

She shook her head and continued, "No one else would have provided the funds in time for me to save my daughter's life. What else could I do?" Without proper support systems in place, the choices faced by poor people are usually uncompromising.

The abominable circumstances in which many families lived and the ailments they suffered from bothered me tremendously. Poor people rarely got a routine checkup and seldom saw a doctor unless their illness became serious. Without nearby hospitals, they settled for substandard care offered by nearby urban clinics that charged low fees. If the prevailing medical conditions were to improve, we would need to offer adequate medical care at affordable costs.

I spoke to my family about the health condition of those living in the nearby villages and emphasized the need for a medical clinic. Thanks to Bijoy's generous contribution, we planned a medical center just two kilometers from Shanti Bhavan, accessible to some thirteen villages. Dr. Maya offered suggestions for the layout, and I worked with an architect to design an airy, three-story building. A staircase and a sweeping ramp rose to the second floor of the building, where a ten-bed inpatient ward, a delivery room, a minor operating theatre, and recovery rooms could be set up.

The ground floor was arranged to provide outpatient services and emergency care, with rooms for examination and treatment, a doctor's office, a laboratory, a pharmacy, an administrative office, and a training classroom. The third floor would house doctors and staff.

In 2001, Baldev Medical & Community Centre began providing outpatient care to the surrounding community of fifteen thousand people in thirteen villages. We came up with the name by combining the first three letters of the two villages closest to Shanti Bhavan: Baliganapalli and Devarapalli. The resulting name had the appropriate and beautiful meaning in Kannada of "Children of God."

We hired a resident medical doctor and nurse, two social workers, and staff to assist the medical personnel and maintain the facilities. Although a modest operation, it was adequate to meet the outpatient and emergency needs of area villagers.

Dr. Maya and I met regularly with the health-care team to discuss our responsibilities. "I think we should focus on prevention and early detection of diseases. We cannot provide inpatient care at this stage, but we have beds to keep patients under observation for a few hours," I shared. Our team members were familiar with rural life in Karnataka and Tamil Nadu, so I felt confident they would recognize the health needs of the villages.

Dr. Maya totally agreed. "Yes, we should be able to provide first aid, emergency care, and basic outpatient services. With a doctor residing at Baldev, we can treat injuries, food poisoning, and minor ailments such as viral fever, diarrhea, allergy, and skin rash. Other cases can be referred to a hospital in the nearest town."

"What about pregnancy and childbirth?" I asked. "These should be an important part of our services." We knew that childbirth commonly occurred at home, assisted by local untrained birth attendants.

"Let's give each mother-to-be a 'delivery kit' that contains a clean blade to cut the umbilical cord, soap, and a towel," Dr. Maya suggested. Worried that women in dire financial situations might sell the delivery kits, we gave them to birth attendants only at delivery time.

"My husband doesn't want a girl child. His parents badly want a grandson. They won't treat me properly if I give birth to a girl," one young woman said. Fearing that some female newborn babies were being killed, I decided to have our nurse present at delivery.

Teenage girls and pregnant women received iron, folic acid, and calcium tablets, as well as protein powder made from locally available grains and nuts for several months before delivery. Baldev organized reproductive health classes for young women to educate them on safe delivery and the importance of good prenatal and postnatal care. Because we had built trust in the local communities, parents willingly sent their daughters to our training sessions. As a result of our interventions, cases of female infanticide and death at childbirth plummeted within two years.

In addition to common illnesses, we addressed nutritional deficiencies, infectious disease prevention, sanitation issues, unclean drinking water, and gastrointestinal ailments. Many villagers went barefoot to the fields for their morning rituals, exposing themselves to unhygienic conditions that led to parasitic infestations from round-worms and tapeworms.

Our staff, therefore, periodically distributed deworming pills to surrounding villages. It was difficult, though, to convince people to take them; they were used to herbal treatment and feared modern medicine. In one village, women flatly refused to take deworming pills, saying, "We heard these pills make our women infertile."

It took considerable time and effort to debunk these beliefs. We collaborated with community leaders to organize health camps and make presentations to explain the need. Several community activities were initiated with the assistance of village self-help groups known as *sanghas*. One such measure was designed to improve hygiene. After meeting and planning with village leaders, we sent a team equipped with a bulldozer and backhoe on a cleanup mission. Villagers and college students from nearby cities joined the effort.

The team removed garbage heaps, cleaned public latrines and gutters, and filled ditches containing stagnant water where mosquitoes bred. Since the villagers had participated, we expected they would continue maintaining their surroundings. Over time, these community initiatives, combined with our preventive care and outpatient services, resulted in measurable improvements in the villagers' collective health and well-being.

• • •

Baldev addressed minor cases, while patients with serious ailments went to local government-run Primary Health Centres (PHCs). Government-assigned doctors from nearby cities attended to patients at PHCs for a few hours every other day. The limited time available to doctors could be better utilized if we streamlined the consultation process. Could we develop a software application to handle patient intake and offer preliminary diagnoses?

I was confident that the software engineers from my former company could build such a system in their spare time if I provided the application design and logic to diagnose illnesses prevalent in our area. It took our systems experts, under the leadership of Dr. Maya, over two years to build the diagnostic logic and specify the treatment protocols for relatively minor ailments within a newly designed software application. We named it EDPS 2000, which stood for Early Detection and Prevention System, and 2000 because its developmental work was initiated that year. The villagers nicknamed it "doctor in the box."

To introduce the system to the public, we invited a group of local villagers to visit Baldev and "talk" to the computer. Most of them had never seen a computer before and considered it pure magic. "This computer wants to keep you in good health," the EDPS operator told the patients. They were flabbergasted when the system, having maintained prior patient records, inquired about family members who had visited Baldev in the recent past.

Each EDPS intake process took less than twenty minutes. A high school graduate, reasonably proficient in both English and the local language, functioned as the operator and translated the questions prompted by the system. Answers to every multiple-choice question generated a more specific question, eventually drilling down to probable diagnoses and prescriptions for over-the-counter medication, lab tests, or referral to a physician.

We initially offered free consultation and medicine to all patients, but when we discovered that even landlords and others with sufficient income were visiting our clinic, we introduced a three-tiered "health equity" model to assess their financial capacity. Our staff visited houses to gather demographic data such as age, number of family members, monthly income, and assets. We considered the families' financial needs for items such as dowries for their daughters of marriageable age and expenses for pending surgery.

Our software application analyzed the collected data and placed each patient into one of three categories based on their family's overall financial status: the very poor, who couldn't afford to pay; those with moderate ability to afford limited charges; and those who had the means to pay the entire cost for our services and medicines for them.

EDPS could address most of the ailments prevalent in the area. A medical team from Johns Hopkins University studied EDPS and validated many of its results. To our delight, most of the diagnoses made by the program were accurate. Further, the medical history of patients gathered by the system was valuable to doctors for diagnosing and treating illnesses. EDPS 2000 seemed to have a bright future.

Our next task was to get the state government's buy-in to implement EDPS 2000 at its PHCs. Despite our reluctance to work with government agencies, we recognized they were integral to delivering health-care services to rural populations. After some persuasion, we received the government's permission to implement EDPS at four PHCs.

At each PHC, we met stiff resistance from doctors displeased that EDPS recorded pending cases they hadn't yet addressed. Most doctors weren't turning up for work regularly to be at their private clinics and didn't want it to be known. They rejected the suggestion that EDPS could handle cases without their involvement.

The health secretary for the state government of Tamil Nadu

finally allowed the foundation to comanage its PHC in Bagalur, a rural town nearby, which served over seventy thousand people. Our staff worked closely with the doctors assigned to this PHC to demonstrate that EDPS could lower their workload.

Patients were equally pleased with a streamlined process that collected detailed information on their ailments. We would have liked to see the project expand to other PHCs, but given our other priorities and the effort required to overcome major political and bureaucratic hurdles, I was not prepared to invest my energies toward such an effort. We were satisfied with our limited success and waited to see if the government would show any interest. In the meantime, our clever little "doctor in the box" continued to serve Baldev's needs for a few more years.

• • •

Village women sought steady jobs but could find only seasonal work as farm laborers. As a result, their incomes couldn't support their minimal needs. Without financial stability, they couldn't become independent of abusive marriages and the patriarchal hold. I sought solutions from village leaders to help the women, but they didn't offer any. Instead, they asked me to persuade the panchayat to improve public transport, roads, and government-run schools. None of their suggestions, though essential, appealed to me, as they didn't address the welfare of the poor and instead were focused on construction projects that would inappropriately benefit the village leaders and officials.

"If we purchase or lease land, we can grow bananas, which are in high demand. The farm can provide steady employment at fair wages for hundreds of women," Jude proposed. I hadn't considered farming, but if we offered steady employment, especially for women, it would free them and their children from bonded labor. In the long term, with profits generated from the venture, the foundation could enable families to own cultivable land. Until then, their subsistence would be limited to our year-round employment.

Lasting improvement on a larger scale could be accomplished only by empowering poor people. If much government-owned land could be available for cooperative farming, and the required initial capital was provided, they could cultivate and have permanent employment. With agribusinesses in rural areas, a ready market for their produce could be found. The promotion of agriculture and its ownership by the rural poor would be a viable alternative to employment as laborers in urban industries.

I gave the go-ahead to cultivate over one hundred acres of land adjoining the school campus, some of which would be leased. Our social workers informed the villages that farm employment would be available at good wages. A requisite for employment at Baldev Farms was that workers' children be enrolled in school instead of working in landlords' houses. Several laborers already had their children studying at Shanti Bhavan, and others sent their children to local government schools. These were no small achievements for women in abject poverty not offered the opportunity to navigate their way out.

These measures weren't well received by the upper castes, who feared they would no longer be able to find cheap labor for their farms. Village heads demanded that Jude source laborers only with their consent, but we politely refused. Even our own staff found it somewhat perplexing to see me venture into one project after another, despite the objections of powerful community leaders. They saw me as a quick decision-maker and a doer, and they were excited to be a part of whatever project I undertook.

The women working for landlords on seasonal jobs were very excited. Our farm was close, so they could easily walk to work and return home early enough to take care of their household chores. They were accustomed to long hours of physical labor and highly motivated to earn. They possessed the knowledge and skills of traditional farming and raising livestock. Instead of training them in a new trade, it was much easier to familiarize them with modern farming.

I was pleased to see how quickly the women picked up the needed additional skills. To increase crop output, we introduced superior technology, such as deep plowing, drip irrigation, and precise fertilization. Tractors and other equipment replaced much of the work previously done by hand. Women laborers and supervisors were trained in modern agricultural techniques and practices such as resource conservation, land and crop management, organic and chemical fertilizer application, and the safe use of pesticides.

When harvest season approached, we introduced the workers to post-harvest processing, packing, and marketing. As they and their supervisors gained experience, we steadily increased the area under banana cultivation to nearly two hundred acres. At its peak, Baldev Farms was among the most extensive banana plantations in South India, producing over twenty tons of bananas daily.

"It is so exciting to see the so-called poor man's fruit being shipped in lorries in such large quantities!" I exclaimed to Jude, watching trucks being loaded with bananas.

He beamed. "The laborers are happy."

Most plantation employees were women. Every morning, senior

managers would meet with the supervisors who directed the farm laborers. Some supervisors were as young as twenty but had been selected due to their high school education. The older workers initially resented young women giving them instructions, but over time grew more accepting as they saw that the younger ones could read the irrigation and fertilization schedules.

I joined these meetings regularly to encourage workers and address concerns like inadequate plant growth, shortage of specific nutrients, pest infestations, and diseases affecting crops—fungal, viral, or bacterial. We reviewed the use of correct quantities of water and fertilizers, as specified by an Excel program I had developed after studying best practices in the industry.

The labor force worked hard, even in the stifling summer heat. I was surprised by their ability to withstand the scorching sun, laboring as diligently as they did. We implemented health interventions to increase their energy levels and physical stamina. I recall Ralph Nader, the well-known champion for consumer safety and onetime US presidential candidate, asking me in one of my meetings with him in Washington, DC, "Abraham, I have read about management techniques to improve agricultural output. How do you ensure good worker productivity on your farm?"

"The formula we have adopted is simple: Deworm the workers every six months, give them iron tablets daily for a while so they are no longer anemic, offer high-protein powder made from local grains and peanuts, and shelter workers from direct sun with a wide Mexican-style straw hat. These cost very little," I explained.

Mr. Nader burst out laughing at our simple ingenuity. "That makes sense," he replied. "You don't need economists to tell you that."

From my frequent interactions with the village women working on our farm, I learned that their families benefited steadily from our initiatives. The health-care costs for their families were subsidized when they visited our Baldev Medical & Community Centre. Our workers were paid higher than the prevailing wages in the area, and we introduced a savings plan wherein participants contributed a small amount to the program each month. "We have never seen this much money before!" one beneficiary exclaimed at the prospect of what she would receive through the savings plan.

Although the amount received was small, nearly one hundred other single women who wouldn't otherwise have saved any money participated in the savings plan and continue to do so. With the money they received at the end of the term, some bought a cow or two for milk and raised goats to be sold for meat. Over time, many could pay off debts, improve their houses, and afford an education for their children beyond high school.

Their well-being improved with such assistance; they could finally afford better food, get healthier, and be more energetic at work. I often wondered how private-sector companies could be motivated to improve the living condition of the poor without having to forgo their profitability.

Our contribution to the welfare of poor people was minuscule compared to the need. In India, over two hundred million lived in abject poverty, and another four to five hundred million earned below five dollars a day per family. Many in rural communities resided in broken-down houses without running water, sent their children to nearby substandard schools, and lacked adequate health care. Through it all, the suffering they endured was indescribable.

The state-implemented remedies were insufficient to significantly improve the living conditions of the poor. To supplement what governments do, the private sector needs to be involved in addressing the problem. That will happen only when the broader society undergoes civic and cultural reforms focusing on general welfare rather than personal prosperity. The emotional drive to build an equitable world must come from a much broader national populace.

CHAPTER 18

FORMIDABLE CHALLENGES

H AVING MADE THE DECISION to move on to the next phase of my life, I was in a hurry to unwind all my business activities in the US and complete any unfinished tasks. Yet, despite a busy schedule, the unfamiliar absence of professional responsibilities left a vacuum in my daily routine. I was at SunGard for two years subsequent to selling MCM, most of which gave me ample time to work on another book on international finance titled *Protecting Shareholder Value: A Guide to Managing Financial Market Risk*. I didn't realize until I typed the last line of the manuscript in the wee hours one morning that this was my last act in a much-cherished business career spanning twenty-five years. Overcome with mixed emotions, I teared up as many unforgettable memories passed through my mind.

I shuttled between India and the US, spending eight months a year at the school to ensure its progress. Twenty-four preschoolers were admitted each academic year, increasing the school population and the demands on my time. I worked closely with the various departments—administrators, teachers, caregivers, and the facility oversight team—offering them leadership and managerial skills.

When the staff consulted me, I asked questions and responded promptly with suggestions or directions. I was decisive and quick, an upshot of my military background. I followed up later and, if necessary, altered the course of action. I didn't brood over my past decisions and instead focused on how to proceed.

From the start, I was concerned about maintaining a green campus and living in an environmentally sustainable manner. To that end, we implemented several measures: jute bags rather than plastic ones, chemical-free laundry detergents, and cow dung and poultry manure as fertilizers. Decomposed plant material kept the soil moist. Extract from *neem* seeds was combined with other herbal plant material and fermented to create an all-natural pesticide. Sewage water was recycled for irrigation.

"Teach the children to do one small thing every day, like planting a tree or watering the shrubs," I told the staff, encouraging a sense of environmental stewardship and sustainability.

My time running MCM had sensitized me to the importance of motivating my staff and being conscious of others' needs. Decision-making authority was assigned among lower-level supervisors and managers. I based my decisions on the answers to three questions:

What is the best course of action right now?

Is it right or wrong—fair, ethical, and moral?

Will my actions or decisions harm or hurt someone else?

If the answers satisfied me, I proceeded.

I guided Lalita in administrative tasks, such as recruiting teachers and caregivers and designing training sessions. With the support of Lalita and Beena, our newly appointed vice principal, we developed a sound program for an all-around education. We selected a well-recognized curriculum offered by the Council for the Indian School Certificate Examinations. Besides academics, we emphasized leadership qualities and nurturing humane values.

The council required English as the medium of instruction and mandated national-level examinations in the tenth and twelfth grades. We worried whether our first-generation learners could reach the high standards. "It is up to us to motivate them to be high achievers in a competitive program," I told my staff.

Psychologists had warned us about the deleterious consequences of poverty and the traumatic events students might have faced in their early childhood. Serious attention disorders and learning difficulties showed up among some students as they entered a formal classroom environment after kindergarten. Despite teachers' one-on-one attention and careful guidance, as well as remedial sessions, a few could not keep up with the rest of the class. Given our limited resources, we couldn't offer them long-term specialized care.

Ultimately, we let go of a few who couldn't meet the school's academic demands, despite our best efforts over prolonged periods. Deeply saddened, I grappled with this decision. Like me, the teachers and caregivers struggled: They had become emotionally attached to these children. It was a hard reality for parents, and I didn't blame them for resenting us or feeling let down. We placed the children in government schools and programs elsewhere that could meet their special needs.

Critics of our dismissal policy failed to recognize that quality institutions must not lower their standards, regardless of a family's low economic status. I realized that compassion alone could not be the decisive factor in our efforts to help others.

Unfortunately, a few parents abruptly pulled their children out of our program for various reasons. Initially, I didn't appreciate their rationales, but as time passed, I recognized their limitations. Pressured by financial difficulties, they needed to put their sons and daughters to work to earn for the family, even from a very young age. Our efforts to convince them otherwise fell short.

In one instance, the staff introduced me to a young single mother who was visually impaired in both eyes. "Thank you for taking care of her, sir," the mother told me. Taking both her hands in mine, I replied, "One day, you will be able to see through her eyes. She will take good care of you."

But this mother unexpectedly pulled her child out of school a few years later. The mother needed the young girl at home to assist her in getting around and bringing in an income. I was initially unhappy with the mother for being selfish but realized not too long after that her life offered her no other choice. Jude tried to keep my spirits up, saying, "Heartbreak comes with this job."

I tried hard not to let my optimism dampen. I realized that for abjectly poor people who daily lived hand to mouth, marking time for seventeen years of schooling and then college for an uncertain future was too much to ask. I was promising a bright future without any guarantee; I was expecting them to take a chance that wasn't realistic in their circumstances.

Only with time would it become easier to convince the parents that waiting for their children to finish their studies at Shanti Bhavan and later at universities would produce far more significant benefits, both in terms of their children's happiness and the long-term earning potential for the family.

. . .

I engrossed myself in creating a forthright culture, the most crucial aspect essential to the children's development and the staff's conduct. In doing so, it isn't enough to set principles and rules; they should be enforced daily. Otherwise, they quickly fall apart in practice, and exceptions will come to steer policy.

However, there was no meeting of the minds on religion. Lalita insisted on holding catechism classes for Catholic children, but I argued vehemently against giving special consideration to any religion. While rituals and beliefs might offer hope and comfort, I believed Shanti Bhavan ought not promote them but instead guide our children to follow the right path. I emphasized to the children that prayers might provide opportunity for self-reflection; however, adherence to religious practices to purify oneself or receive God's blessings does not replace our responsibility to help those in need.

Appreciating religion's important role in people's lives, I suggested two spiritual initiatives. First, I worked with Lalita to compose an official school prayer—a simple statement of love and peace that captured a universal wish. It ended with "Help us to know right from wrong, to be honest and truthful, kind, and peaceful. Help us to do our best each day and to love, honor, and value all that we have. Namaste." I asked them to follow right conduct that comes from right beliefs.

Next, we built a prayer hall facing north to avoid religious preferences. Holy texts like the Bhagavad Gita, the Quran, the Bible, the Torah, and others were prominently displayed. Anyone could pray silently there, but singing, chanting, or reading aloud from religious books were not allowed.

Most visitors accepted this arrangement and enjoyed the prayer hall's peaceful, silent tranquility, but a few maintained that Shanti

Bhavan was a "godless place." One blogger attacked our practice by writing, "It is a terrible crime to bring up children without a firm religious foundation. Hindu children should be taught the Vedas and the teachings of the Ramayana and Mahabharata." I am sure many Christians felt the same about the Bible as Muslims did about the Quran.

We prohibited parents from extending some traditional practices to Shanti Bhavan, such as shaving their children's heads as part of a religious ritual for pilgrimages or funerals. We explained, "It is not good to have a child appear different from the rest. Such distinctions will lead to divisiveness." Similarly, boys and girls from Christian families were required to wear cross necklaces tucked inside their blouses or shirts.

I remained convinced that the only way to ensure harmony among the children and staff of different faiths was to avoid openly practicing religious preferences. I did not want the children to grow up distinguishing from others based on their faiths. Some staff members argued against this policy, but I wouldn't relent to pressure, and many of them could see the merits of our approach.

I expected Lalita to carry out the rules consistently for staff and children, even in my absence. Much to my dismay, despite orienting the staff to the significance of their nurturing role, some displayed undesirable behavior carried over from their own upbringing—coercing children into obedience by spanking, using demeaning language, and raising the dreaded specter of dismissal. They still believed the best way to discipline children was to inflict harsh punishments like beating them or depriving them of meals. They considered fear to be more effective than encouragement in inducing behavioral change. Some staff members ridiculed the children's backgrounds and their parents' occupations: "Your mother is just a housemaid" or "I don't know why Dr. George has come here to raise kids like you. He's wasting his money on you."

When I learned of these troubling instances, the caregiver or teacher was either warned or dismissed. "I don't care what you might have experienced yourselves as children. We won't permit this here," I sternly reprimanded them. We could manage temporarily with fewer staff, but we couldn't afford to retain anyone who physically or emotionally harmed the children.

Similarly, I was troubled by some of the children speaking in a subservient tone and avoiding eye contact with those in authority. The children said a warden instructed them to do so. I was angry at the conditioning, counter to what I believed in. "Raise your head. Look up! Be confident," I repeatedly urged the children.

The prejudice meted out by adults increased the children's troubling lack of self-worth and trust in their potential to excel academically; they internalized shame and helplessness. To combat this diffidence, I repeatedly assured the children that they were just as beautiful and intelligent as anyone else and that their family's condition didn't make them any less.

I believe the children's inferiority complex resulted from observing their families constantly demeaned by upper castes in their villages. Living in secluded sections reserved for the lower castes, they felt lesser than others. Not being allowed to fetch water from the village well until late evenings and being forbidden to worship at the same temple as the upper castes were two instances among many that diminished their self-worth.

I knew the children might view their social status as destined or ill-fated. I explained to our staff and children that there was no such thing as a divine curse or blessing, as these beliefs were propagated by those who consider themselves superior in caste and self-importance.

"Although your families have patiently borne the notion of low caste as your fate for generations, you must not accept such a status. Your families are treated inhumanely based on other people's false sense of superiority. Everyone is born equal, with equal rights. Being born poor is an accident of birth. Do not accept the notion of caste," I repeatedly told them. However, parents likely found these concepts alien when their children voiced them at home.

Similarly, when I heard about children of darker complexion being bullied by their peers, I advised them, "Beauty is defined by the person you are, not by your skin tone." I pointed out that dark skin color, often associated with lower caste, didn't make them any less, and they shouldn't let themselves be treated unfairly or unjustly.

Bringing up children in a coed environment isn't easy. In their teenage years, they are highly driven by sexual curiosity and tempted to engage in intimacy. Our guidance and frequent conversations on the dangers of sexual relationships aimed to persuade them from making poor choices. However, as adults, we needed to recognize that it was natural for teenagers to feel strong fondness for another, and enforcement of strict rules could prevent unwanted incidents.

Sound parenting style and stable caregiving in a secure environment are fundamental to the children's social and emotional well-being. To that end, I wouldn't let a child pass by me, anywhere, without making eye contact, smiling, or softly expressing my affection for them. I hoped assurances of my love and my confidence in their abilities would help them overcome their lack of self-esteem and self-confidence.

The children were encouraged to follow world events to broaden their outlook and gain global exposure. We enhanced their world-view by welcoming individuals from diverse walks of life from India and elsewhere—scientists, musicians, journalists, lawyers, and others. Over a dozen volunteers from other countries served at any given time, enabling children to appreciate and develop a multicultural outlook. The children observed the volunteers' manners, etiquette, speaking styles, and enthusiasm, anxious to emulate them. Some even tried to imitate their accents.

Among the exciting guests who shared time with children were renowned journalist Thomas Friedman of *The New York Times*; Mark Tully, a director at BBC; I. K. Gujral, the former prime minister of India; and Sandra Magnus, a senior NASA astronaut. The NASA team was accompanied by both the husband and the father of the late astronaut Kalpana Chawla, who had died in the explosion of the space shuttle *Columbia*. The interactions with eminent people, I hoped, would inspire children to study hard in school and aspire to promising careers.

I constantly thought of ideas to enhance the quality of our program and the children's experiences. I was confident that our consistent efforts would bear fruit incrementally over the years.

CHAPTER 19

NEW EXPEDITIONS

"ANIYAN, YOUR FATHER AND I have a project for you to consider in India," Ammachi said, motioning me to join her and Achachan at the breakfast table. "We have seen how poor artists struggle in India. We would like you to build a museum to promote their artwork," she continued without waiting for me to settle in my chair.

I hadn't seen this coming. All along they had been worrying about my getting involved in one expensive venture after the other, and now they were proposing I plunge into an unfamiliar field.

"We are prepared to give a part of our savings as capital to get it going," my mother said.

"Rural artists can display their work in this museum," my father added. "Then they may sell their pieces at good prices in galleries."

My mother nodded. "We can collaborate with artists from other countries to blend different art forms. Our museum should exhibit curated collections of traditional and contemporary paintings and sculptures." Clearly, the two of them had already discussed this at length.

My mother then detailed her concept of an arts village surrounding the museum. "Most artists are poor. We should house talented artists on the premises. That way, they can live there comfortably and create excellent artwork."

"That's a fantastic idea, Ammachi. Give me some time to think it over," I said.

Though it diverted from our primary mission of addressing poverty and social injustice, promoting rural art excited me. My exposure to the Indian arts, however, was limited to the stone carvings in temples of Hindu gods and goddesses and sculptures depicting characters in legends and epics. I recalled, as a child, attending an exhibit of Ravi Verma's celebrated portrait paintings in Trivandrum, which had triggered my interest in visual art.

From my inquiry into the state of rural arts and crafts in India, I discovered that modern art forms were threatening traditional creative expression. Consequently, many skilled craftsmen and artisans were forsaking their age-old traditions and talents to earn a livelihood in other professions. An arts project in a rural area could employ gifted artists from the villages who were struggling to make a living.

I discussed the idea with other family members and Jude, and they, too, were excited about it and wanted me to get started. We chose an elevated piece of land adjoining the main campus of Shanti Bhavan for the museum.

The arts colony near the museum would be equipped with indigenous and contemporary materials and tools for exceptionally creative artists who might not have yet received public recognition. I thought of inviting reputed artists from other countries to interact with those residing in our arts village. Together, they could produce a variety of sculptures of wood, metal, and clay in a new form of "fusion" art.

With the help of V. Kiran, a talented architect trained in New York, we drew up blueprints for a modern building with parquet wood flooring, a winding staircase with a majestic interior, and a circular contour. The grounds outside would have a reflecting pool. Large glass panels would admit abundant natural light, complemented by interior focus lights. The building's stark bluish-gray walls would thrust up from the earth in a rocky outcropping silhouetted against the sky. The multitiered and rounded shape of the building prompted Kiran to call it the "Little Guggenheim," after the iconic New York Museum. I christened it "Tillany," as suggested by a friend who said it meant "explosive energy" in Sanskrit.

In January 2001, the first exhibit opened. Some people declared it the finest museum building in India. My parents, who attended the inaugural festivities, were delighted. I recall Ammachi saying, "The museum is a wonderful structure. It can exhibit art pieces beautifully."

Achachan's loving nature was on full display during the evening ceremony. With the help of a walking stick, he approached the microphone, discarded his prepared script, and raved about Ammachi and her love for the arts. The audience laughed affectionately at his heartfelt tribute to his wife. My mother, seated in the front row, was utterly flustered. "Why does he have to praise me instead of talking about the museum?" she asked with embarrassment and feigned irritation.

• • •

The needless troubles our foundation endured over the years revealed how ingrained corruption was in the system. Charitable projects, in particular, attracted intermediaries who sought money for themselves, especially if the projects received public funding. I expressed my frustration at staff meetings with these words: "Ineffective, dishonest undertakings are among the reasons for poverty and slow economic progress."

A vigilant and free press could help expose ineffective policies, poor management, and corruption. If citizens were well informed, sufficient public pressure might drive systemic change. Greater awareness could improve governance and strengthen India's democratic values and institutions.

My frustration with the Indian media heightened following a troubling exchange with two newspaper editors during the Kargil War between India and Pakistan. Militants from Pakistan had occupied several mountaintops in India-controlled Northern Kashmir, leading to a major border skirmish. Newspapers published the casualty count of Indian soldiers as a few hundred dead and over one thousand injured, though live coverage of overloaded trains transporting wounded soldiers to military and civilian hospitals throughout North India told a different story. A doctor friend in Calcutta told me of receiving hundreds of injured soldiers in his city alone on the eastern side of the country, far removed from the northwestern battlefront.

As a former military officer, I was certain that a significant operation requiring mountaintop assaults would result in more casualties than what was officially reported. War correspondents on the ground could have verified and attested that the government was deliberately undercounting. I questioned the veracity of the coverage, observing that reporters weren't examining the army's tactics or assessing the failure of the country's leaders, who were constantly playing to the public's fervent patriotism and offering empty promises of a quick and decisive victory.

"Am I supposed to buy your newspaper knowing full well that

you are lying to me?" I asked the mid-level editors I invited to the Bangalore Club to discuss media reporting of the war.

"Everybody knows those published battle casualty numbers are lower than the real ones. We can't contradict the government in times of war," one editor argued.

"Then you are a mouthpiece for the government!" I retorted.

"Hmph! *The New York Times* does the same thing," he replied.

I didn't respond.

I had lived through the Watergate break-in that led to President Richard Nixon's resignation, and I was aware of the critical role the investigative press had played in exposing political wrongdoing. The journalistic integrity and courage of *The Washington Post* investigative reporters Bob Woodward and Carl Bernstein, as well as their chief editor, Ben Bradlee, exemplified the highest ideals of truthful reporting.

My conviction on press freedom being central to democracy and social equality motivated me to start a journalism college called the Indian Institute of Journalism & New Media (IIJNM) in Bangalore. The college would offer a postgraduate diploma in print, online, and broadcast media to train students in investigative and truthful reporting. The college would remain autonomous, although nonmonetary collaboration with major media houses was desirable so that we could work together toward improving press quality.

Our focus on promoting investigative journalism appeared unrealistically ambitious. I knew press freedom wasn't received well in certain circles, and truthful media might not be acceptable to those being criticized. If we were to train journalists to cover corruption and wrongdoings, the college could face repercussions from those involved. It might also become difficult to hold events designed to share different viewpoints through lively discussion forums and debates among journalists.

To circumvent such possibilities, we needed an influential partner, perhaps a significant religious leader, to prevent external interference. Not wishing to align with any political party or individual, I was advised to contact one of Karnataka's most prominent Hindu spiritual leaders, His Holiness Balagangadharanatha Swamiji, who was revered by the farming community. No political party in the state could win an election without his public support.

I met him at his *mutt*, a monastic residence—albeit one with a palatial appearance. A community leader ushered Jude and me into Swamiji's presence. Two or three men in white robes—presumably his loyal assistants—stood by in the room to take his instructions or assist him. Unaccustomed to the traditional greeting of a holy man—kneeling and touching his feet—I bowed my head and offered a "namaste."

The community leader who acted as the translator introduced me: "This is Dr. George. He's come from New York."

Swamiji smiled in welcome and gestured for me to sit near him.

"Swamiji, I am very much aware of your humanitarian work—feeding the poor and running schools for the blind. I, too, am involved in social endeavors but on a smaller scale," I began, pausing every so often for the translator to convert my English into Kannada and to gauge Swamiji's reaction.

"It would benefit the country if you would join me in starting a journalism college. Citizens need an honest, unbiased press," I said.

He listened patiently, occasionally smiling and nodding.

From what I observed, except for me, no one in the room made eye contact with the holy man while speaking to him. I was as friendly and respectful toward him as I would be with anyone else, and Swamiji appeared cordial, apparently not minding my casual style and straight talk.

"I feel that our current press fails to report the news accurately," I continued. "It is important to train journalists to be truthful and ethical. I humbly seek your partnership and collaboration to establish a journalism school in Bangalore." Expecting questions or perhaps resistance, I paused again.

A broad smile spread across Swamiji's face.

"When can we start?" he asked without any inquiry.

I hadn't expected such a quick decision. With great excitement, I thanked him for his immediate decision. "Once we find the land, I estimate it will take a year or more to build and equip the college."

"You shall have sufficient land within a month," he declared immediately. "I will see to it."

It appeared we had established an emotional connection. Swamiji saw value in my proposed venture; Jude thought that Swamiji might have liked the prospect of gaining the support of the press. True to his word, Swamiji arranged to transfer ownership of over eight acres: four for academic spaces and four for the student hostel. It was a suitable location, with easy access to public transport for students to cover city news. I would cover construction and operating costs and assist the mutt financially in some manner for its social projects. And so began a close and rare association between a prominent Hindu religious leader and an NGO headed by someone with a Christian background.

We established a new nonprofit trust called the BS&G Foundation, combining the first letters of our names—Balagangadharanatha Swamiji and George. I envisioned a college dedicated to the highest principles of the profession and ethics in its work. In the following months, a twenty-thousand-square-foot college was built on beautiful grounds surrounded by rolling hills, an hour from central Bangalore. I worked with a celebrated architect to design a modern, appealing building for the college, with expansive hallways and an outdoor amphitheater.

A sophisticated media lab, a library, a television studio, radio recording stations, and auditoriums would complement its classrooms. Jude and Frank oversaw the college and hostel construction while I focused on hiring the staff and organizing the institute's day-to-day operations.

"IIJNM should start a program in Kannada, George," Swamiji suggested when I met him next.

"That's not a good idea, Swamiji. Students will have more opportunities throughout India and abroad if they learn to communicate well in English," I politely argued.

He saw the merit in this and didn't bring up the subject again. His Kannada-speaking devotees in the room might have been unhappy, but seeing that Swamiji agreed with my position, they didn't show any outright displeasure.

I traveled home to New York and met with Tom Goldstein, then dean of Columbia Journalism School. I sought his advice in developing our curriculum to meet the highest journalistic standards. Tom was enthusiastic and assigned one of the college's faculty members, Sree Sreenivasan, to assist me.

I convened an international advisory board of well-known journalists, business executives, and academicians, including Goldstein and Michael Golden, vice-chairman of The New York Times Company, to guide and direct IIJNM's management. IIJNM held its first advisory board meeting in the boardroom of *The New York Times*—a great honor.

In January 2001, IIJNM welcomed its first class of students. At the inaugural ceremony, I passionately spoke of what the institution stood for: "The ideals of social justice and economic fairness the country embraced when it became independent over fifty years ago are constantly being eroded. It is our mission to strive for those noble goals by fulfilling our responsibility to the public."

Kanchan Kaur, a distinguished professor, told the students, "We strive to offer the best education and training for you to address critical issues and make a good start in the profession."

I was confident that our program would graduate students who would adhere to those ideals and report courageously to expose corruption, poor program planning and implementation, environmental concerns, and other troubling issues plaguing the country.

In my opinion, a weak press has been one of the main reasons for the failure in developing and implementing effective policy measures to address poverty. The press fails to follow through on leads on corruption and serious misdeeds by companies that harm citizens. The headwinds being faced by the journalism profession comes from a fear of personal safety of its reporters and the threats faced by media establishments.

• • •

I frequently received invitations from Swamiji to join him in his Hindu religious ceremonies and partake in the rituals. He always greeted me at his mutt with a warm smile and asked me to sit beside him. Swamiji would introduce me first and praise my work if any guests were present. Our starkly different personal backgrounds didn't diminish our respect for each other; our mutual interest in serving the poor united our two distinct worlds. We had transcended our religious "barriers" and forged a strong friendship.

Swamiji knew well that my humanitarian work was not easy and came with deep disappointments. He cautioned, "You might do good things for the poor, George, but you can't expect their undying loyalty or gratitude. You are always in the company of children. Isn't that enough of life's blessings?"

He appreciated my efforts, and I valued his kindness toward me. He told me of his respect for Christianity and showed me a picture of the Last Supper in one of his rooms. I was initially surprised at his acceptance of other religious faiths, but as I got to know him, I felt the expansiveness of his spirit.

On one occasion, I attended a midnight procession with Swamiji seated atop a chariot several stories high. His followers pulled two long ropes to roll the heavy granite wheels while others ensured the chariot didn't topple over on its side.

When nearing the large artificial lake by the mutt, Swamiji's attendants helped him descend and led him to a waiting boat. Just as he was about to step aboard, he turned and asked, "Where is George?" His disciples looked for me in the crowd and brought me to the boat. The only others allowed on the boat were a few favored followers to pole the vessel forward with long bamboo sticks.

I stepped onto it and sat beside Swamiji's throne on the open deck, visible to the large crowd gathered on the banks of the lake. We presented a study in contrasts—a holy man of India blessing his devotees by raising his folded hands and an ordinary man beside him, embarrassed by the grand ritual. Our shared mission and genuine respect for each other broke through religious barriers that could have kept us apart.

Me on my mother's lap.

George family photo, 1964.

Me when Captain in the Indian Artillery, 1967.

Academy No. : 4441

Name: M ABRAHAM GEORGE

Service: ARMY

SQN: I

Course: 26

My army service record from the NDA website gallery.

The road to Sela Pass.

The Indian army at a skirmish with the Chinese military in the Northeast Frontier, 1967.

A medium-size gun battery near the Pakistan border with India, 1967.

At the battleground near Pathankot, 1966.

Leaving for the US as a civilian, 1968.

Mariam and me at our wedding.

Receiving Hind Ratan Award from late Prime Minister of India, Mr. I. K. Gujral.

Primary sponsors of the conference from Left to right: Dr.H. Falk(CDC), Mr. W. Nitze(USEPA), Dr. A. George(TGF), Mr. K. Alam Khan(Governer), Dr. Y.Schrinding(WHO), Admiral O.S Dawson(TGF) & Mr. R. Ackermann(World Bank)

Lead conference held in Bangalore with the primary sponsors.

An aerial view of the Indian Institute of Journalism & New Media (IIJNM).

The Tillany Museum.

An aerial view of Shanti Bhavan.

Bananas ready for harvest at the Baldev farms.

The Baldev banana farm adjacent to Shanti Bhavan.

Chatting with the children of Shanti Bhavan.

Lighting a ceremonial lamp with the Hindu religious leaders.

The Baldev Medical & Community Centre.

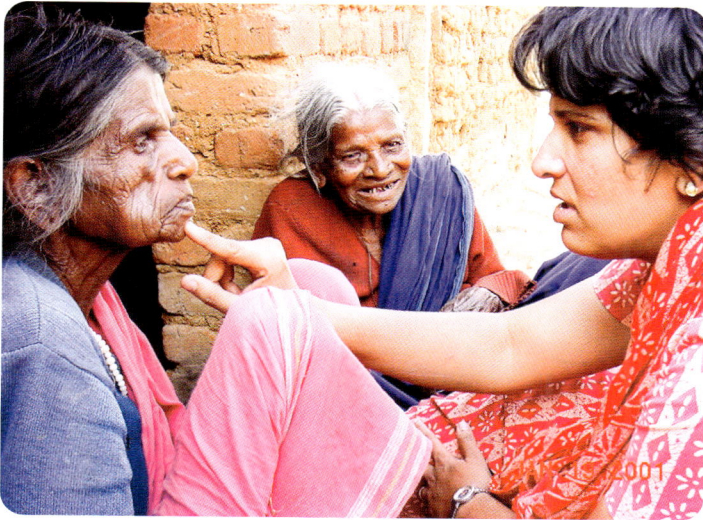

A Baldev medical doctor examining village women.

CHAPTER 20

PROGRESS AT LAST

T HE BEST PART OF MY DAY at Shanti Bhavan was my interactions with the children, especially in my meetings with grades six
and above on a variety of topics of interest to them. I often concluded
my talk by saying, "This is my opinion. Now, freely form your own."
I didn't want them to unquestioningly believe or accept my views
without developing their own perspectives.

"What have I become, Jude? I sound like a preacher, dishing out
lessons and advice," I once remarked.

Jude chuckled. "They love your stories."

My army days in the Himalayas and my childhood in Ayyampilly
interested them most of all. They asked many questions about my
life experiences, eager to learn where and why I had succeeded and
failed. Describing the setbacks MCM experienced and the struggles
I had endured to make my company successful, I acknowledged that
defeats also offer valuable insights. It was up to us to learn from them
and go forward undaunted.

I was gladdened as the children grew more comfortable with me.
A few were still nervous in my presence, which I attributed to my

role as the founder. Over time, they opened up about their compli-
cated home lives. A frequent struggle was sibling rivalry at home
and survivor's guilt for escaping the hardships that entrapped their
brothers and sisters. I empathized with their situations but pointed
out that, through their triumphs, our children could eventually
better the lives of their siblings. Of course, that didn't completely
resolve the dilemma.

Most children had encountered one or multiple traumatic events:
parental abandonment, alcoholism, theft, emotional neglect, suicide
in the family, sexual abuse, witnessing domestic violence, generational debt and harassment by moneylenders, and homelessness.
These experiences adversely impacted their mental health, their focus,
and their happiness while at school. We addressed their trauma by
following advice from external psychologists. Children needing psy-
chiatric intervention for depression, anxiety, and PTSD were taken
to St. John's Hospital in Bangalore for professional help.

I spent hours talking to them on handling their difficult
experiences and assured them of protection at Shanti Bhavan. Additionally, through science classes and sex education, they learned
about consent, different forms of sexual abuse, and ways to guard
themselves. "If you don't feel safe at home during your holidays, call
us up and we'll come and get you," we reminded the children before
they left for summer and winter breaks.

In one shocking case, a five-year-old girl who had been home-
less since birth was sexually abused by her ten-year-old stepbrother
when she visited him at an orphanage over the school break. The
horrors she had suffered troubled me greatly. Her foster family was
called and informed, and the child was not sent home during vacations until we were assured of her safety. She remained guarded and

scared of adults but over time became more trusting of those who cared for her.

In another incident, even after learning that an older male cousin was sexually molesting their daughter, a teenage girl's parents brushed it aside callously, telling her, "What does it matter? You're going to marry him soon anyway." We heard about such incidents from the child, but the parents would not admit it when questioned.

In this part of southern India, village girls are often married off as soon as they come of age. Being aware of this practice, we encouraged the girls to seek our support and intervention in dealing with family members who might have this intention. Some children were ashamed to reveal it or get their parents into trouble with us.

In Shilpa's case, she was fourteen when her grandparents expressed their wish of her marrying their youngest son, her maternal uncle. The young girl didn't initially consent. Still, to my shock, she gradually yielded to family pressure for unconditional loyalty and obedience.

"You don't have to agree with your family when they are wrong. After being in Shanti Bhavan for ten years, how can you not see what is good for your future?" I scolded her. She broke down in tears, confused and helpless. At the time, my empathy didn't extend far enough to understand that she inhabited two deeply conflicting worlds and was distraught at choosing between her driving need to appease her grandparents, whom she loved, and her desire for a better future. Her parents and grandmother were called for a meeting with us on multiple occasions and were firmly dissuaded from ruining Shilpa's life.

The normalization of sexual abuse and consanguineous marriages appalled me. On hearing about these incidents, I angrily rebuked the parents at our biannual meetings. "The children trust you to protect

them. How can you allow them to be harmed? We can't accept this."
My reprimand was usually met with tense silence and guilty looks.

I questioned whether I had the right to scold the parents, and
I wondered how they saw my role in their children's lives. Were
they silent because of the benefactor–beneficiary relationship, or
did they recognize that the staff and I were genuinely invested in
their children's welfare? I like to think it was the latter.

Everyday life at their homes ran counter to the culture cultivated at Shanti Bhavan. Most families didn't adhere to the virtues we
taught their sons and daughters. The children saw their parents lie,
and were even instructed to do so to meet their family's needs. As one
mother told her child, "Truth alone can't put food on the plate." Loyalty, gratitude, and honesty were seldom emphasized. "To be grateful
is the most graceful act," I explained to the children, asking the staff
to teach them to appreciate the kindness shown to them by others.

The "character backlash" from families who considered the values
taught at school as "impractical" for poor people hindered our ability
to mold the children. "Those two months at home undo what we
advise them in the ten months they are with us!" I exclaimed in exasperation. Their ability to succeed depended on how the staff and me
countered the adverse effects of their home lives. When the children
consistently observed our proper conduct, they emulated it and offset
what they witnessed at home.

Regardless of what they might have learned at home, I understood
they would first have to choose what they wanted for themselves
while navigating their two worlds. In the initial years of a child's
development, I emphasized "globally shared values"—honesty,
personal integrity, and transparency—which everyone could easily
understand. I brought them up as I thought best, which I recognized

may not have met everyone's approval. When a child got into trouble, their initial reaction was often to hide the truth for fear of punishment or loss of face. My approach to correction varied depending on the seriousness of the situation and the child's ability to self-reflect and feel remorse.

Nevertheless, I pointed out that their faults didn't define them, if they accepted responsibility and expressed remorse. "You are not a bad child. You made poor decisions, and I trust you will change." Hearing this, children usually changed their ways.

What mattered was that the child recognized what went wrong and tried not to repeat the same in the future. How they overcame their faults was integral to self-improvement. Through it all, I have realized that the best one can do for a child is to never give up on them.

While I didn't expect them to be perfect, I held them to a high standard and wanted them to improve. This demand was not only for their academic progress but also for their character formation and moral development. I gently corrected their minor mistakes, but serious bad behavior was dealt with strictly. They knew that I didn't hold resentment toward them for long and would forgive their mistake if they made attempts to improve.

• • •

The year 2010 saw the publication of my book *India Untouched: The Forgotten Face of Rural Poverty*, which chronicled my experiences as a philanthropist. Social work in India was "emotional quicksand," I explained. I had been pulled toward several issues equally deserving of thoughtful attention: a school for children from poor families, farming to empower women, health care for people with low incomes, opportunities for deserving but poor artists and artisans, elimination of lead poisoning, and improving press quality. These were not all preplanned but rather the outcome of a natural progression.

By 2006, Baldev Farms faced severe operational difficulties. Rainfall had become increasingly scarce, and additional water sources had to be tapped. We leased small parcels of land in the nearby village of Devarapalli to drill more wells. Five kilometers of pipelines were laid along the roadside to transport water—quite an engineering feat.

As for Shanti Bhavan, water conservation became imperative with scarce rainfall. Initially, we met our relatively small water requirement by pumping from shallow wells with generators. With groundwater levels falling and the campus population increasing, we drilled deeper ground wells. Today, these wells provide over 60,000 liters of water daily for residents, kitchens, ornamental gardens, vegetable farms, and fruit orchards.

To minimize freshwater usage, wastewater is channeled into a central tank and processed through three charcoal-and-sand chambers. The resulting partially clean water reaches a larger tank where a solar-powered pump aerates it to boost oxygen content and reduce bacterial levels. This processed water is then used for ornamental and fruit trees.

The Tillany project was challenging to pursue, though novel and exciting. A team of artists and artisans from Bangalore and elsewhere were approached to help design the arts village around the museum. Developing the concept proved especially tough because of differing ideas about how the arts village should look and function. Unable to reach a consensus, much to Ammachi's disappointment, I deferred the construction of the arts colony and the formal start of the Tillany project to a future time.

Among the projects, Project Lead-Free was an immense success. While environmental health issues were not part of our original mission, I didn't want to be an idle spectator, knowing that lead was causing immense harm when relatively simple solutions were within the state's available financial resources.

I found that, even as a layperson, I could attract the cooperation of renowned experts if they witnessed my commitment. It gratified me immensely that my efforts contributed to a healthier environment for hundreds of millions of people, especially children, in India and possibly other countries.

IIJNM steadily progressed by offering a superior program each year. Kanchan Kaur rose to the position of dean, and under her leadership, the institute attained new heights. We placed hundreds of graduates in the Indian media, trained in the core principles of journalism. Some educational journals hailed IIJNM as the best post-graduate college for journalism in India for its excellent program, international faculty, and student performance. Media organizations in India sought our graduates, who were uniformly commended as highly competent, objective reporters.

Our alumni made their mark in mainstream media and other outlets addressing social issues. For instance, a story about the LGBTQ+ community was published anonymously by one of our graduates in *INK* magazine, an online forum on changemakers. The article, which triggered a global discussion in liberal circles, talked about an infant abandoned by her parents after they learned that a transgender person had donated blood for her serious medical condition. This was only one of several investigative pieces our graduates authored in a marked departure from conventional news stories in the Indian media.

His Holiness Swamiji passed away in the twelfth year of IIJNM's operation. His death was a personal loss, as I had grown quite fond of him and he of me. Perhaps Swamiji liked me because, unlike those with whom he most frequently interacted, I dared to counter his assertions if I disagreed. I felt comfortable sharing my views openly with him and didn't engage in pointless or disrespectful arguments.

Among my memories of our time together, the most prominent one is his arrival by helicopter on Shanti Bhavan grounds, much to the children's delight. He spent the day with us and visited our banana farm, where he planted a sapling and then headed to the local villages. He called on the village leaders who had come to receive his blessings. At a village gathering, he said in a firm tone, "I will protect George if anyone tries to harm him. Remember, Shanti Bhavan is not simply where your children live and study. It is where the gods live."

Over my initial twelve years in India, I encountered successes and failures in equal measure. Each project had unique challenges that called for leadership, problem-solving skills, and winning over different groups of people and organizations—children and their parents, staff in various projects, villagers, farmworkers, worldwide volunteers, and government officials. As a team, the foundation made substantive progress with creativity, initiative, and flexibility.

The demand on my time, leadership, and resources was significant, but the novelty of our activities excited me, and the improved lives drove my actions. I trusted that, with grit and grace, much could be accomplished over time. I was happy and woke up each day with purpose and pursuit.

PART IV

CHAPTER 21

THE STEEP FALL

IT WAS 2006, AND ACHACHAN was ninety-six years old and steeply declining in health. Ammachi, approaching her late eighties, could no longer look after him by herself, so for the first time, I decided to skip my biannual visit to India.

I entrusted Jude with the responsibility of operating Baldev Farms. Until then, I had controlled the foundation's finances, personally authorized all payments, and limited the transfer of money from the US to correspond to the operating and capital needs of projects. But in my prolonged absence, handing over the check-signing authority to Jude to operate Baldev Farms's bank accounts became necessary. I was confident he could manage it in good faith.

I drove from Penny Lane to my parents' condominium every morning to spend time with them until late evening. I would sit beside Achachan on the sofa, talk for hours, and share stories of my adventures in India until he drifted off to sleep. I would then make regular telephone calls to India to monitor ongoing projects.

One day, concerned about my finances, Achachan asked me,

"Aniyan, do you make enough profit from the bananas to run Shanti Bhavan?"

In my usual silly way, I replied, "No, we don't. I eat up all the bananas, Achachan."

My father probably didn't find that funny, but Ammachi, who was listening in, burst into laughter.

Achachan grew increasingly frail and dependent on others. His appetite decreased, and coaxing him to eat took some effort. Constantly short of breath, he frequently got up from his chair and walked. I would hold his arm to help him up and then support him as he hobbled around with his walker. This activity seemed to ease his breathing a little during the day; at night, he slept with an oxygen mask.

As the days passed, Achachan's complaints of drowsiness and fatigue grew more worrisome. He would sometimes say, "I am just a burden to others. Why should I live any longer?"

Ammachi chided him sternly when he repeated this. "All these years, you promised to always be there for me; now you want to go away."

To this, Achachan instantly replied, "No! No! I don't mean to go now. I want to die only after you. I will take good care of you."

Ammachi struggled to hold back her tears at his sweetness.

My two sons adored their grandparents, and they returned the sentiment. Achachan called Ajit *nalla paiyan*, a "fine young man," and referred to Vivek as *ponnumon*, meaning "golden boy" in Malayalam. When Vivek decided to spend a year volunteering at Shanti Bhavan and Baldev Farms, we feared Achachan wouldn't be around when he returned.

On the day of his departure, Vivek struggled to bid farewell to his grandfather, teary-eyed and fighting conflicting emotions. With my help, Achachan rose from his recliner and slowly approached his grandson.

Vivek, choked with emotions, asked, "Achachan, do you have any words of wisdom for me?"

"Oh, no! I have no advice for you," my father replied gently, gripping his walker. "I want you to be safe. That is all I want."

But Vivek wasn't satisfied and insisted that his grandfather impart some words he could hold onto. He persisted, and Achachan finally replied, "What can an old man like me tell you?" He paused momentarily and added, "Work hard and be good."

"Is that all?" Vivek inquired. "Yes, Monu," Achachan replied.

Not long afterward, I asked Achachan for his advice. "When you look back, what do you think is the most important thing in life?"

This time, he responded immediately. "When you reach my age or anywhere close to it, you should be able to say with a clear conscience that you harmed no one."

One morning, I noticed my father wasn't eating breakfast. He insisted he wasn't hungry, so I helped him from his chair at the dining table and returned him to his recliner. Hiding my distress, I lovingly chided him, "Achachan, you never listen to me. Won't you please eat something?"

He replied, "Monu, I always listen to you. When have I not?"

A minute later, he relented. "Okay, then. Bring me something to eat."

Relieved, I ran to the kitchen and returned with a slice of bread spread with butter and jam. He broke off a small piece, put it in his mouth, and, with some struggle, swallowed it.

Late that night, he started throwing up blood. We didn't know what to do—fear overtook all of us. Bijoy frantically called for an ambulance, and we rushed him to the hospital. My siblings and I waited anxiously outside the emergency room. I was overwhelmed by so many memories of my father.

Shortly, the doctor informed us that Achachan had succumbed to internal bleeding. I was expecting this news, but it was not something I wanted to hear, and deep sadness washed over me. I wondered how the family would go on without him.

I returned to the apartment and clasped my mother's hand. My voice shaking, I whispered, "He is gone."

Ammachi burst out in uncontrollable sobs, saying repeatedly, "Oh no! Oh no! He was so good to me."

It was the first time I ever saw her weep openly.

Both my parents had expressed their wish to be cremated and to have their ashes buried on Shanti Bhavan's ground, a place they had embraced as their haven of peace. My three siblings and I had assured them we would respect their decision.

At my father's burial ceremony, I was surrounded by Shanti Bhavan children and staff. Grief-stricken, Vivek cried while recounting some favorite memories of his grandfather. I couldn't hold my tears back, and struggled to get through the eulogy. Everyone stood in silence for two minutes at the end of the ceremony. The school choir sweetly sang a rendition of "I Believe in Angels."

In the following years, the family took comfort in sharing stories about Achachan's absent-minded ways. Ammachi laughed along with us, but suddenly, her cheeks would tighten, and her eyes would turn moist. But then, she would compose herself in no time. Having silently endured the trauma of her mother's terrible condition, I could tell she had learned to hide her sadness, never to burden her loved ones.

We all knew that Achachan had been Ammachi's emotional anchor for over seventy years of their marriage. He had counseled and stood by her in every major decision she'd made, and she'd thrived because he understood her. She couldn't have accomplished all she had without his support and stability. Losing the man whose love and devotion she had relied upon was unbearable.

I fondly recall the earlier years when Ammachi went shopping alone. Achachan would look out the window and impatiently wait for her. If she didn't return within what he thought was a reasonable time, he would anxiously call out, "Aniyan, what is taking her so long?"

On his daily walks, he would pluck a flower or two from our garden or someone else's and give it to Ammachi without saying a word. Neighbors complained that Achachan had repeatedly helped himself to their flowers—a ritual he practiced throughout their long marriage.

As he lay on the recliner in his last days, I remember how his eyes followed Ammachi. Every time she went upstairs out of his sight, he panicked. "Where did she go? What is she doing?" I tried to reassure him she had just gone to fetch something, but he wouldn't accept my explanation. Once, I refused to let him go upstairs to look for her. "No, Achachan. You might fall and hurt yourself," I said in a loving but firm voice.

He broke into an angry outburst in Malayalam. "You are a bad son. I curse you!"

I was stunned into silence.

Fortunately, Ammachi came downstairs just then, and Achachan calmed down. He turned to me and apologized. "Monu, I didn't mean what I said. My curse has no value. How can I curse you?"

I laughed it off, knowing he would never wish ill upon anyone, especially his son. His devotion to my mother and his love for his family were uncompromising lessons I carry to this day.

For my father, his family was his world—my mother was his life, followed by his children, especially his two daughters and grandchildren. He was too shy to express affection for anyone outside the family. Looking back, I realize the profound impact Achachan had on our family through his caring, honesty, and simplicity. I never heard him speak vindictively about anyone; he had upheld and lived his last words of wisdom. He was gentle and loving toward everyone in the family and gracious toward others.

Despite his concerns about my finances, I knew he was supportive and proud of my philanthropic endeavors, and that was what I needed. The troubles I would experience shortly after his passing would have worried and disappointed him immensely. I was relieved he didn't live to see his son's steep fall.

• • •

In the aftermath of 2005's Hurricane Katrina, property values of beachfront houses and condominiums dipped sharply. Soon after, the entire real estate market in the US plunged during the subprime mortgage crisis, dragging me down with it.

Until then, the stock market had been doing well, and my investments appeared safe. However, when stock prices began to decline the next year, I didn't want to sell them, hoping that there would be a turnaround soon in the market. Instead, I put up for sale my four real estate properties on the Gulf Coast of Florida and by the Hudson River in New Jersey.

The subprime mortgage market entered a steep downward spiral, with increasing homeowner defaults caused by predatory lending practices and loans to less-than-creditworthy individuals. The sharp drop in property values adversely impacted mortgage-backed securities, affecting large US banks and other financial institutions.

By the second half of 2008, a rapid stock market fall matched the steep decline in house prices. I had waited too long, hoping stock prices would turn steady, but losses mounted quickly. With a 50 percent drop in technology stocks, I liquidated them at a considerable loss, as I hadn't yet sold any of my real estate properties. I frantically borrowed from relatives, close friends, and a board member of the foundation to meet expenses in India. My guarantee of repayment, fortunately, was enough assurance for them.

The front pages of newspapers carried stories of multimillionaires and billionaires falling victim to market declines. Economists were comparing this financial turmoil to the Great Depression. I was compelled to delay my biannual trip to India, again, to address my rapidly declining financial situation.

To add to my horror, I found out that Jack Barnard, who had been involved in my family's real estate transactions for the past twenty years, was deceiving me. He had been the family's trusted broker for our real estate properties, and was a part of our family events, spending Thanksgiving and Christmas with us. Over time, he had become more of a family member than a business acquaintance.

Jack had been working on a condominium development in Marco Island, Florida, for a while and had invited me to be an early investor. Not familiar with such ventures, I had turned him down, but he later persuaded me to purchase two apartments and a piece of land by the ocean as investment properties.

A few years into his condominium project, Jack said the developer had removed him from the venture and swindled him out of his investment. After that, he began asking me for money while he sued the developer, promising to pay me back once the case was settled. Our close family friendship prompted my help. Over the years, I loaned him substantial sums at his request, especially for his family's well-being and to cover the cost of the lawsuit.

He kept delaying repayment on the pretext that his lawsuit hadn't concluded, and continued borrowing from me. By 2008, he owed me nearly two million dollars. My secure financial status until then led me to neglect his failure to repay, confident that he wouldn't renege on his word. But now, with my finances tight, I insisted Jack meet his obligations.

"Show me the tax statements of your business," I demanded, struggling to control my anger when he gave me excuses for not repaying. This time, I wouldn't let him go without proof.

Finally, Jack confessed, with a guilt-stricken face, "Sorry, Abraham. I lied to you. I had no choice. I'm sorry." Everything had been a lie—the real estate deals, the court cases, and the promises of repayment. His revelation stunned me.

Seething anger turned to horror. "Jack, why did you cheat the one helping you and your family?" I asked, feeling betrayed.

Unable to answer, he looked away.

I walked him out of the house and shut the door behind him.

My heart pounded. After much contemplation, I saw no way to recover any money from him, even with litigation. I resigned myself to the fact that a trusted friend had defrauded me.

I was knee-deep in trouble on several fronts. I couldn't wait for property sales to meet my cash needs. Frantically, I called Ajit. "Please come home immediately."

"What's wrong, Dad?" he asked anxiously.

"Just please come over quickly," I repeated.

Within an hour, Ajit was at Penny Lane, and I divulged the painful details, of both my investments and Jack's deceit. "Our investments are worthless with financial markets and real estate prices this low."

"I can't believe this, Dad," Ajit said, his face filled with horror.

He had no clue what I had been facing. All along, I didn't want to worry my family about our finances. I was accustomed to making all financial decisions in my professional and charitable endeavors, and I thought I could come out of this crisis, too. And up until then, I had been successful.

"We must inform the whole family," he advised.

I wanted Mariam to hear from me firsthand what had happened, so I asked her to come home early from work.

Mariam burst out crying. "What are we going to do? What's going to happen to us?"

Holding her by the arm, I settled her into a chair and handed her a glass of water. What had I done to her? Fighting my anxiety, I assured her, "Mariam, we will get through this somehow. Just give me some time."

I had brought this situation upon myself for a variety of reasons. For one, I was overconfident about handling any difficulty I might face. I should have been more careful about my investments and taken steps early enough to avoid steep losses. My inherent optimistic nature prevented me from considering all possibilities, especially the extreme scenarios that could destroy me.

We made phone calls asking my siblings to gather at Ammachi's condo that evening. Facing my family would be one of my most embarrassing and painful moments.

"I would have cautioned you about Jack long ago. Why didn't you trust me?" Ammachi asked outright, hurt and disappointment in her eyes. I tried to respond, but she cut me off. "We have always planned everything together. How could you leave me out of this?"

"Why did you have to give him such huge amounts?" Mariam asked angrily, aware I had been lending money to Jack for years. She had questioned him herself on occasions, without being able to tell whether he was lying. I had no explanation to give Ammachi or Mariam except that I had been gullible.

Aware of the mortgage crisis and the world's financial turmoil at the time, everyone could understand how I had lost so much money in real estate and the stock market. But there was no denying that I should have sold my properties much earlier. Not expecting the shocking decline in real estate prices, I risked waiting for the stock market to bounce back.

My siblings and their spouses questioned me to understand the depth of my financial quagmire and what was at stake. Bijoy inquired, "How much is your loss in the stock market?"

Roughly assessing it, I replied, "Most of my stocks are less than half their value now. Some are leveraged."

Everyone knew that liquidating my stock holdings might be necessary, but it wouldn't generate the needed cash. Lekha joined in, her face drawn with deep worry. "Will you be able to run Shanti Bhavan, Kochetta?"

"I don't know," I replied, my thoughts scattered.

"What are you going to tell the children? How will you face their parents, Aniyan?" Mariam asked. "You have made so many promises about their future."

Her words cut through me. The horrifying thought of letting the children and their families down made me sick to my stomach. "I will handle this when I return to India. I will have to go back soon, Mariam." From their expressions, I could see no one was satisfied with my answers.

They hadn't expected me to be in this situation—it was so unlike me. I wasn't sure whether they thought I was arrogant, careless, or foolish. No one commented about it, either.

"How will you repay the loans you guaranteed, Kochetta?" Vinita asked.

"I will talk to each of the lenders and buy some more time. Profits from the sale of stocks and properties will cover them."

"You'll have to get their consent quickly," Bijoy urged.

I agreed. I urgently needed a coherent plan, but there was no certainty that I could sell the properties at current prices. Even if I could, there wouldn't be enough savings to run the projects by myself much longer. As painful as it was, the family gradually acknowledged the gravity of the situation, and we met weekly to discuss the ensuing troubles. Ajit was present at the gatherings, but Vivek was still in India, overseeing Baldev Farms, and had little knowledge of his father's problems.

"In the future, we need to seek donor contributions. You take the lead," I told Ajit. I could tell he was nervous about it. He had no experience in fundraising, but he immediately took charge of it.

• • •

Days blurred into months of chaos and crippling uncertainty. The fall was too sudden and devastating, overwhelming me with helplessness. I couldn't think of a way out, and there were moments when it felt like the end of the road. Anxiety attacks persisted throughout my days and even in my sleep, gripping me with a constant feeling of impending doom. The recognition that I had sacrificed my family's security in pursuit of my personal mission troubled me deeply.

To add to my anguish, in August 2008, my dear friend and mentor Professor Hawkins unexpectedly died. His impressive legacy was apparent in his distinguished professional career and lasting accomplishments in public life through the guidance he offered. He was among the first to encourage me to follow my dream of creating Shanti Bhavan. He had been concerned about the opposition I faced from those in power but happy to learn about all the projects I had undertaken. I lost one of my best supporters, but I was relieved he didn't know about my situation, as that would have disappointed and worried him.

The news that I was in deep financial trouble spread quickly. Acquaintances phoned to inquire about what had happened; some questioned if Shanti Bhavan would close, while several others assumed it had already. Some believed I had been overconfident or arrogant in undertaking too many projects without seeking external support.

Shortly afterward, Mariam and I attended a function hosted by the Kerala Association in New York. In the past, people had approached me to discuss my activities or to seek advice. This time, no one did. Hesitant to walk around and greet others, I stood alone in a corner. My good friend Joy Nampiaparampil came over to keep me company.

When we returned home that evening, Mariam teared up as she relayed that one of her friends had asked her, "How could Abraham do this to you? Anybody else would have reserved a portion of their wealth for their children as an inheritance before dishing it out to strangers." Another advised her to persuade me to abandon the projects in India and return to the US for good.

They had a point, but my reason for not setting aside money for my sons in their names was a combination of two things. First, I had been confident that if my children were financially pressed, I could easily provide for them. After all, we had considerable physical assets they would eventually inherit. It had never occurred to me that the markets—both real estate and financial—could collapse simultaneously, leaving me with few resources.

Second, I had already given my sons the ability to earn and support themselves through an excellent education and proper upbringing. I expected them to work hard and make it on their own. I knew we would help them if they needed it.

With Mariam's good position as a vice president in a major insurance company, we could manage our lives in America. Still, I could no longer solely finance Shanti Bhavan and the multiple projects in India, which were operating at a cost of well over $1.5 million annually. But I didn't entertain the thought of shutting Shanti Bhavan down—walking away from the children was not something I could even imagine when their well-being, aspirations, and futures were tied to me.

Selling off everything I owned in India and living a quiet life in America wasn't an option I would consider. I had to find the money to keep Shanti Bhavan running. The first priority was to repay my recent loans and scale back all projects. It didn't take much time to jointly decide with Mariam to sell practically all our assets in America—both stocks and real estate—to generate money to pay off debts and finance Shanti Bhavan until we could find willing donors for the school.

With heavy hearts, we sold Penny Lane, our beautiful home for over twenty years. I didn't think much about the delicate furniture, antiques, original paintings, and beautiful statues we had collected over the years that had filled the house's three floors. They were either put up for sale, given away to my siblings, or kept in storage. As we packed our favorite items in large cartons into the early morning hours, Mariam kept breaking into uncontrollable sobs. It was devastating to lose a home that carried precious family memories.

I tried hard to not break down in front of her. Wanting to be strong for us, I said, "I promise we will get back to a good life, Mariam." But my words fell short. I sensed she no longer had the same confidence in my ability to set things right. Neither Mariam nor I knew what the future held. I agonized over what I had allowed to happen.

The beautiful condo where Ammachi had been living was put up for sale. She moved in with Mariam and me into a house owned by Vinita and her husband, Sabu. Ajit gave up his apartment and came to stay with us too. I was glad that at least one of our two sons would be with us to discuss every step.

As if things weren't grave enough already, Denny, Jude's sister who had been working at our head office in Bangalore, called one morning to inform me that Jude had made a series of mistakes and had incurred enormous debts. She said, "Dr. George, he claims he borrowed money to finance the losses Baldev Farms has accumulated during your absence."

"What! How could he do that, Denny?"

I frantically called my key staff, but they could only tell me that Jude had been dealing with a group of investors in land development. No one could definitively answer my questions, and there was no point in trying to investigate over the phone. I decided to leave for India immediately to assess the situation, even though there was still considerable unfinished business at home. I felt miserable leaving Mariam and Ajit to handle the ongoing pressing issues, but they bravely took up the unfamiliar tasks.

As always, I spent time with Ammachi on the day of my departure. She had recently suffered a heart attack, and her mental state was drastically affected, leaving her disoriented most of the time. My siblings and I took turns keeping her company and attending to her while Ajit managed her daily medications and routine.

I sat by Ammachi's side and held her hand. We discussed family matters and my plans for the three months I expected to be in India. Both Ammachi and I feared we might not see each other again. I couldn't fathom how I would go on without her. Throughout my life, she had been my staunchest supporter, someone I could lean on in every situation. Fighting a thousand conflicting emotions, I told her, "Ammachi, I don't think I can leave you like this," ready to reverse my travel plans.

"Monu, go. It is more important that you go. I can take care of myself."

She had always been decisive, and I knew she wouldn't allow herself to be the reason for my not doing what she thought was essential, especially now when the school needed stability. When the time came for me to leave, I kissed her and held her for a moment. I feared what might happen in my absence, and the thought of not being there for her when she needed me most was heartbreaking.

Struggling with her walking stick, she followed me to the front door and watched me enter the car.

"Bye, Ammachi," I called out. I badly wanted to look at her one more time.

She gave a gentle smile but didn't wave. Fighting back tears, she remained composed. She surely wanted to give me the strength I badly needed. I wondered what thoughts were running through her mind at that moment. I was filled with terrible sadness at the emotional pain I had caused her. Despite her rapidly deteriorating physical condition, my mother had sacrificed her need to have me beside her. Her quiet courage deeply touched me, and I prayed I might possess her selflessness and strength.

I was faced with crises in not one but two continents, both converging simultaneously. If there had been one problem, I could possibly have come through, but that was not the case. The realization that everything around me was spiraling out of control frightened me to the core. I was crushed by the unexpected, violent forces that left me gasping for breath beneath the rubble. There was nowhere to turn, no escape, and the anguish was unbearable. I had always been the family's problem-solver; now, I had become the problem.

CHAPTER 22

CONFRONTING THE UNFORESEEN

The flight from New York to Bangalore seemed endless as I feared what awaited me in India. Unrelenting anxiety attacks made it hard to sit still; at times, I wanted to jump out of the plane.

Immediately upon arrival, I called Jude and Denny to my apartment in the city. Seated at the dining table, I confronted Jude right away. "What do you owe?" I asked sternly.

Gazing down and appearing embarrassed, he remained silent. I demanded an answer. In a nervous tone, Jude gave me a figure in rupees equivalent to nearly three million dollars.

"Do you have any record of these transactions? You must have repaid a considerable amount from banana sales, right?" I leaned forward, hoping for anything positive.

"Yes, Dr. George, but the borrowed amount has tripled. The interest rates . . ." Jude struggled to complete his sentence.

"No. I can't believe what I am hearing. This can't be happening," I said, looking at the ceiling.

"I took loans only to cover the losses incurred by Baldev Farms. The interest charges were exorbitant, but I was confident that I could repay the loans with improved banana sales," Jude explained.

I looked away and ran my fingers through my hair. The situation was worse than I had expected, and it took all my strength to control my anger. I couldn't risk Jude shutting down and not revealing what had transpired. Taking a deep breath, I willed myself to keep calm and focus on what had to be done.

The foundation might not be legally responsible, but we couldn't ignore the situation. Overcome with conflicting emotions, I told Jude, "I have to let you go. I can't have you working for us any longer." He didn't protest or deny his share of the blame.

"You must help me resolve this terrible mess you have gotten us into," I pleaded.

"I will sort this out somehow," he promised.

I saw no option but to shut down the entire farm and cut our losses. I met with Vivek immediately. "I'm sorry, Monu. We must uproot the farm, including your vineyard. We are losing money. The vineyard won't be productive for at least three more years, and we can't hold out that long."

Vivek was appalled. "This wouldn't have happened if you had been more careful with your investments, Dad. Now you're making another mistake!"

My decision was firm. "Tomorrow, I am closing the farm. It ends now."

"Dad, you can't do that. The vineyard will take time to be profitable." He had diligently overseen the vineyard's operations for nearly a year, but the losses were cutting into the school's financial needs, and I had to be decisive. I felt guilty for letting my son down, but I felt I had no choice, as saving Shanti Bhavan was my priority.

Before night fell, I left for the school campus. There was only one way to handle the situation: being transparent with the children and staff. Lalita and Beena were anxiously awaiting my arrival to know about the prospects for Shanti Bhavan. The questioning gazes of the children and staff that evening told me that word of my financial troubles had already spread.

I gathered the staff separately and spoke to them about our predicament. "I can't fully finance the operation of Shanti Bhavan without external support. Until we find sufficient funding, all of you must take salary cuts." No one argued or showed anger. Denny, Beena, and some others graciously expressed their willingness to forgo 20 percent of their yearly salaries. I didn't blame those who wished to leave.

A week later, I summoned the children and their parents to inform them of the school's precarious status. I dreaded this encounter, but it had to be done. As usual, the gathering rose respectfully as I entered the assembly hall. Their polite gesture had always made me uncomfortable, but this time, it gave me a pang of guilt. Mustering courage, I announced, "Shanti Bhavan may have to close. I lost most of my money in what I was doing in America."

Shocked gasps broke the deafening silence. The troubled faces of the boys and girls were haunting. Questions followed.

"What will happen to my daughter's future? We were hoping she would one day save us from our suffering."

"My son will have to work for the landlord."

"We have three other children. How can we look after another with the little we earn?"

Worried parents found their children's fates in peril. Families who couldn't afford school would most definitely put their boys to work, and girls might be married off early. Denny and Beena did their best to console and control the worried crowd, explaining we were doing everything possible to set things right.

I tried to calm the parents, but not having figured out how things would turn out, I couldn't quell their fears. All I could tell them was that I was trying to find the resources to run the school. However, I alluded to the possibility that if I failed, their children would have to return.

"Could we pass a basket around to collect money, sir?" an anxious father asked, and an eager chorus joined in support. It warmed my heart to see that those with so little were willing to give what they could to keep the school open.

"It's considerate of you," I said appreciatively. "Instead of giving money to the school, why don't you consider buying your child some clothes, a pair of sneakers, or toiletries? That would be helpful." I wanted them to be a part of the solution, no matter how small.

In the past, eager mothers and fathers would flock around me before leaving to express their gratitude for looking after their children, but this time, they trickled out of the auditorium in a disconcerted gloom. It astonished me when one mother came over to say, "We will pray for you, sir." I fought back tears.

There was some relief in having spoken to the parents and having told them the truth. But it didn't negate the pain and terror I had caused them. All these years, I had raised their hopes by promising them their lives would improve through their children's professional success. Parents were earning very little as quarry laborers, sex workers, ragpickers, and doing other menial jobs, and they had pinned their hopes on their children.

I couldn't demand their understanding of the present situation after having raised their hopes earlier. I couldn't give them any assurance, as I didn't know my next steps. My choices were limited, and the agony of defeat was insufferable. How could I drive the children back to a world of poverty and oppression? How could I even expect their forgiveness?

That night, alone in my room, I cried out, "You are a cruel god. Why do the children have to pay the price for my mistakes?"

• • •

Sadness overwhelmed me as Vivek returned to the US with his own grief and a sense of personal failure despite his commitment to the success of the vineyard. I learned from the farm staff that he had taken great pains to oversee the vineyard, researching and visiting other farms to learn how to grow good grapes. Each time it rained heavily at night, he would go out alone to inspect the farm, flashlight in hand. With his youthful optimism, he had been determined to make the project successful.

Mariam informed me six months later that Vivek had taken out a student loan and enrolled in the MBA program at NYU's Stern School of Business. He kept his distance from me for over a year, seldom speaking to me. Though heartbroken, I understood his hurt and couldn't blame him. Until that point, my sons had trusted my decisions and thought of me as one who couldn't make mistakes, but that image had shattered. I had fallen short as a son, a husband, and a father. Dejected, I constantly mulled over what had happened to put the pieces together in my mind. I reviewed the sequence of events and how things had reached their present turbulent state.

Starting in 2003, the banana crop output was high; a bunch

yielded a relatively large quantity of about forty kilos. As Jude expected, it had turned out to be a profitable business. But over time, an acute shortage of rainfall in the area depleted the groundwater. The fifteen bore wells we depended on for water mostly dried up. Baldev Farms demanded over a million liters daily, and even after tapping additional water sources by deepening the present wells, there wasn't enough. As the water supply dwindled, the fruit size diminished until a bunch produced fewer than twenty kilos. Worse yet, bananas no longer fetched a decent price in the market.

Jude was embarrassed because growing bananas had been his idea in the first place, and he didn't want to admit defeat. He converted fifty acres of the banana plantation into a grape vineyard, as it required lower water consumption. An eternal optimist, he had hoped this move would improve the situation, but the new venture only raised expenses.

Panicked, Jude borrowed from local land developers to cover the deficit. Given his standing in the organization, he had no difficulty getting funds in his name, especially by guaranteeing that the foundation would repay if he couldn't. It never occurred to me that he would operate outside the dictates of the board. My lack of involvement in the operation of Baldev Farms during the two years I was in America and venturing into a large-scale farming project without sufficiently assessing obstacles had been colossal mistakes. There was nothing I could do about the past, and I resolved to find a way out of my predicament.

Expenses ran high, with salaries for workers, substantial fertilizer and electricity usage, and capital costs for machinery, pumps, and miles of drip lines that had to be periodically replaced. Despite using revenues from banana sales to make periodic loan repayments, including some interest charges, loan liability more than tripled from high interest rates during the two years of my absence. Debt and accrued interest accumulated to a point where Baldev Farms's financial status became untenable.

Having taken loans from illegal private lenders, Jude couldn't obtain any receipts or acknowledgments for repayments and had no official record of the transactions. Consequently, we had to look for other evidence to discover all transactions with lenders. We had to follow every lead to determine precisely how much Jude had borrowed, when, how much had been repaid thus far, and the interest charges. I considered repaying the principal, but Jude having already paid considerable interest charges, I would not make any further interest payments.

Hoping that wealthy businesspeople in Bangalore might partner with us to run Shanti Bhavan as a charitable venture, I invited some to visit us. If our mission wouldn't be compromised, I was prepared to even rename the school in their honor and offer naming rights to classrooms and other facilities to smaller investors. Two wealthy investors from Bangalore visited, and I assumed they would be interested in teaming up with me to save Shanti Bhavan. I didn't initially realize that they hoped to convert the expanse of land into a commercial venture, such as a luxury resort. I naively believed they would value the humane nature of our work and would want to ensure its continuity.

How could I convince these well-off individuals in India to help raise the status of the underclass? Could I expect them to appreciate that the happiness derived from improving lives and communities would be a much greater reward than any commercial monetary gain?

During a similar visit, a staff member overheard a businessman remark that Shanti Bhavan was a sinking ship. Following that, I decided not to discuss our financial troubles with potential partners, as no one would want to be involved in a failing endeavor. The parade of potential partners, the endless speculation, and the school's uncertain future had already unsettled the children. Our older boys and girls in high school frequently asked me if I would sell Shanti Bhavan. "I don't want to, children. I promise I will keep you updated," I assured them to ease their anxiety.

But I could tell from their worried looks that they feared investors might not be interested in their futures. Clearly, I should not have single-handedly taken on the sole responsibility for the lives of so many children and staff. Right from the start, I should have sought donor funds to build and operate the school and the other projects. My excessive self-confidence in my ability to go alone might have been the unfortunate result of my past successes.

Short of teachers, I pitched in to hold accounting and economics classes for the higher grades and guided them on their class projects. Not being sufficiently familiar with the Indian system of teaching, I would frequently drift into the bigger picture of the topics covered, often ignoring the details required to perform well in the public examination.

I had hidden my birthday from the children, but Vivek revealed it by mistake when he was volunteering at Baldev, much to my annoyance. The children secretly planned a grand celebration, as they wanted to express their affection for me and enjoy the birthday cake and a special dinner. Their exuberant displays of fondness were embarrassing but touching. There was no way I could leave them helpless when they had so much love for me.

• • •

Compounding my troubles, the villagers saw me as weak and alone. When we fired some laborers for stealing farming supplies, landlords used this as an excuse to stir up trouble. They incited our on-site cleaning staff, who hailed from their villages, to demand a raise. When I refused, the cleaning staff locked up the children's dorms and the main gate to the campus.

"Tell them they can't treat this place like a factory. They must open the dorms immediately," I commanded in a firm tone. Denny and Frank conveyed my disappointment. Fully prepared to act decisively if they didn't comply, I told my senior managers, "They have just one day to decide whether they want to return." Not waiting for a response, I picked up a broom and started sweeping a pathway, plucking weeds, and joining the children in doing their laundry. I hid my anxiety and asserted myself as a leader who wasn't frazzled by this troubling situation; any sign of weakness on my part could be exploited.

When the cleaning staff observed the children joyfully completing their daily chores, such as tending the gardens, washing dishes in the kitchen, and sweeping floors, they realized they were not indispensable and stood to lose their jobs. To add to their defeat, they were taken aback to see me join in the work. They returned to work that evening after failing to get me to negotiate a salary increase.

When I next encountered them, I asked, "Why did you do this? I am only trying to help you and the children." It was met with silence and embarrassed looks. I sensed that my troubles with them were far from over. I couldn't understand how the cleaning staff could try to shut down the school that was looking after children from poor families like theirs. Their outrageous behavior in joining their landlords to create trouble at Shanti Bhavan hurt me emotionally. Considering how good I thought I had been to them, there was no explanation for their offensive behavior.

But upon reflection, I could see why they were "ungrateful." They probably hadn't experienced meaningful loyalty from others to know what it meant. They might have considered the banana farm as a business venture to profit only me, though it was solely to employ and benefit them at considerable cost to the foundation. But I couldn't expect them to understand that when I hadn't yet earned their trust. I calmed myself by accepting that their crushing dependence on powerful landlords and moneylenders might have compelled them to act this way at their urging.

Not too long after, Shanti Jayanthashree, or Shanti J as we called her, the head of our facilities department, sternly reproached a woman on the cleaning staff for tardiness. Shanti J was not popular with the workers she supervised, so this stern, or at least ill-timed, rebuke riled up the male supervisors and female laborers who couldn't stand taking orders from an assertive woman in a senior managerial position. Even Lalita had been a source of antagonism for some of our laborers, staff, and villagers. The female cleaning staff got together with some of our male managers and dragged Shanti J out of her office, barricaded the door, and wouldn't let her back in. Reasoning with them failed. Shaken, she left for her daughter's place in Bangalore.

The workers' unacceptable behavior infuriated me, but I saw that Shanti J didn't have the support of her staff, and I had to let her leave. However, my loyalty to her wouldn't allow her defeat. I told our team, "She's been a hard worker and is committed to Shanti Bhavan. I have an alternative arrangement for her; she will head up our fundraising activities in Bangalore." This newly created position was better suited to her temperament and skill set and invaluable to the foundation, but my support of her angered the male managers and workers in the facilities department.

Late one night, I awoke suddenly to a loud bang. My head throbbed. Someone had hurled something hard through the window, which bounced off the headboard and hit my head. My military instincts took over as I threw myself onto the floor and crawled behind the dresser. I reached for the switch, turned on the light, and lay still on high alert in case the attacker struck again. A piece of rock, half the size of a brick, lay on the floor.

My mind raced with questions. Who could have done this? Should I call Denny in the middle of the night and ask for protection? Whom do I trust? Deciding not to alarm anyone, I remained on the floor for the next few hours until early morning, pressing a towel against my head to stanch the bleeding. I knew I wasn't hurt badly but feared that I might have many enemies who wanted to hurt me.

At dawn, I called a manager to come to my room with the school nurse, who cleaned and bandaged the wound. The bleeding had been heavy initially, but I didn't think it was severe enough to rush to a hospital. Moreover, I didn't want to display any weakness by being seen leaving the campus. I did my usual campus routine all day, wearing a cap to conceal the bandage. Hearing about the rock attack, the children were concerned for my safety, and some of the older boys volunteered to stay awake and guard my residence at night. It was an offer I couldn't accept, but the warmth of their affection was a comfort.

I didn't tell my family about the attack for a long time. Ammachi and Mariam would have insisted that I keep guards around me at all times or that I wind down the projects, hand them over to someone else, and return home for good. These were not choices I was willing to consider, as I had already made up my mind to remain with the children. However, I understood the need for personal protection. It pained me tremendously that I could no longer freely go about the campus and that the very people I was committed to could turn against me.

Only one or two trusted senior staff members, like Denny and Beena, knew where I was at any time or when I planned to travel. Whenever I left campus in my car, I had a security guard ride ahead on his motorbike to check the country road for any suspicious activity. There was always a chance that a landlord with a grudge against me could arrange for gangs to block my vehicle and set it ablaze. I wouldn't take unnecessary risks just to prove my courage.

Until that incident, I hadn't thought much about the implications of my social work or foreseen any danger to myself. I had misgauged the power dynamics dictating justice, law, and order in rural India. Those who held authority in the village dictated whatever they wished and punished those who didn't comply; even in the midst of poverty, power and cruelty seemed to go together. Moreover, I should also have known that poor people's loyalty toward outsiders like me was short-lived, as they were concerned mostly about the present and not the past or the future. They worked at our farm and the school to meet their immediate necessities, while the domination by landlords was inescapable and permanent. The choice between us and landlords was clear to them.

CHAPTER 23

TURNING THE CORNER

IN THE SUMMER OF 2010, to my shock and disappointment, Lalita resigned as principal of Shanti Bhavan, causing more instability. A part of me felt she had lost respect for me after my financial loss and left a pioneering project I thought was a shared dream for everyone involved. Feeling let down, I tried hard not to turn pessimistic about human behavior. Her absence left a vacuum that had to be filled quickly.

I was faced with several challenges: Raise staff morale and run an effective organization, pay off all debt incurred by Jude, cut costs where possible, generate immediate funds to meet current operating needs, and create revenue sources for longer-term operations. Given the urgent need for on-site leadership, I took up the role of school principal, overseeing both academic and residential responsibilities, which required my daily involvement. Even though I was unfamiliar with running a boarding school, I was confident that I could learn quickly. At first, the children seemed intimidated by my presence in their daily activities, and I could sense their nervousness.

We were confronted with another major decision concerning our first batch of children soon graduating from high school. They were anxiously awaiting our decision on whether we would support their college education. After bringing them up through elementary, middle, and high school for fourteen years, I felt obligated to offer them a college education and see them through to their first careers. In the past, my financial strength provided me sufficient courage to pursue any venture, but now I worried about overextending myself again. I had to tread carefully and plan for outcomes that could seriously affect the school's financial stability.

The senior managers agreed that a college education for our graduates was highly desirable but pointed out that funding it by ourselves would mean taking on another significant obligation when our fundraising efforts were still nascent. We were not sure we could fund their entire college fees and residential expenses.

At a team meeting, it didn't take long for Ajit to assure everyone, "We will find the means to cover their tuition fees and living expenses at colleges. We will convince the donors."

"I am happy to see your confidence, Ajit. With a college education, they would have the background to compete in the marketplace for well-paying jobs," I said. Having made the decision to go forward with it, Ajit and I sat down to plan how to motivate donors.

The first priority was to generate sufficient cash to continue Shanti Bhavan. With no time to wait for better deals, I quickly concluded the sale of our two Florida and two New York properties. From the proceeds, I paid off outstanding mortgages on our properties and other loans, setting aside the balance to meet Shanti Bhavan's immediate operating needs. My life's earnings were being liquidated in a flash.

The sale of Penny Lane was taking too long, however. Despite cutting the price to one-third of its assessed value, there were no takers. Too many large houses were on the market. Since a turnaround didn't seem likely any time soon, I asked the bank to sell the house to satisfy its mortgage of a million dollars and that the surplus to be given to me. My earlier expectations of my investments' values, both in real estate and stocks, turned out to be an illusion.

"This is what happens when you do wrong," Ammachi remarked, likely referring to when I moved her and Achachan from Penny Lane.

Furthermore, I needed to sell my real estate properties in India to settle the debt Jude had incurred. The first sale was my comfortable apartment in Bangalore. I also sold three other condos I had bought for rental income. Uncultivated farmland and machinery, such as bulldozers, tractors, and other farming equipment, were also sold.

Baldev Medical & Community Centre was scaled down to a strictly outpatient clinic, with only one nurse, an assistant, and cleaning staff. One of Baldev's former doctors was contacted by phone when medical advice was needed. Patients who required a doctor's physical attention were directed to a hospital forty-five minutes away.

School operating expenses had to be reduced or held in check. With a conflicted heart, I delayed recruiting a new class of preschoolers for the next two years. "This is the only way we can take care of the two hundred and seventy children already in our care," I reasoned with Denny and Beena. They unanimously agreed.

Since leaving MCM, I had earned income only from share profits and dividends, but this ended when I sold my stocks. We had to conserve remaining money to meet Shanti Bhavan's ongoing needs until we found sufficient financial supporters. Ajit and I hoped potential donors would appreciate what we had achieved and would step forward to help the school. Whenever Ajit saw me disheartened, he would cheer me up. He once said, "Dad, you will come through this stronger. And when you do, you will have accomplished far more than you did in your twenty-five years with MCM."

I was surprised he still had confidence in my ability to turn things around. Hearing those words, the "doer" in me came alive, determined to fight seemingly overwhelming hurdles. Just as I began feeling optimistic, the gravity of the situation pulled me down again.

"There are only two options for us, Dad. Either lie down and die or go forward and find the money," Ajit would say to lift my spirit. I admired his inner strength to face defeats and his intellectual capacity to find solutions.

Ajit's relatively new fundraising campaign had gotten off to a slow start. He was often met with rejections, and I was worried whether he would be disheartened. I cautioned him, "In marketing, you can expect ninety-nine failures before one success."

While waiting for his efforts to bear fruit, I turned my energy to making our journalism college profitable. With only three months left before the start of the next academic year, we launched a robust recruitment campaign to increase enrollment by 50 percent. This target, if met, would help generate surplus funds that could be used toward Shanti Bhavan.

Dean Kanchan and other faculty members held workshops in major cities throughout India. Advertisements appeared online, as well as in newspapers and magazines. The school website was quickly improved, and newsletters were mailed to a long list of journalists and colleges. Denny diligently oversaw the promotional effort and directly interacted with applicants and their parents.

In the meantime, Sreedhar Menon, ten years my senior, who had held influential positions in banking, was among the first of several friends to offer assistance for Shanti Bhavan. Although I had previously borrowed a substantial amount from him and had taken some time to repay it, he remained generous and understanding. Other wonderful souls like Mary-Mitchell Campbell, a Broadway music director; Michelle Miller, a professor of music who had volunteered at the school; Janet De Penning, the founder of the De Penning & De Penning law firm; and Tammy Tibbetts and Christen Brandt at She's the First, an NGO supporting girls' education worldwide, were among those who stepped up initially to save the school. The Indo-German Chamber of Commerce based in Bangalore also lent their support.

My mother's life savings of over a million dollars helped ease the situation considerably. Her assistance to Shanti Bhavan in my time of great difficulty was indispensable, and I hoped to return the money when my financial situation stabilized. Nevertheless, I felt guilty about having sought her help when she had other plans for the family.

· · ·

Our first Shanti Bhavan class graduated from high school in June 2010, a remarkable milestone. Not wanting to miss celebrating their accomplishment, Mariam flew to India to attend. The children's parents were overjoyed to see their first family member complete high school and move onto college.

As I shook their hands and took pictures with them, one mother said, "Thank you, sir. You have been their true father. We only gave birth to them, but you have given them life." I was moved by this sentiment and comforted to see that they still had faith in me.

Donor contributions made it possible for the foundation to financially support students' undergraduate degrees at top colleges. They opted for business, engineering, law, biotechnology, psychology, and other majors. Female graduates received admission to well-established all-girls' colleges like Mount Carmel and Jyoti Nivas, and their male peers opted for Christ University and St. Joseph's College.

Shanti J and Denny served as their guardians, guiding them through personal conflicts, monitoring their academic performance and conduct, and, most importantly, providing emotional stability. A considerable number of former volunteers of Shanti Bhavan remained closely connected to the children and provided one-on-one mentoring. Every few months, I met with the class at our head office in Bangalore. I inquired at how they were doing and assured them of my love and involvement in their future.

Following their years in a protected environment, it was daunting for our graduates to suddenly face the "real world." With their newfound independence, they could quickly go astray. "The stakes are too high. You can't afford to fail. Your family is counting on you," I cautioned frequently, not wanting them to jeopardize a promising future.

Unfortunately, a few students didn't work hard or adequately adjust to the new environment and fell through the cracks. Such losses were sad and disappointing, but I hoped they would eventually find self-motivation. We kept in touch with them and brought them back into college when we sensed they would remain steady.

We encouraged Shanti Bhavan graduates to set realistic short-term goals and achieve them through hard work. They selected academic majors that would help them pursue careers soon after earning their bachelor's degree to generate sufficient income. Most wished to take up business and technical fields, and a few expressed interest in music, painting, sculpture, sports, marine, wildlife, and other exciting pursuits.

I worried that careers in fine arts might not meet their family's financial needs. Since we could not offer the requisite training early enough to advance their skills in these arts and other "creative" professions, we asked our children to take them up as a hobby or pursue them later.

Regardless of whether I was in India or in America, I would wake up every morning to long phone calls with Ajit and Denny on our action plan. Sometimes, I struggled to find the energy to get out of bed and confront my emotional setbacks. It was hard to come to terms with Jude's transgressions, as he had been my confidant in implementing all projects, having worked shoulder to shoulder with me to make Shanti Bhavan a reality. I proceeded cautiously but was pleased to see that he was sincere. He kept his word and negotiated with moneylenders to address the troubles he had with them; his willingness to set things right comforted me.

On the home front, I hadn't pacified anyone's disappointment. Vivek still hadn't made up with me. Although this grieved me, I understood he needed time to heal from his hurt. Ammachi and Mariam regularly called me to check how I was doing and inquire about the children. It was hard to shrug off my guilt at having failed all of them.

"Ammachi, can we talk about the future?" I once asked her when she mentioned my having kept her in the dark on my troubles.

Ammachi snapped back, "What future? I have no future! I only have the past." Her words startled me. It hurt to see my mother, who always planned for our family's future and had been the shining optimist, sink into helplessness. She was in her nineties and declining in health. I didn't want her to spend her last days thinking I had been a failure. I had to act fast.

The children's implicit faith in me and the trust that I would pull through motivated me to persevere. I was moved to hear from the caregivers that the children gathered every night before bed to pray for me. I had to stop dwelling on the past. There was no sense playing the victim or being too hard on myself. I mobilized all my strength to return to the man I knew I once was: the risk-taker and the caring provider.

With this resolve and without waiting for our financial condition to stabilize, I soon addressed the morning assembly. "Children, no matter what happens, we will not shut down Shanti Bhavan. We will grow what we need for food on our land, and those staff members who wish to continue working here will look after you and teach you." Thunderous applause followed. No one had expected this outcome. Children hugged each other and shouted joyfully. Watching their exuberance, I was overcome by an intense optimism I hadn't experienced since the troubles began, but worried if I was feeding them false hope. I vowed I would not let them down again.

Realizing that potential investors and wealthy individuals in India hadn't embraced our mission, we quickly abandoned seeking their collaboration. Instead, we sought the support of individual donors from abroad, particularly those in the US, and companies in India whose contributions were part of their corporate social responsibility. They contributed toward sponsoring the children for a year or more, meeting capital expenses for the construction and renovation of buildings and other infrastructure projects, and establishing an endowment fund that would meet our expenses perpetually from the interest earned.

With increased student enrollment, IIJNM began generating surplus funds each year to partially finance Shanti Bhavan's unmet expenses. "My investment in the journalism college has contributed in more ways than one, beyond improving the quality of the press," I told Dean Kanchan and Denny. With equal satisfaction and relief, I expressed my deep appreciation to them and their team for their hard work and commitment. Surplus revenues from the journalism school, funds raised from the sale of properties in India, financial assistance from my mother and a few large donors, and my remittances from the sale proceeds of properties in the US, all combined, would help weather the difficulties faced by the foundation in the next few years.

In addition to his fundraising responsibilities, Ajit joined me in India twice yearly to direct Shanti Bhavan's activities in his new role as director of operations. By 2012, his steady and persistent efforts had attracted donors who valued our foundation's mission and its potential to create generational social impact. With newfound success, his confidence in facing challenges steadily improved. His deep conviction in Shanti Bhavan's mission motivated him to strive harder.

Reflecting on the significant mistakes that had brought about this crisis, I recognize my limitations and shortcomings. I should have known that the money I had made in my business could vanish if I encountered an unexpected major financial crisis. My tendency to take excessive risk without heeding worst-case scenarios was instrumental to the unhappy outcome.

CHAPTER 24

A NEW ROAD MAP

PAINFUL MEMORIES OF EARLIER SETBACKS still lingered, but they no longer affected my optimism. My anxiety subsided, and a renewed determination took hold. From my corporate background, I knew everything boiled down to good management at all levels. I set out to motivate my staff, assign goals, monitor progress, and quickly address problems. To heighten staff performance, I acknowledged those who took the initiative and went the extra mile. Relatedly, we strove to provide fair salaries, comfortable accommodation, and healthy meals. Most importantly, we treated all employees with dignity and sensitivity. As a result, most staff have remained with us for a long time, some over twenty years. Continuity of employment is essential to maintaining the organization's culture and practices.

"What the children need most is to feel loved and cared for. Rather than punishing them, explain what went wrong. Encourage them to do the right thing," I advised the staff. The children's progress is inextricably linked to the efforts of our staff. With small and big successes, students would gain self-confidence to embark on complex challenges.

From the outset, I felt the need to establish a community comprising of our children and staff, who worked together and cared for one another. Only then would everyone focus on general welfare over individual gain. This requires constant dialogue, listening to others, and questioning ideas and beliefs. Interpersonal relationships through interaction with each other couldn't be accomplished remotely; hence, children's access to social media was banned in the school from a young age.

The staff began to consider themselves surrogate parents, guardians, mentors, and counselors. I worked closely with Denny, Beena, and the various department heads to ensure the children's physical and mental condition. I gave particular attention to the children's personal needs such as orthodontics, which helped improve their self-esteem and personality. Over time, I noticed a steady improvement in the spirit of teamwork and enthusiasm among the staff and the children's well-being.

From the start, we strove to develop critical thinking in our children. This entailed reflecting, discussing, and debating—instead of merely memorizing study material. They were taught to examine and combat practices of sexism, racism, and social prejudice. We introduced teaching methods such as putting on plays, organizing activities, and undertaking research projects. Children were encouraged to take charge of organizing festivities like Diwali, Halloween, Thanksgiving, Christmas, and graduation to enhance their leadership potential.

High schoolers took turns in groups watching the evening news on television and presenting it at the morning assembly with the rest of the school. Besides learning current affairs, they overcame stage fright and improved their public speaking skills. Children in middle and high school participated in community work, such as cleaning grounds, watering plants, and removing weeds amid the dozens of vegetables and lentils grown on the six acres previously used for banana and vineyard cultivation.

On Saturdays, I watched movies with them, coached them in soccer, and advised them on how to deal with the challenges back home. Every year, we organized a match between the mixed teams of girls and boys of the school and our college students—a much-anticipated event.

I shared my vulnerabilities with the children in the hopes that they would consider that I am far from perfect and to humanize our relationship. My efforts to build a bond with them improved their willingness to share more of their lives. Many children told me that their utmost desire was to improve their families' living conditions. They had witnessed their parents being frequently subjected to harassment and threats by moneylenders for not repaying loans on time. The children wanted to clear those debts as soon as possible, so their families could live peacefully. Additionally, they desired to educate their siblings through college and fulfill the dowry requirements for their sisters' marriages. I reassured them I would be by their side to guide and help them through until they settled into their professional careers.

Supplementing our internal efforts, noncommercial organizations emerged to support our academic program. UWC ISAK, a well-reputed boarding school in Japan, sponsored six children to study in its International Baccalaureate Diploma Program. Northwestern University, Illinois, began hosting two of our seniors for a dance competition annually. The University of California at Santa Cruz invited some of our children to participate in a seven-week science workshop. Artists from Broadway for Arts Education, New York, conducted two weeks of on-site vocal and instrumental music training every year.

Major companies like IKEA and Ernst & Young invited our children to visit their Bangalore offices to get acquainted with business and interact with employees. General Motors, ExxonMobil, and others conducted technology and management workshops at the school as part of their employee engagement program. Corporate-assisted initiatives included a STEM curriculum for science students desiring careers in technology-based companies. Larger donor contributions every year enabled us to hire more teachers and introduce computer applications and learning tools to improve the academic program.

These engagements broadened our curriculum, enhanced our children's exposure and skills, and helped them understand the importance of innovation, good business practices, and professional conduct. We expected them to thrive in any setting with their diverse experiences and perspectives and grow into global citizens.

Members of my extended family helped out in different ways: Lekha mentored the older children in English, and Bijoy took up teaching yoga online. Vinita became my confidante in matters related to school administration. My family was relieved to see the turnaround in the school's progress.

· · ·

I made time on the weekends to travel to Bangalore to meet up with our graduates in their first, second, and third year of undergraduate studies. Occasionally, I attended the alumni association meetings to learn about their job experiences. They shared with me exciting stories of being on the college football team, running for class president, and making new friends outside of their Shanti Bhavan circle.

I learned also about their struggles with discrimination directed at their economic and social status. Subtle instances of demeaning treatment followed them in communities where their backgrounds were known to others. Not having faced any form of prejudice while at Shanti Bhavan, adapting to a caste-based society outside was uncomfortable and hard.

One of our graduates recounted that a professor, upon seeing that she had a cell phone, mockingly remarked, "Oh, see how technology has reached the masses!" Laughter broke out in the room, but a few students were upset and expressed their disapproval privately to our graduate. She told me that she regretted having disclosed that she had studied at a school that helped poor children—something most of our graduates are reluctant to reveal.

Rena, one of our recent graduates, said she was only four when she first learned about caste differences. It happened when her family went to fetch water from a tanker operated by the government. While waiting in line with others in the village, Rena excitedly ran to the front to put her hand under the running water. A wealthy-looking woman had just readied herself to fill her jar, but Rena hadn't noticed her, as she was in a separate line. The woman pushed her aside roughly and emptied the water that had fallen into her jar before continuing to fill it. Hearing Rena's cry, her mother ran up and carried her away. The woman yelled at her mother, calling Rena a filthy child and demanding, "You all stay away from us while we collect water. The government should install another tap to prevent contamination by people like you."

Later, Rena asked her mother why the woman had shouted at her and she hadn't yelled back. Her mother told her not to argue with such people and stay close to her. Rena realized that some people had greater privileges and considered themselves superior.

The first lesson Dalits learn is their place in society and to accept their social status without questioning. Rena didn't remember her parents ever expressing unhappiness over the discrimination they faced, as it had always been this way for them and their ancestors. Her family was uneducated, worked in the fields for landlords, and lived on meager wages. If they violated village rules, they wouldn't find employment and could be castigated; it was safer to avoid confrontations with those of upper castes.

Caste continues to be India's "hidden apartheid." Nearly 70 percent of Indians identify themselves as belonging to Scheduled Castes and Tribes and Backward and Most Backward Classes—among the lowest in the social hierarchy. Their accounts reveal what it is to live as outliers in the forgotten fringe of society. The class structure is inextricably woven into the fabric of life in India, with little possibility of meaningful change soon.

To improve the living conditions of those belonging to lower castes and economically weaker sections (EWS), the government has instituted guaranteed quotas or reservations in public-sector employment. Those in the EWS category are allotted a 10 percent quota for admission to private and government colleges. Since most lower caste individuals fall into the EWS category, they, too, receive the same preferences offered to the broad EWS category. Yet they lack opportunities for quality education during their years in school, hindering their ability to obtain admission to superior colleges or obtain professional jobs.

Rena's experience in Shanti Bhavan was different. "I never thought about the caste system while at school. We were treated as equals and given the same opportunities as all other children, so my self-esteem remained intact. My classmates and I sat around, ate, and played together without considering each other's caste or religion."

Rena said she was not ashamed of her impoverished background or caste status.

"With the excellent education and the sound values I have acquired, I am confident of breaking the cycle of poverty and providing a better future for my family," Rena said. She recognized that social equality for her parents might not be possible in their lifetime, but she could aspire to it for herself through her success. She said she and her friends frequently brainstormed ideas for improving the world.

Today, when Rena returns home during vacations from college, villagers notice and admire her self-confidence and polished manners. Girls in her neighborhood talk to her and express their desire to follow her path. They want to know what she has learned and how she interacts with boys in her class. They are astonished at the ease with which she speaks with village adults. She is now an example for other girls, giving them the confidence to aspire to professional careers.

Like Rena, Ashwath also came from hardship. His family had lived in a single-room hut beside a sewage drain on the outskirts of Bangalore. Having understood what professional success could bring, he was determined to improve their condition as soon as he started working. Ashwath was a top student in his class at Shanti Bhavan, and after college, he got an entry-level job in a major accounting firm. Subsequently, he was hired as a general manager of a small fabricating company that made picture frames for Dutch customers. He later joined a human resources management company in a middle-level position.

Ashwath set out to relocate his family to a better neighborhood in a house he built with his savings. He paid off his father's loans and stabilized his family's financial status. With money put aside each month, he purchased food rations and clothing for everyone at home. Their improved economic condition allowed the family to live with respect and dignity in their new community. Ashwath is now educating his siblings through college, so they will not have to endure a life like their parents.

Sainath, another graduate of Shanti Bhavan, had a painful story to share. At fifteen, his mother had married his drunkard father and had endured constant physical abuse until she poured kerosene on her body, set herself on fire, and died. Sainath didn't know about it until he turned seventeen, when his uncles revealed the sordid details. Until then, he thought the woman whom his father had remarried was his birth mother. He despised his father, who fed him only one meal daily when he was home on vacation. As a Dalit, Sainath's father couldn't work inside landlords' homes as a servant, so he cleaned cow sheds and sewage pits for a living. His father was always in debt, having taken loans at high interest rates from moneylenders and been unable to repay on time. Constant threats and insults from landlords ensued, and the major topic at home almost every evening was how to handle the situation. There was no way out but to save whatever money they could, even if it meant forgoing meals.

After college, Sainath secured a good starting job at a multinational company. He decided to put the past aside and help his father repay the family's debt. He built an adjoining bathroom to their single-room house, so his parents didn't have to walk to the woods. Every month, he sends money to his father to buy food provisions and continues to improve their living conditions with items such as mats, cooking utensils, and house repairs. Sainath hopes to assist others in similar circumstances and work toward ending child marriage in his village. With his proper upbringing and excellent education, he is able to assimilate with others at his workplace. He has gained sufficient self-confidence to move about comfortably in any social circle.

Having witnessed the deplorable conditions in which their parents and siblings live, Shanti Bhavan alumni have a burning desire to improve their lives. But until they are gainfully employed, poverty and social prejudice will remain with them. Even with better living conditions, their families will take a while to find respect within their communities.

· · ·

In the earlier years, our school children were not self-motivated to aspire to college education or successful careers. Some parents didn't encourage their children, because they didn't believe in their ability to become professionals. But now, seeing that many have already completed their college and secured well-paying jobs in top companies, most parents are motivated and hopeful for their children's futures.

Parents are most eager to have their children earn money quickly to help their families burdened with debt. Their houses are usually crowded and in poor condition, with leaking roofs, no toilets, and a lack of other necessities. When unexpected medical emergencies arise, their financial situation becomes untenable. Employed graduates have the economic power to address their families' essential needs. The parents are amazed that within three to five years of starting their first jobs, their sons and daughters have already earned more than what they have in all their years.

Some parents are unhappy about not being able to exert control over their children's finances. They ask their children to hand over to them all their earnings or purchase for them houses and cars, among other expensive items. Their families' unrealistic expectations and demands place pressure on their children, who have only recently taken up jobs. Some parents claim that their children owe their financial success to the family's decision to send them to Shanti Bhavan, but I do not agree that decision obligates their children to turn all of their money over to their parents.

With several fathers being alcoholics, it is not prudent to give cash as assistance; instead, I advise the graduates to arrange for provisions to be delivered home monthly, directly pay the contractor for refurbishing the house, take out medical insurance for their parents, and negotiate and settle with moneylenders to whom their families are indebted.

Our girls take on leadership roles in their patriarchal society, where it is uncommon for daughters to be breadwinners in a family. They do not see a difference between their responsibility to their parents and that of their brothers. Disregarding the tradition of early marriage for girls, they strike a balance between their professional and personal goals. Education has enabled them to seek equality with men in their society. I am proud of their courage to break away from centuries-old practices and live their lives the way they want.

CHAPTER 25

UNFATHOMABLE DESTINATION

AMMACHI'S WEEKLY CALL on the early morning of July 31, 2016, was unusual. She always asked how I was doing and whether all was well at Shanti Bhavan. "Are the children happy, Aniyan?"

I kept my answers brief, more interested in knowing how she was.

She mentioned being constantly tired but added, "Don't worry. This is normal for someone ninety-six years old, Monu."

There was something strange about her voice; it was weak and barely audible. Alarmed, I asked, "Are you all right, Ammachi?"

"Monu, from your youngest days, we have done so many things together for the family. You have been a good son and a friend." This was unusual; she hardly ever spoke to me like this.

I could hear her taking a deep breath. "I love you," she said. Pausing for a moment, she repeated, "I love you. Goodbye, Monu." The phone clicked. She had hung up.

Her words rung in my head. Was my mother trying to bid me goodbye?

Denny was the first person I called in times of personal difficulty. I asked her to book me a flight back to the US the following day. Grasping the gravity of the situation, she got me one for that evening. Upon arriving in Newark the next day, I rushed to Lekha's house, where Ammachi had been living for the past three years. I found her asleep in bed. Her face was visibly swollen and unrecognizable. I sat on the bed and whispered, "Ammachi." She didn't respond.

I gently stroked her face, and she opened her eyes partially. "Oh, it is you! It is you!" Her voice, though feeble, carried joy.

I reached out for her hands and clutched them tightly to my chest.

"How did you come here so quickly, Monu?" Ammachi asked, still unable to believe I was there just a day after her call.

"I came as soon as I could get a flight, Ammachi. I knew you wouldn't ask me to leave the children and return." For a few moments, we sat in silence, grateful to be together again.

"Will you be with me for a few more days?" she asked.

I assured her I would.

"Then I won't be afraid," she said.

I discussed her condition with Vinita's husband, Sabu, who recommended giving her water pills to drain excess fluid. Each morning, I made a special glass of orange juice with extra sugar, salt, and potassium as electrolytes to compensate for the minerals lost from taking water pills. Ammachi appeared slimmer each day, and in three to four days, she returned to her earlier size and could sit upright in bed.

Being very frail, my mother required constant attention. Everyone in the family pitched in to look after her. Lekha made her dinner, and Bijoy and Vinita came over to help and keep her company. Mariam prepared Ammachi's favorite foods and brought them when she visited her on weekends. Vivek, Ajit, and their cousins phoned her frequently.

By six o'clock each morning, I would leave my apartment in North Bergen, New Jersey, to get to Ammachi before she woke up. Several times a day, I would gently lift her from bed and help her to the toilet or to the sofa to rest awhile. We would spend hours reminiscing about our days in India and the life we had built for ourselves in the US. She told stories I had heard many times before; nevertheless, I enjoyed hearing them again. I shared news about Shanti Bhavan, and she inquired about the children and staff she knew by name.

I reflected on how she had shaped my siblings and me. Ammachi's courage and determination gave me the self-confidence to take on challenges, no matter how formidable. She had pushed us all toward being independent and free thinkers and expected us to choose what was right. Her unique blend of artistic sensibility and scientific thought cultivated our resourcefulness to pursue our aim. Her ambitious outlook became a part of me. The freedoms my parents provided, their expectations of me, the initiatives I took, and the adventures I had experienced during my early years laid the foundation for my willingness to take risks.

Ammachi was very charming; she could win over anyone. Emulating her, I picked up some of her skills in dealing with others. Her forthright manner and the values she and my father lived by each day set the stage for my evolving convictions on moral courage, kindness, and honesty. My siblings and I grew up knowing we wouldn't indulge in misdeeds that might tarnish the family's name or reputation by lying, drinking excessively, swindling, or being wasteful.

Family meant everything to Ammachi, and loyalty topped the virtues our community embraced and revered. She emphasized the importance of listening to our conscience. She taught us that wealth and sophistication do not necessarily lead people to do the right thing and act sensitively toward others. Her courage to go alone to a distant land as a young woman and build a successful career shaped the destiny of our entire family for generations.

It was hard to accept that my mother, who had been the strong matriarch of our family for as long as I could remember, was now in her current state. As she napped, I would sit by her side, watching over her. At times, I retreated to the porch and cried with overwhelming sorrow.

· · ·

One morning soon after, Ammachi asked me to connect her on the telephone to friends and relatives in America and those back in India. I gathered the telephone numbers from her small diary, which she had maintained for decades. She spoke to only three or four people daily, each call lasting barely three minutes. She would recall special incidents in her relationship with them and wish them well. I took the phone from her after she spoke to each one and told them softly that she was thanking them for their friendship and saying goodbye. I could hear gasps at the other end.

One of the calls she made was to the children of the graduating class. After briefly inquiring about them, she concluded the conversation, saying, "One day you will be successful and in high positions. But remember, when you have the power, do not misuse it. Be humble and do what you can for others."

Constantly dreading the inevitable, I prayed for yet another day with her. I asked her, "Ammachi, what will I do after you are gone?"

"You'll get over it. You'll be all right."

"I don't know that, Ammachi. I don't know if I'll ever get over it."

"No, Monu. You will be all right."

I didn't see how that would be possible. Years ago, I had written an email to her, saying, "I don't think the umbilical cord ever got cut, Ammachi." She was a pillar of strength and a loving mother throughout my life. The thought that she would no longer be there was sheer agony.

One day, Ammachi said, "Monu, I am glad things have worked out for you." Knowing that I had recovered reassured and comforted her. She was relieved that I hadn't allowed financial troubles to let the children down and that they were doing well in school and college. I felt deeply grateful for finally having had the chance to set things right for her.

As weeks passed, Ammachi's condition deteriorated steadily: Her breathing grew shallower and labored and her fatigue severe. Sensing that the end was near, I chose to sleep beside her at night. I ensured her oxygen mask was correctly placed over her mouth and nose. If I sensed any movement in the middle of the night, I immediately attended to her.

Sure enough, one night, Ammachi was sitting on the bed, preparing to go to the bathroom in the dark without disturbing me. I gently scolded her for not alerting me and then helped her. After that incident, I lined up a heavy chair and sofa on her bedside so she couldn't escape alone.

"You are too tricky, Ammachi," I said, hiding my amusement.

"No. What trick am I doing? I don't want to trouble you."

Shortly after that, I had a midnight conversation with her, which had become a regular occurrence by then, but this time it seemed more urgent to her.

"I want you to promise me something, Aniyan," my mother began.

"What is it, Ammachi?"

"The four of you shouldn't fight among yourselves. You promise me that," she said, referring to us siblings.

"We won't, Ammachi," I promised.

As she prepared us for her absence, she seemed most concerned about the closeness of the family and our being there for each other. But she had other concerns as well. "Ensure that the children of Shanti Bhavan are looked after well."

"You can be confident of that, Ammachi."

"I have no regrets for giving my wealth to Shanti Bhavan. All four of you can take good care of your families without it." Ammachi concluded our brief conversation, "I raised my children to be good people and was blessed to have your father, the most wonderful man in my life." After a pause, she added, "I have accomplished everything I wanted to."

I was happy that she was content.

My mother's breathing deteriorated sharply the following day. I found her gasping for air, rolling frantically from side to side, and struggling to raise herself from bed. "Give me air! Give me air!" she pleaded as if she were drowning. I panicked and clutched her hands in mine, tears rolling down my face. I called Sabu and urgently sought his advice. He prescribed medication to calm her so she could breathe easier.

When my mother's breathing slightly improved later that afternoon, I sat on the bed, took her hands in mine, and asked her with overwhelming sadness, "Ammachi, if your breathing difficulty becomes severe, can I get you something to relax?"

Without thinking twice, she replied coherently, "Yes, you can."

After a few more attacks of breathlessness, the situation turned critical. Ammachi was now in terrible distress, unable to take in sufficient air. Her forehead had turned blue, and her eyes were closely shut. I asked my siblings if I could give our mother the tablet Sabu had prescribed, and they agreed that the most important thing was to bring her as much comfort as possible.

I asked Ammachi to open her mouth, telling her the tablet might help. I placed it under her tongue and gave her a glass of water. In a normal situation, this medication would have relaxed her, but in her case, she fell asleep quickly. I was relieved to see her chest moving up and down. Waiting by her bedside, I nervously watched for any adverse reaction to the medication. Her breathing grew strained and louder at times, but she didn't wake up or struggle as before.

I slept by my mother's side, not releasing her hand. As usual, I woke up at midnight to check if she wanted to go to the bathroom but found her still sound asleep. I hoped she would wake in a few hours and talk to me as she had done the last few nights, but she didn't. Comforted that she was not struggling to breathe, I anxiously sat beside her and waited for sunrise. As she slept undisturbed, loneliness and sorrow washed over me.

By morning, I could no longer hide my mental anguish and needed some time alone. Bijoy had stayed overnight, and I informed him of Ammachi's condition. He took over immediately, and I stepped outside to the porch. Memories flooded my mind as I contemplated the world without my beloved mother—my best friend and a constant source of encouragement.

A little later, Bijoy's wife, Angelica, came running. "She is dying!" I ran back inside. Ammachi had just taken a deep breath, but there was no sound of an exhale. I placed my hand under her nose, hoping to feel some sign of breathing. There was none.

Ammachi had moved on.

CHAPTER 26

TO GREATER HEIGHTS

WITH MY PARENTS GONE, I recognize that my time in this world is limited, and I am in line for the inevitable. The company of loving children and a purposeful life sustain me. Hearing their cheerful chatter and laughter makes me feel wonderful; seeing them wave to me from afar or run up to hug me lightens my steps.

We are immensely proud to see our high schoolers graduate and move on to college every year. In their final year in college, our support teams in the US and India assist them in finding employment. With strong academics and excellent interpersonal skills, our college graduates shine at interviews to gain starting positions in major companies at attractive salaries.

Most graduates have taken up good entry-level jobs at multinational companies like Morgan Stanley, Ernst & Young, Mercedes-Benz, Google, Amazon, and Deutsche Bank, to name a few. Some graduates are now married and have their own families but continue in their jobs after a brief break.

Amuda, from the class of 2011, worked at Goldman Sachs for five years before pursuing her MBA in a joint program between the

Asia School of Business in Kuala Lumpur and MIT in Boston. In the meantime, she has been supporting her mother, a single parent, by covering all her living expenses.

Manikaran, another graduate of 2011, went on to work for JP Morgan & Company. With his earnings, he cleared the family debt incurred by his late father, who was said to have committed suicide because of financial pressures. This young man paid for his sister's college education and continues to support his family as its head.

Vyshali, a tea vendor's daughter who had graduated from Shanti Bhavan, was honored by *Glamour* as one of their "Glamour Women of the Year 2014." I was proud to hear her address thousands of guests attending a star-studded gala at Carnegie Hall in New York City. Her hard work subsequently earned her a full scholarship to study sciences at Grinnell College in Iowa.

Shilpa's maturity and aspirations for a better life made it easier for our staff and me to convince her to make wise personal decisions. She ultimately opposed her family's wishes to marry her maternal uncle and was self-driven to build a meaningful life for herself. She completed two master's degrees and is now on a scholarship to pursue a PhD in clinical psychology at Hofstra University in New York. She also authored a best-selling memoir, *The Elephant Chaser's Daughter*, which has received wide acclaim.

These are just a few outstanding accomplishments among others. They have already shattered the constraints of the long-entrenched caste system, not only for themselves but for future generations of their families—an achievement that has no precedent elsewhere on a wide scale.

To our delight, *Daughters of Destiny* debuted on Netflix in July 2017. Seven years earlier, Academy Award–winning filmmaker

Vanessa Roth had approached us to film a documentary on Shanti Bhavan. Although she shot footage of both boys and girls, an editorial decision was made later to feature only girls. This direction addressed the gender bias Indian girls typically experience and showed how their upbringing at Shanti Bhavan helped them overcome it.

The film received the Television Academy Honors award, an accolade the Academy bestows on "television with a conscience," recognizing its contribution to "leveraging the dynamic power of television to inspire social change." Hundreds of thousands of viewers worldwide learned about Shanti Bhavan's transformative impact. Several wrote encouraging words, complimented our work, and offered donations. I felt gratified by the public's appreciation of our mission.

For Shanti Bhavan's twentieth anniversary, we hosted a beautiful fundraising gala at The Bowery Hotel in New York City on November 9, 2017, attended by over four hundred guests. Shilpa, Preetha, and Manjula, three of the girls featured in the documentary, formally spoke to the gathering. They served as our ambassadors, sharing their past and their future plans. I smiled proudly, watching them present their stories and hopes with confidence and elegance.

Padma Lakshmi and Hasan Minaj were among the gala celebrities in the crowd. It was gratifying that so many had come together to crusade for the replication of Shanti Bhavan and fulfill a shared dream. Ajit spoke passionately at the gathering. "Think of the generational impact of Shanti Bhavan's model. Our children are the first in their families to break the cycle of poverty. With their financial progress, they carry their families forward. We expect they will eventually change society and the nation." I wished Ammachi and Achachan had been there to witness Ajit taking the helm and pushing our endeavors to greater heights.

An impressive $1.2 million raised that evening was earmarked to create a second Shanti Bhavan school. I couldn't believe how far we had come from the depths of financial crisis just over a decade earlier that threatened Shanti Bhavan's survival. In the months following the gala, with Jude's assistance, we identified and bought thirty acres of property close to Bangalore.

Since purchasing the land, thousands of beautiful ornamental trees have been planted already on the grounds to complement varieties of fruit trees that will in a few years offer the children their special snack. Building construction will go on for the next several years, and when completed, it will be a special place for children to grow up healthy in harmony with nature. The challenge is in ensuring that the second school carries the same culture as the first.

It is heartwarming that the number of donors is increasing steadily, contributing to the mission's success. I am profoundly thankful to all of them. Now, the crucial task is long-term financial sustainability. We will accomplish this when our endowment fund sufficiently covers our ongoing annual capital and operating costs from its interest income. Kindhearted friends and supporters like Sreedhar Menon, Bobby Abraham, K. Balasubramanian, and Karan Ahooja contributed toward the initial capital. Since then, we have made considerable progress toward an endowment generating sufficient interest income for the present school and hope to meet our goal for the second one within the next five years.

The power of community and shared dreams is the best way forward. It is evident from the assistance received, both from those who have visited Shanti Bhavan and those who have not. Volunteers from around the globe share their time and expertise with our children for one or more months. Donors' support and concern about the welfare of our children have been extraordinary, and I owe them my immense gratitude.

· · ·

With growing financial stability for Shanti Bhavan, I revived some of the essential services we previously provided to local communities but at scaled-down levels. The Quality-of-Life Project we embarked on to meet some of the essential needs in a home substantially improved the living conditions in the seventeen villages surrounding Shanti Bhavan.

Our first initiative was reinstating services once provided by Baldev Clinic, such as deworming and outpatient care for minor illnesses, wounds, snake bites, and food poisoning. Dentists from Italy and physicians from the US volunteered their time to Shanti Bhavan and nearby communities for short periods each year. Patients with minor illnesses and injuries began visiting Baldev Medical, and Sister Sheila, our in-house nurse, offered treatment as best she could.

To this day, we provide midday meals to the sick and elderly in the villages who don't have families or close relatives to care for them and hence depend on others' generosity. It is sad but heartwarming to see them gather at a specified location, usually in the shade of a large banyan tree, waiting for our vehicle to arrive with lunch. Occasionally, in a show of respect and affection, our eldest children accompany our delivery staff to help serve the meal.

For as much as the behavior of the cleaning staff amid our earlier troubles disheartened me, I couldn't show spite toward them and walk away. We decided to build houses for them after ensuring that the land they lived on was registered in their names on the official records. We replaced their broken-down huts with model homes constructed of cement blocks, concrete roofs, and tiled floors. Wire mesh windows provided cross-ventilation and kept the entire residence free of smoke, rodents, flies, and mosquitoes.

At about three hundred square feet, each house features a small room for living and dining, a bedroom, a separate kitchen, and an attached bathroom, all at a construction cost of under seven thousand dollars. The space may not sound like much, but to families crowded into one room with a mud floor and a thatched leaking roof, it is an island of calm and comfort. We continue to expand the housing project to include those living in dilapidated homes, recognizing that proper housing remains the biggest need of poor people.

In early 2020, when the COVID-19 pandemic engulfed the world, many low-income people in surrounding villages lost their jobs, adding to their already severe hardships. Shanti Bhavan immediately supplemented their government rations. Every month, we supplied nearly five thousand neighboring people with quality rice, dhal, lentils, spices, cooking oil, and bathing soap. This practice continues to this day but only once per quarter.

Our contribution enables those who are most needy to cope with their difficult situation. We improve the quality of their lives with items such as mattresses, blankets, cooking utensils, pressure cookers, steel plates and tumblers, towels, buckets, and footwear. Our modest help sustains them during these challenging times and has garnered considerable goodwill toward Shanti Bhavan. Through these efforts, we demonstrate to our children the significance of being a good neighbor.

As it was unsafe, we decided not to send our children home as usual for their summer holidays during COVID-19. Although the campus was closed to outsiders, we continued to care for and teach our children uninterrupted, avoiding the pitfalls of remote learning. We met our residential needs with the fruits and vegetables grown on our farm and the dry rations delivered to our gate by the provisions shop. While schools across India were closed during this period, Shanti Bhavan took a different path to benefit all its residents.

• • •

In 2021, when the world was locked up by the pandemic, four of our graduates took the SATs for admission to American universities. They scored above the ninety-fifth percentile on the tests and, after interviews, waited for their admission results. When the notifications arrived, I was overcome with joy, as all four received multiple acceptances with full scholarships to top-tier universities to select from, including Dartmouth, Duke, Middlebury, Princeton, and Stanford. Their accomplishment is a triumph over adversity to fulfill our dream.

As they told me their exciting news, I could hardly hold back my tears of joy. Its confirmation brought me inexpressible satisfaction and jubilation. Up until that point, my conviction from the start that our graduates would be among the best in the world was only a dream. The wait has been long, but finally, the children have proven themselves, despite all the odds of their family's circumstances. My expectations for them, which I had spoken about thirty years ago at the first board meeting of the foundation, were realized!

Since the first group of four children joined American universities, eight more from further batches have been admitted on merit to The University of Chicago, Carnegie Mellon, Princeton, University of Rochester, Swarthmore, and UCLA, to name a few. The excitement of watching the graduates go to America to study encourages our high schoolers to aspire to similar opportunities.

The children of Shanti Bhavan are encouraged to believe they can accomplish their goals with hard work. Their journey equips them with the skills and resilience to navigate life's challenges. They understand that their education is a powerful tool for empowering and elevating them. Their humble beginnings don't stop them from exuding confidence in their potential to achieve their dreams.

I often tell the children, "Money is a good thing as long as you make it the old-fashioned way—honestly." I expect them to persevere and succeed in whatever they do professionally or in business. With the excellent education they have had, they will have the capacity to participate in India's industrial and technological progress. Their accomplishments will hopefully inspire hundreds of thousands of young people from similar family backgrounds to aspire for and work toward a rewarding future.

Our children have witnessed the struggles faced by their communities and yearn to be catalysts for change. Obstacles encountered by their families might have once seemed insurmountable, but now they are determined to overcome them; some have already gained the capacity to help their parents and siblings. They also envision a future when they can make a tangible difference in the lives of countless victims of the caste system. Their dreams of assisting those less fortunate reflect the ethos and values instilled in them at Shanti Bhavan. Over time, they will help solve society's intractable problems.

Donors have asked whether the children are expected to pay back what they have received. Though they are not obliged to Shanti Bhavan for what they have gained, they should not forget the kindness others have shown toward them. Undoubtedly, they have been beneficiaries of others' generosity and concern for them. Their recognition of those who were integral to their success must be demonstrated by upholding the promises they made while studying in Shanti Bhavan to contribute generously to worthy causes.

Some criticize me for pressuring the children by holding them to our ideals and their early naive commitments. It is true that I ask them to strive for professional success and later help others in whichever ways they wish. That has been my vision from the beginning, and I will not lower those expectations.

In this regard, I have suggested to our alumni that they allocate a small percentage of their income to support the future children of Shanti Bhavan who are yet to pass through its gates. I assume that their kinship with the younger children will motivate them to reach out within their means. This solemn obligation extends beyond blood relationships to strangers as well; it is an act with no human boundaries.

Unfortunately, human desires and self-interest often overshadow our best intentions. As mature adults, our graduates will have many needs. They will understandably desire to own a house, buy a car, and enjoy other comforts. When selfishness takes over, and excuses and indifference cloud a clear conscience, earlier promises might go unmet. Giving money to humanitarian causes might not be their immediate concern, and consequently, they might postpone it to future years when they might become prosperous and willing.

By the same token, the desire to undertake something of major significance might cause a delay in taking small steps and building on them. But I expect our graduates to assign a high priority to this moral imperative and not treat it as an act of charity or as a favor to consider doing at a later time. Good intentions are not a substitute for inaction.

Regardless of how the future turns out, I hope their inner voice will persuade them to act as early as possible. If and when they fulfill this duty and encourage others to do the same, the resulting multiplicative impact will be enormous. With thousands of Shanti Bhavan graduates in prominent positions, their economic status and influence will one day root out the caste system totally from society.

From their earliest days at Shanti Bhavan, I have tried to gently push the children from indifference to sympathy to empathy. Empathy might go a step further in connecting us viscerally to another person's predicament by putting ourselves in their shoes, but that, too, is not enough. "Can you understand another's pain?" I question the children. "The poor do not seek others' sympathy or platitude for their suffering, as it doesn't help improve their condition."

Most important of all is compassion. It leads to a positive emotion that motivates and drives us to make life better for others—compassion *in action*. Its singular purpose is to improve the condition of another with genuine caring. Helping another brings fulfillment and happiness to the giver and the recipient alike. There is no greater joy than reducing suffering and bringing comfort to another's life where all hope is lost. One must pursue this virtue and act on it; excuses for inaction are unconscionable.

I wish our children would remain kind and sensitive toward others. "Don't let yourself be hardened by greed. If you wish to change the world, be generous and offer your service. When you have the power to do good, do it," I frequently emphasize to them. If they choose collective well-being over excessive personal affluence, they would be fulfilling their moral duty. I prefer to see idealists among them who act on their dreams, rather than pragmatists who are overly cautious.

I help them understand what I have realized firsthand: "Wealth offers you the freedom to work toward something more satisfying and fulfilling. That satisfaction is not necessarily dependent on the amount of wealth you possess, but instead on what you do with it to make life better for yourself as well as others." It is rooted in actions and experiences not consumed by self-centered desires but by caring toward others. In a world of so much suffering among so many, there is no excuse for being indifferent. The duty to serve is fundamental to one's existence.

If they become immensely rich one day, I hope they would think of their good fortune not as an entitlement but as an opportunity to do maximum good. Their excess wealth beyond what is needed for a comfortable life must be thought of as resource for helping others who need their assistance. Making money for personal prestige or power or as the purpose in life has no meaning. To set aside huge amounts of wealth for their children as inheritance has no moral justification. Instead, they must be agents for change to bring comfort to the suffering.

I often emphasize the need for our children to cultivate good relationships with family members, friends, and colleagues, and remain sensitive in their interactions with everyone. Further, by doing the right thing at all times and being kind toward those who need help, they will find happiness in their own lives. When the alumni write to inform me of the progress in their careers or to convey their best wishes on special occasions, I use the opportunity to remind them to live by the values they learned at Shanti Bhavan. "Your credibility is your biggest asset," I remind them, and ask, "What kind of person do you want to be?"

I have often told the children that they will discover the purpose to their lives if they follow the right path and lead by example. No human being experiences a sudden realization or enlightenment.

These outcomes arise from long introspection and deliberation, culminating in personal conclusions that are still far from certain. Hence, they have to discover for themselves the right way to live.

"It is important to carry forward what you believe in. You will set good examples for others with your character, ideals, and service. When you become such individuals, then you will have upheld what this institution stands for in your lives and in the lives of those who will follow you," I told them at a graduation ceremony. I frequently advised them to follow their conscience and do the right thing at all times.

On Thursday night formal sessions and other occasions, I explained to the higher-grade children the lessons learned from major world events of the past and the ideas presented by great thinkers. If they would embrace some of the ideals they have learned, and make their own contributions, the impact would be insurmountable. I hope they will have the "indomitable spirit" that the famous anthropologist Jane Goodall talks about in her book *The Book of Hope* to act unselfishly to create a better world.

CHAPTER 27

AN ODE TO PURPOSE AND HOPE

ONCE BARREN, THE GROUNDS of the first Shanti Bhavan have become picturesque: Bougainvillea and hibiscus sprawl over the landscape in various shades and hues, complementing the colorful trees initially planted, which have now grown tall and lush. The symphony of birdsong and the boisterous laughter of children wafting out of the dorms bring forth the spirit of life.

My week is divided between overseeing both Shanti Bhavan schools. The second school has already sprung up in the village of Chikkahosahalli, in Karnataka State, and has welcomed its first sixty preschoolers and kindergartners. Nestled in a valley of rolling grounds and surrounded on all four sides by the rocky Makalidurga Hills, the new campus offers a breathtaking presence.

When it rains there, water gushes down the hills to be channeled through ravines and gullies to two large artificial ponds. Whether it is the sunrise over the horizon or the sunset with glowing colors over the surrounding hills, a profound sense of wonder permeates this place. Those who live here feel the warmth of humanity and a sense of belonging.

I am blessed to have a loving family that has stood by me over these arduous years. With Mariam at work in the US, we could live together only a few months a year in the initial twenty-six years of Shanti Bhavan. She endured my long absences, looked after the family, and encouraged and supported me through challenging times. She recently moved permanently to India and is now involved in the school's administration while teaching children with learning difficulties. We both enjoy living on campus and plan to spend the rest of our lives peacefully with the children and staff.

I am thankful for the love and support of our sons. Ajit is my right hand, working hard and following the mission to take Shanti Bhavan to new heights. Vivek is very affectionate and encouraging of what we strive for. He keeps up with the children's progress and assists them through his mentorship. I couldn't have asked for more from them.

I realize that relationships with colleagues and well-wishers are a lasting source of joy and satisfaction. I am strengthened by the goodness of the people I work closely with and by our deep love for each other. I am especially indebted to Beena and Denny, who have remained loyal and dedicated to our mission for the past twenty-five years.

Those seven weeks with my mother before her death were moments of great richness, even amid the grief of watching her fade away. I am thankful I had the chance to be there for both my parents in their last days. I constantly remember my father's advice to "work hard and be good"—a philosophy to live by—and I convey these ideals to my sons and the children of Shanti Bhavan.

The lessons from my parents, my time in the army, and my years as a businessman in America formed an appreciation of a purposeful life. In my search for doing something meaningful for others, I concluded that building on compassion is the right way to live my life. This consequential act—to revere every individual life—removes any excuse for indifference or inaction and brings spiritual fulfillment.

The 50-50 game plan I set for myself—to devote the first half of my life to professional ambitions and personal goals and the second half to service to humanity—keeps me persevering. Consistent with this plan, the course I mapped out decades ago has been largely fulfilled, although it has been smaller in scope than I initially envisioned. Despite unexpected stumbles, I have dared to dream and forge ahead. I am immensely grateful to all those who have supported us through the years.

Shanti Bhavan has been an extraordinary pioneering effort among all my social endeavors. It has been demonstrated that children from the lowest socioeconomic strata can succeed through the power of an excellent education and a nurturing environment. In one generation, our alumni have dramatically altered the course of their destinies and freed their families from the constraints that had held them back for centuries.

My years with the children have tempered my business demeanor and softened my ways. Bringing them up and watching them grow into affectionate and motivated young adults has been a tremendously rewarding experience. I love them as my own and always strive to be true to them. I hope they will remember me for having done my best for them.

I am hopeful that in the next decade, we will establish more Shanti Bhavans across different states. These schools will turn out cadres of graduates who will be high professional achievers with a drive for social service. With their notable educational, social, and leadership skills, they will be changemakers to benefit society. In turn, they will enjoy prosperity and multiply their impact through the assistance they provide. Then the cost of running these schools will only be a small fraction of their tremendous contribution to humanity.

The most pressing issue is how best to transition the current leadership to the next generation. With that in mind, we have begun training managers to take on top-level responsibilities. Those committed to humanitarian causes and who appreciate what Shanti Bhavan stands for might lead and extend its impact. I am confident our alumni and the younger generation of friends will take the mantle when their turn comes.

Over the past thirty years of social work in India, I have learned a great deal from the people we serve. I am humbled that they let me into their lives and received me with kindness. In their simplicity, I have seen order; in their beliefs, I have found faith; and in their suffering, I have gained compassion.

Fate took me to places where some thought I didn't belong, and I made them my home. From the mountains of Se La to the rural village of Baliganapalli, I traveled a path wrought with risks, triumphs, and defeats. Through the trials and tribulations of the varied social ventures I embarked on, my story played out like a billowing fabric of disparate threads woven together.

I am deeply grateful to all those who stood by me and contributed to our efforts. Your generosity enabled me to strive in the face of all odds. Your kindness taught me the beauty of forgiveness and trust. The success we have had in accomplishing our mission was the result of the indispensable contributions of every participant. The good we do in the time we have will live on long after we have crossed the final mountain.

NOTES

Chapter 16, page 182: "A study of vegetables grown near Delhi showed dangerously high lead levels in spinach, but no environmental laws addressed soil contamination by lead particles."

SOURCE: S. Singh and M. Kumar, "Heavy Metal Load of Soil, Water and Vegetables in Peri-Urban Delhi," *Environmental Monitoring and Assessment* 120, no. 1-3 (2006):79-91, doi: 10.1007/s10661-005-9050-3.

Chapter 24, page 282: "Nearly 70 percent of Indians identify themselves as belonging to Scheduled Castes and Tribes and Backward and Most Backward Classes—among the lowest in the social hierarchy."

SOURCE: S. Government of India, *Census of India 2011: Maharashtra, District Census Handbook, Ratnagiri*, Series 28, Part XII-A, 2011.

Chapter 26, page 297: "The film received the Television Academy Honors award, an accolade the Academy bestows on 'television with a conscience,' recognizing its contribution to 'leveraging the dynamic power of television to inspire social change.'"

SOURCE: Television Academy, "Honors Call for Entries," news release, December 12, 2018.

ACKNOWLEDGMENTS

I AM IMMENSELY THANKFUL to my wife, Mariam, who reread the manuscript several times and offered valuable suggestions, and to Shilpa Anthony Raj, a graduate of Shanti Bhavan, for greatly assisting me throughout the evolution of this book. Having been one of the children who grew up under my guidance, Shilpa was uniquely positioned to tell me the perspective of the children and my role in their lives. Without her help, I wouldn't have fully understood the complexities faced by the children who have been navigating through two different worlds—one of poverty and the other preparing for a modern, successful life.

I am eternally grateful to all those who worked closely with me to improve the lives of those we serve. A good part of my story is theirs as well, as we strove together every day for the past many years to accomplish our mission. I also can't thank enough all those who extended a helping hand with their generosity and kindness.

Finally, I wish to thank Lou Ann, who assisted me with the early versions of the manuscript; my son Ajit, who encouraged me to embark on this book; Brianna Provda, for efficiently managing the promotional process; and the editors and business managers at Greenleaf Book Group for diligently preparing it for publication.

ABOUT THE AUTHOR

DR. ABRAHAM GEORGE began his career in the Indian army as an artillery officer stationed at the Se La mountain pass on the India-China border, the highest battleground in the Himalayas at that time. Following brief military service, he moved to the United States and earned two master's degrees and a PhD in business administration from New York University. For nearly twenty-five years, Dr. George pursued a successful entrepreneurial career before returning to India in 1995 to address deep-rooted discrimination and economic oppression faced by the country's social underclass.

Among the initiatives he embarked on in India are a school to provide high-quality education to children from socially and economically disadvantaged backgrounds, a premier postgraduate institution aimed at fostering a free and independent press, and a rural hospital to serve the health care needs of fifteen villages. His pioneering work in environmental health played a pivotal role in the removal of lead from gasoline across India in April 2000, a milestone achievement in public health.

Dr. George is the author of three books on international corporate

316 | Mountains to Cross

finance and two on his social work. Over the years, he has championed social justice for the underclass in India, offering their children economic opportunities through a unique educational model. He has served on prestigious boards including Human Rights Watch and the International Center for Journalists and has been honored with several awards, including the Hind Rattan Award.